SIN, ORGANIZED CHARITY AND THE POOR LAW IN VICTORIAN ENGLAND

Sin, Organized Charity and the Poor Law in Victorian England

Robert Humphreys
Department of Economic History
London School of Economics and Political Science

St. Martin's Press

© Robert Humphreys 1995

All rights reserved. No reproduction, copy or transmission of this publication may be made without written permission.

No paragraph of this publication may be reproduced, copied or transmitted save with written permission or in accordance with the provisions of the Copyright, Designs and Patents Act 1988, or under the terms of any licence permitting limited copying issued by the Copyright Licensing Agency, 90 Tottenham Court Road, London W1P 9HE.

Any person who does any unauthorised act in relation to this publication may be liable to criminal prosecution and civil claims for damages.

First published in Great Britain 1995 by
MACMILLAN PRESS LTD
Houndmills, Basingstoke, Hampshire RG21 6XS
and London
Companies and representatives
throughout the world

A catalogue record for this book is available from the British Library.

ISBN 0-333-63379-2

10 9 8 7 6 5 4 3 2 1
04 03 02 01 00 99 98 97 96 95

Printed and bound in Great Britain by
Antony Rowe Ltd, Chippenham, Wiltshire

First published in the United States of America 1995 by
Scholarly and Reference Division,
ST. MARTIN'S PRESS, INC.,
175 Fifth Avenue,
New York, N.Y. 10010

ISBN 0-312-12755-3

Library of Congress Cataloging-in-Publication Data
Humphreys, Robert.
Sin, organised charity, and the poor law in Victorian England / Robert Humphreys.
p. cm.
Includes bibliographical references and index.
ISBN 0-312-12755-3 (cloth)
1. Charity Organization Society (London, England)—History.
2. Charities—Great Britain—History—19th century. 3. Poor laws-
-Great Britain—History—19th century. I. Title.
HV245.H88 1995
361.7'63'0942109034—dc20   95-14318
                                                        CIP

To Paul and Adrienne

Contents

List of Figures		ix
List of Tables		x
Acknowledgements		xi
Abbreviations		xii

1	Introduction	1
2	*The Poor Law Crusade against Outdoor Relief*	14
	The 1834 Poor Law Amendment	14
	Poor Law administrative changes, 1834–1869	17
	National development of the crusade	21
3	*The Provincial Crusade: Results and Reactions*	29
	The selection of Poor Law unions for analysis	29
	Anti-outdoor relief unions and their specific rules	32
	Results of the crusade in anti-outdoor relief unions	36
	Unions adjacent to provincial centres with a society practising methodological charity	41
	Discussion on the mixed responses to the crusade	44
4	*Victorian Ideology, Early Attempts to Organize Charity, and the Beginnings of the Charity Organisation Society*	50
	Reforming ideas, the persistence of outdoor relief and the formation of the COS	51
	Early attempts to organize charity	55
	The formation and development of the London Charity Organisation Society	59
5	*The Emergence of Provincial Charity Organisation Societies and Responses, 1870–1890*	64
	The development of provincial Charity Organisation Societies	64
	The provincial COSs and Poor Law guardians	83
	Relationships with other charities	87
	The COS and the clergy	90
	Provident dispensaries	93
	Relationships with the London COS	95

6	*The Activities of Provincial Charity Organisation Societies, 1870–1890*	101
	Categorization of applicants and comparative relief values	102
	Dividing the deserving poor from the undeserving	110
	Methods of COS relief to the deserving	114
	Exceptional distress	130
	The undeserving: cautionary procedures	133
	Lack of COS volunteers	136
	Organizational finances and administration costs	138
7	*Ideological Change in Late Victorian Britain: The Response of the Provincial Charity Organisation Societies and the Local Government Board*	144
	COS adherence to principles	144
	Changing circumstances and attitudes	146
	The COS and the LGB: objectives and achievements	159
	Discussion	164
	Summary and conclusions	171

Appendix General Notes on Poor Law and Organized Charity Data — 175

Notes — 177

Bibliography
  Archive collections — 204
  Unpublished theses — 207
  Parliamentary Papers — 208
  Nineteenth-century publications and pamphlets — 209
  Contemporary newspapers and magazines — 211
  Secondary sources — 212

Index — 220

List of Figures

2.1	Numbers of outdoor paupers per 1000 population (England and Wales 1849–1869)	19
2.2	Direct expenditure on paupers (England and Wales 1849–1869)	20
2.3	Metropolitan outdoor adults (excluding lunatics, the insane, etc.) (1860–1869)	21
3.1	Paupers: England and Wales (average of daily counts 1870–1889)	30
3.2	Brixworth Poor Law union (average of 1 January and 1 July day counts 1870–1890)	37
3.3	Brixworth outdoor paupers (average of 1 January and 1 July day counts 1870–1890)	38
3.4	Manchester Poor Law union: outdoor paupers and workhouse inmates (1870–1890)	39
3.5	Manchester Poor Law union: adults on outdoor relief (1870–1890)	40
3.6	Manchester Poor Law union: out-relief – adults and children (1870–1890)	40
3.7	Birkenhead Poor Law union: outdoor paupers and workhouse inmates (1870–1890)	42
6.1	Organization chart for medium-size COS	103
6.2	Procedure recommended for Provincial Charity Organisation Societies following receipt of an application	113

List of Tables

2.1	Adult able-bodied paupers in receipt of relief in England 1872	23
2.2	Outdoor relief and outdoor paupers in England and Wales 1861–70	25
6.1	Numbers relieved annually and value comparisons between provincial COSs and Poor Law unions	105
6.2	Annual values of Poor Law outdoor relief and the annual values of relief provided by a nearby COS to the average deserving applicant	107
6.3	Percentages of total applicants who were assisted, not assisted and referred by various provincial societies	115
6.4	Types of relief provided by provincial Charity Organisation Societies	117
6.5	Manchester and Salford DPS Convalescent Home, Southport: number of admissions and their categorization	128
6.6	Birkenhead COS Provident Department: details of deposits	129
6.7	Manchester and Salford DPS: Savings Department details	130
6.8	Provincial COSs: annual income and administrative expenditure	139

Acknowledgements

There are so many good people who I should acknowledge but regretfully can here only touch briefly on a few. I am particularly thankful for the long-term kindness and encouragement of Paul Johnson. His constructive support and ever perspicacious comments have been the main pillar of strength throughout the research leading to this book. My grateful thanks also to Eddie Hunt for his scholarship and helpful advice during my research.

The enthusiastic erudition passed on by other members of the Department of Economic History at the London School of Economics and Political Science during many stimulating discussions must also be gratefully acknowledged. For their unflagging camaraderie I must especially record my gratitude to Dudley Baines, Max Schulze, Kirtida Parikh, Mary Morgan, Francesca Carnevali, Peter Howlett, Tim Meldrum, Linda Sampson, Ann Morris and Wendy Willson. The many whose names I have ungraciously omitted remain in my appreciative thoughts.

Since becoming involved in economic history I have been moved by the generous and patient help ever available from my numerous contacts whether in universities, libraries, public record offices or other learned institutions. My grateful thanks to them all.

August 1994

Abbreviations

AR	Annual Report
BPP	British Parliamentary Papers
COR	*Charity Organisation Reporter*
COReview	*Charity Organisation Review*
COS	Charity Organisation Society
CRS	Central Relief Society (Liverpool)
DPS	District Provident Society (Manchester and Salford)
LGB	Local Government Board
PDA	Provident Dispensary Association (Manchester and Salford)
P and DS	Brighton Provident and District Society
PDS	Provident District Society (Liverpool)
PLB	Poor Law Board
PLC	Poor Law Commissioners
£	pound sterling = twenty shillings
s. or /-	shilling = twelve (old) pennies
d.	(old) penny

1 Introduction

The national ambience in the 1860s was one of confidence. Britain's dominance as a world power was at its apogee with prominent middle-class factions convinced that the nation's economic and political success, of which they had been the essential part, was their God-given right. It provided fertile ground for reformers who claimed that the poor also would benefit from a stiffening of their morals and character brought about by charities newly organized using the principles of scientific methodology. As a result, the first Charity Organisation Society (COS) was formed in 1869 London at the mid-point of Victoria's reign.

These would-be radical reformers of poor relief were not to know that the 1870s and 1880s would result in exceptional social and economic change together with fundamental shifts in political processes. For the first three-quarters of the century there had continued to be broad acceptance that free market principles were inviolate. Laissez-faire ideas had been translated successfully into the popular idiom by Samuel Smiles and Harriet Martineau with emphasis on the commendable individual values of character, morality, diligence, discipline and deference.[1] But during the 1870s these concepts began to be challenged with new ideals under the intellectual prompting of those such as Henry Sidgwick, Thomas Hill Green and Alfred Marshall. The new Idealists argued that a modern industrial nation could no longer leave the well-being of the individual to the unrestricted market mechanisms responsible for Britain's early success. Rapid population growth and burgeoning industrial urbanization were seen to have brought human problems not easily solvable by traditional rural paternalism.

Two centuries earlier the liberalism of Thomas Hobbes had laudably attempted to define a private sphere for the individual independent of the state in a civil society where personal, family and business life was free from political interference. Hobbes, and those like John Locke, Adam Smith and Thomas Malthus who followed, had understandably sought to restrict the involvement of the state to that consented to by 'free and equal individuals'. Then, from the 1870s a paradigm shift in political philosophy began to take shape when Green and other Idealists developed the concept of the 'common good'. This was to transform the early liberalism with its protection of sectionalized interests to one which argued it was essential for the retention of the socio-economic status quo that the general well-being of the community should be nurtured. The traditional belief that the state should be kept at bay to permit each individual an untrammelled life now gradually gave way to a state which recognized that for its own preservation it must accept wider social responsibilities.

There was also a further spur to the state arising from the revolutionary successes on the continent of radical-minded liberals and socialist movements. The British establishment wisely recognized the need to yield a measured amount of political ground without confrontation so as to maintain the socio-economic equilibrium which had been the bedrock of national success. New Idealists provided the solution whereby it was only necessary to 'abate' the essentials of the existing political class framework for it to be preserved. It was shown to be quite feasible to satisfy citizenship demands through a wider franchise because votes for the masses would create a special form of status, distinct from class in being intrinsically levelling. As a consequence enhanced voting rights would strengthen Britain's greatness by ensuring that those responsible for its past dominance through effective control of the nation's wealth would continue relatively unhindered in their accumulation of capital.

The state was encouraged to show it was interested in redressing the existing ills of poverty and disease with growing involvements aimed at developing more meaningful interpretations of words like 'freedom' and 'equality'. These were viewed by Idealists as hollow possessions for all those who were struggling for existence in badly-built inadequately administered environments with little education, health care or job prospects. Now there was a perceived need to be seen to do more to provide social environments for the masses capable of supplying living conditions and opportunities to encourage individual self-fulfilment. The negative role of the liberal state with its protection of individual freedoms was moved sensibly in the late Victorian decades to the restrained interventionism essential for its continuance.

The advent of the new ideologies was paralleled by subtle adverse drifts in Britain's economy. Although the 1851 Crystal Palace exhibition had twenty years earlier provided some slight doubts about Britain's future global industrial competitiveness, the international challenge had become sufficiently apparent by the 1870s to reflect on most levels of society. Even the seemingly impermeable confidence of the middle classes began to be eroded by deceleration in national prosperity growth. Although the increasing number of items coming into British ports were still more than balanced by exports, there were signs of slippage in unit selling prices and manufacturer's margins. The industrialization of other countries through investment in sophisticated modern equipment had guaranteed their productive efficiency and encouraged further technological advance while marooning Britain's fixed capital in relative obsolescence. Slackened demand for UK steel exemplified these constraining economic forces as indigenous railway expansion faded and industrializing economies overseas competed effectively for world rail demands. When nations like the USA and Germany erected tariff barriers, British producers had little alternative but to hawk their goods around unfamiliar, restricted and less-profitable markets.

Along with the dampening of their own ebullience there was broader willingness amongst the better-off to appreciate the worsening plight of the poor in difficult times with urban environments providing a useful focus in which to express this enhanced awareness. Town accommodation for the poor was arguably no worse than had been the rural cottages abandoned by agricultural labourers mobilized by the attraction of higher factory wages. It was the sheer weight of numbers now herded into confined areas which humiliated by their unwanted intimacy and transgression of human decency. Expanding towns and cities had been blighted with unsanitary acres offering nothing better than back-to-back housing, shared street taps and communal middens. Short-time working, factory lay-offs, illness or a debilitating accident often forced workers to take a paying lodger or further sublet their already meagre living space. Poverty and disease were all too often integrated by inadequate sustenance.

Commentators describing the plight of the Victorian poor in a particular locality have often assumed that the social malaise they unearthed was unique and have failed to recognize its typicality. For example, Simey believed that Liverpudlian 'poverty was more desperate, housing more squalid, social distinctions more cruel, the state of health more shocking ... than elsewhere' without recognizing that the abhorrent conditions were all too common in Victorian towns.[2] London itself was no exception. A contemporary described how in the late 1860s the poor were housed 'for the most part in pig-sties ... sleeping and working amid bad air, nourished by dear and adulterated food, and exposed to damp, darkness and overcrowding'.[3] Charles Booth was to later famously quantify London's squalor, as was Seebohm Rowntree in York, but long before these surveys apparently startled the middle-classes John Rae, when Provost of Edinburgh University, had revealed that:

> large classes of working people in towns are too poorly fed to save them from what are known as starvation diseases ... with no prospect in old age but penury and parochial support ... one-third, if not indeed one-half, of the families of the country are huddled, six in a room, in a way

... quite incompatible with the elementary claims of decency, health or morality.[4]

Although many amongst the middle classes managed to avert their gaze from the intimate details of nearby degradation, there was wider acceptance that poor people could occasionally suffer misfortune which deserved help and guidance from their betters. Joseph Chamberlain's municipal improvements in Birmingham are a well-documented example of how the New Liberalism began to express itself in practice. In addition to acceptance of more interventionism from state and local authority there was also indication of strengthening in the Victorian virtue of charity whereby uneasy consciences were prepared to recognize that wealth and status carried moral responsibility for the poor. A whole miscellany of charities mushroomed with each responding unilaterally to their particular concern with little reference to those around them.

What distinguished those reformers who were to attempt the nationwide expansion of organized charity from 1869 was their intransigent rejection of the change in contemporary opinion which occurred through the 1870s and 1880s. Transgression of the individual spirit through the haphazard provision of relief whether from state or charity, without prior searching investigation, was seen by the would-be reformers as evil, mischievous and abhorrent. They remained dismayed as year after year their message for organization was largely ignored while thoughtless do-gooders continued to flit irresponsibly among the poor disbursing their alms regardless of whether the character of the recipients deserved support. Those wishing to rationalize relief steadfastly maintained that capricious benevolence did nothing for the poor but weaken morals and nurture inherent sin. They were convinced that although irresolute moral fibre was often to blame for inadequacies in the condition of the poor, their problems were compounded by the boundless careless profligacy of meddling philanthropists. According to these relief progressionists, regardless of environment those among the poor who they judged to be deserving would, when aided by appropriate encouragement from their social betters, possess the innate character to soon fend for their families instead of grovelling for hand-outs. They dismissed arguments that the plight of the poor may sometimes have association with socio-economic disequilibria characteristic of their individualistic philosophies. Malthus's advocacy about the fear of want being an indispensable spur towards self-reliance and improvement was interpreted by the reformers as confirmation that haphazard charity was against the recipient's best moral interests because it removed fear short-term.[5]

As mentioned earlier, it was with the purpose of scientifically rationalizing existing charitable inconsistencies that various reforming elites got together during the late 1860s, allegedly for the moral good of the poor, with the common purpose of co-ordinating and controlling voluntary disbursements. They agreed that relief should be provided only after the case had been rigorously investigated to ascertain the applicant's worthiness.[6] Those judged to be deserving would then receive scientifically measured assistance whereas those exposed as being undeserving would be despatched to the nearest workhouse.

The reformers eventually combined on 29 April 1869 to form 'The Society for Organising Charitable Relief and Repressing Mendicity', soon known as the 'Charity Organisation Society', and colloquially as the 'COS'. The emergent Society committed themselves to stem the widespread moral deterioration resulting from traditional charities being hoodwinked by the cunning poor so as to cause 'imposture of all kinds' to be 'rampant and triumphant'.[7] This concern was shared by Poor Law President, George J. Goschen who, in a Minute dated 20 November 1869, warned metropolitan guardians about the 'alarm which might arise on the part of the public' if double distribution persisted involving both statutory relief and charity.[8] Goschen concurred with the COS idea that the inferior condition of the poor in England was due 'not to their circumstance ... but to their own improvident habits and thriftlessness'.[9] If the poor were ever to become more prosperous it would be only through self-denial, discipline, responsibility, hard work, thrift, temperance and forethought. There was no remedy for pauperism and mendicancy without the expulsion of the sin of haphazard relief, whether by charity or Poor Law.

Goschen argued that there should be 'opportunity for every agency, official or private, engaged in relieving the poor to know fully and accurately the details of the work performed by all similarly engaged', but was quite clear that the required relief rationalization was a task for a voluntary agency and not officialdom.[10] This was most encouraging for the newly formed COS as such a co-ordinating role was precisely what they had specified for themselves. They were confident that under their influence, scientific investigation, categorization and co-ordination would soon become hallmarks of a composite relief system in which family values would feature at the core of moral activities.

More than a century later similar beliefs have surfaced among influential contemporary social thinkers and politicians on both sides of the Atlantic about what they identify as worsening moral degradation.

Failure of young people to recognize work as being 'at the centre of life' is claimed to be instrumental in eroding the independent spirit and in weakening family values so that moral decline is evidenced by increased crime, single-parenthood, drug-taking, social violence and the inability to hold down a job.[11] They have argued that growth in public transfers also diminishes the act of charity by crowding out private anti-poverty efforts and fundamentally changing the nature of private charity.[12] The social irresponsibility of state assistance is perceived as a major factor which has led to the decline in individual 'dignity, self-esteem, and self-respect'.[13] As John Moore put it when he was Mrs Thatcher's Secretary of State for Social Services, the 'nanny state' engenders 'the sullen apathy of dependence'.[14]

Looking askance at the fractured crime-ridden inner cities of the United States in the 1980s, Charles Murray has argued that the necessary moral improvement will come only from the development of small 'functioning communities' akin to Burkean 'little platoons', where the 'pursuit of happiness' would be encouraged and where individuals facing adversity would not be allowed to deteriorate to the indignity of state dependence. Instead, they would gain self-respect with the help of neighbourly 'prodding' and friendly emphasis on reasons 'why failing to become self-sufficient is a drain on the community.'[15] When leader of the free world, Ronald Reagan believed that the private sector would replace and improve upon the services and supports of the federal government. Reliance on voluntarism and individual initiative were claimed to be the traditional and appropriate responses to social problems. President Reagan launched a nationwide drive to encourage citizens to join him 'in finding where need exists and then to organise volunteer programs to meet those needs'.[16] It is clear that these concepts have obvious parallels with the radical organizing reformers of Victorian Britain who through the COS were also driven by the conviction that moral standards would be improved by curtailment in state aid and by the elimination of character-sapping gratuitous charity.

There is a wide range of contemporary and twentieth-century accounts about how London COS set about applying their scientific methodology towards the rationalization of poor relief and their activities are summarized in Chapter 4.[17] In contrast, the historiography of the charity organization movement in the provinces is sparse. Historians have usually depended on the impressions generated by the COS Council in London and echoed by their 'official' commentators. A received notion of vigorous national growth echoes Helen Bosanquet's pronouncement that the reputation of the COS lay 'very largely in the hands of the Provincial Societies, while to their co-operation the London COS owes much of its strength and efficiency'.[18] COS branches were 'springing up all over the kingdom' with members intent on solving 'some of the gravest problems of the day ... affecting the entire country'.[19] With the scarcity of other sources, the shrewdly selected information propagated by London COS has been the foundation of twentieth-century historiography. Harris accepts that a 'popular and new voluntaristic social-scientific culture' found expression 'through numerous Charity Organisation Societies'.[20] This followed Owen's view that 'the Charity Organisation movement stands as perhaps the most representative current, certainly the most characteristic innovation, in the philanthropic practice of the mid-to-late Victorian Age'.[21] It has also been proposed that 'the COS represented the main effort of the free market society to solve the problem of poverty without government intervention.'[22] The image of considerable social impact is conjured by Mowat's description of how provincial societies in Britain 'grew rapidly in the 1870s and 1880s'.[23] Young and Ashton agreed that the COS 'had a large public interested in its activities' with their visitors acting as 'necessary personal links between guardians, the COS and other organisations'.[24] There has also been reference to 'the success of organised charity in persuading local guardians to adopt a stricter policy towards "casual" and "outdoor" pauperism'.[25] Vincent believed that 'one of the key functions of the COS from the 1870s onwards had been to organise, centralise, and systemise charity'.[26] Others have described how 'charities were regulated' by the 'effective rule' of the COS, and how COS assistance to the deserving poor would always be 'adequate in amount and time'.[27] In the same vein, Woodroofe explains how COS assistance to the poor was 'hand tailored' with grants designed 'to set a man on his feet'.[28]

This volume shows that contrary to the COS rhetoric, their practical influence on rationalizing charitable disbursements across England was marginal. In reality there was no flourishing national COS network effectively rationalizing relief to the poor. While it is correct that organizing societies were attempted in many English towns and cities during the 1870s and 1880s, it will be shown that the received impression of them forming an effective, vigorous, national movement was illusory. Provincial COSs never became a 'popular culture', they had great difficulty in recruiting voluntary visitors, they rarely achieved formal relationships with local guardians, they had even more frigid responses from local charities, they were treated with grave suspicion by most working clergy and were seen as being even less attractive than the stigmatized Poor Law by many in need. COS assistance to supplicants they did judge as being deserving is shown to have been generally inadequate for the regeneration of independence which ostensibly was the COS's paramount objective.

Chapter 2 emphasizes how for decades succeeding governments schemed for curtailment of Poor Law outdoor relief. Assistance for the able-bodied outside the workhouse had been discouraged by the Poor Law authorities from 1834 because it allegedly eroded the moral fibre of the poor by blunting the urgency of their search for work. These government intentions were frustrated for decades by entrenched opinions, socio-economic pressure groups and outdated legislation. Pragmatic Poor Law guardians conscious of local social tensions largely chose what many saw as the more humane palliative of providing adult doles of a few shillings so that the poor could continue life's struggle in their home rather than being forced into the feared segregated workhouse. The result was that there were commonly more than four times as many outdoor paupers nationally than there were workhouse inmates.

Eventually government considered sufficient legislative change had been introduced to improve the mobility of labour and to so modernize rating assessments that the prevailing social climate provided the chance of success for a national curtailment of outdoor relief. The newly created Local Government Board (LGB) in 1871 expanded Goschen's earlier metropolitan Minute by launching a countrywide initiative which became known as the crusade against outdoor relief.[29] Supported by their forceful itinerant inspectors, the LGB applied persistent pressure on guardians to persuade them that outdoor relief was a demoralizing evil, was economically indefensible and was a vote loser. The mixed success of LGB efforts is debated in Chapter 3 with particular focus on the few 'strict' unions where, with LGB and COS encouragement, guardians persistently squeezed the numbers on outdoor relief through the 1870s and 1880s. Other Poor Law unions examined here in some detail are where nearby reformers expressed intent on organizing relief to the poor.

During its first six years the LGB crusade reduced the numbers of outside paupers nationally by about one-third. Numbers then levelled off across the country despite persistent government pressure. Congratulations heaped upon the 'strict' unions contrasted sharply with the vitriolic LGB brickbats thrown at the majority where legislation was not being applied 'correctly'. The LGB crusade was cloaked in a subterfuge about the alleged need to prevent outdoor doles getting to indolent able-bodied scroungers. In reality robust men formed only a small part of those purged. Disadvantaged categories were those mainly hit including the aged, the disabled, the chronically infirm and widows with dependent children.

Chapter 4 examines the voluntary sector and how adherence to classical economic doctrines, combined with a perceived horror of the evils wrought by haphazard charity, sparked the COS's formation in London. Influential support from Queen Victoria, the Royal Family, members of the aristocracy and other elite groups, together with the recruitment of gifted officials, helped the Society become a dominant voice on matters relating to the condition of the poor. COS propaganda was also buttressed by repeated glowing references to the alleged successes of earlier reforms like Thomas Chalmers' neighbourly experiment in St John's parish Glasgow and the organized social structures at Elberfeld in the Rhineland.[30] It is argued that much of the advantage claimed for these ventures was exaggerated, ill-founded and misleading.

Chapter 5 concentrates on a number of provincial Charity Organisation Societies believed not to be untypical of peer groups elsewhere in the country. Societies analysed most closely are those centred at Birkenhead, Birmingham, Brighton, Leamington, Liverpool, Manchester, Oxford, Reading and Southampton. Some societies such as the Manchester and Salford District Provident Society (DPS) and the Liverpool Central Relief Society (CRS) were established prior to 1870 but eventually joined the charity organization movement. Other provincial COSs with roots in local anti-mendicity groups were so impressed by London COS's theories as to join them in the 1870s. The above nine societies were among the few to become 'affiliated' to London COS as distinct from merely being 'in correspondence'. Affiliation committed them to supplying London COS regularly with activity data and so increased the likelihood that details of their activities were known to the central COS council. Quantitative data and descriptive information about provincial COS activities has been extracted mainly from their published reports and statements, together with unpublished minutes, letters and other documents. The contents of these primary sources have been compared and contrasted with contemporaneous comments made locally and nationally by COS individual commentators, organizations, pamphlets, journals and newspapers.

The COS nurtured the impression that they enjoyed close relationships with local guardians by insisting that 'co-operation with the Poor Law is of primary importance in any good system of charitable relief'.[31] Chapter 5 shows quite clearly that such an impression was unjustified. Provincial attempts to develop ideological harmonies and structured working partnerships with workhouse establishments, as envisaged by Goschen, were usually unfruitful. When occasional rapport was achieved, such as when COS members doubled as guardians in 'strict unions', dissension from other board members generally ensured that co-operation remained tenuous. The response of other charities to COS overtures is shown to have been even less warm. Charitable bodies were not generally enthused by the COS's invitation to fund the organizing activities of these newcomers to the voluntary scene, especially when the intruders insisted on informing the public that traditional 'unscientific' relief was outdated, irresponsible, mischievous and immoral. COS implications that clergy generally concurred with their ideas is also shown to have been misleading. Clerical support was mainly confined to the higher echelons of the established church and to some non-conformist ministers, particularly Unitarians. Work-a-day parish curates tended to join the majority of dissenting Protestants in shunning the COS's judgemental stance which many saw as being alien to commonly accepted ideas of Christian charity. Organizing societies in the provinces are shown to have failed to convince sufficient people for their principles to have had more than a peripheral impact on the provision of relief to the poor.

The investigation and categorization of applicants was crucial to COS philosophy and Chapter 6 analyses data which provides a new slant on these procedures. COS investigation aimed at judging whether applicants were: 'deserving' of direct COS assistance, were 'not deserving', or were worthy of referral elsewhere. Broad provincial consistency is revealed outside the big cities in that the ratios between the three categories was maintained at about 0.5:0.3:0.2. These ratios are shown to have interesting differences from London COS.

COS propagandists referred scathingly to the 'uncharitableness' of the 'small pittance' given in Poor Law outdoor doles.[32] They claimed that, in contrast, 'the bestowal of relief' from charities should always be 'suitable and adequate' such as would 'enable the recipient to rise' to independent respectability.[33] These claims are shown to have been hollow in the light of their own practice. The value of provincial COS assistance was often less than the derided Poor Law dole, both as regards unit weekly value and the period over which relief was provided.

Ample evidence indicates that provincial COS revenues were not usually a match for many traditional charities. The COS explained that their *raison d'être* was not to disseminate alms but to investigate the justification of those who were asking for them. Such excuses about their financial weakness are unconvincing when it becomes known that provincial COSs were embarrassed by their inadequate public support making it impossible for them to succour some of those they had investigated and found deserving.

In spite of their tight financial constraints provincial COSs attempted a miscellany of assistance techniques. A discernible general shift in their relief patterns occurred in the later 1870s when many looked for appropriate circumstances in which to offer loans in preference to grants because the former allegedly possessed great therapeutic value for the poor. It is shown that contrary to COS anticipations, widespread defaulting on loans eventually dimmed their attraction and eroded their use.

In the 1880s another shift occurred in the pattern of provincial disbursements. Contrary to some earlier reluctance within the society, 'special case' pensions, often for 'fallen' members of the middle classes or for the 'cream' of working people, became an important aspect of provincial COS assistance. The institutional problems regularly encountered by COS committees are also discussed. This exposes their persistent failure to attract volunteer visitors and how high COS administrative costs regularly became butts for public ridicule.

Although the COS propaganda machine retained much of the high ground in social debate, the influential calibre of damning critics grew ominously by 1890. When in the late 1860s the Society had first fashioned plans for organizing charity, there were good reasons to expect middle-class support. Unfortunately for the COS, their venture was spawned at a time when public attitudes were about to reflect the need for social change. The notion that from around 1870 fundamental revisions were awakening in British society involving the 'replacement of an assertive individualism' by modest collectivism has been 'propounded by British historians from the time of Dicey downwards'.[34] Whether or not increased intervention was accepted because social conditions deteriorated so intolerably as to prompt the likes of Lord Shaftesbury and Joseph Chamberlain to push for state involvements or whether collectivism followed naturally with the inherent momentum of an expanding Civil Service need not concern us here.[35] What historiography does imply is that during the later decades of Victoria's reign there developed greater awareness and acceptance that modern urban environments had brought socio-economic factors against which the poor were frequently defenceless. Redundancy or short-time working from a factory, at the same time as hundreds of other operatives were being laid-off, was eventually seen as bringing a level of distress to poor families which they found impossible to circumvent unaided. Poverty was now more readily recognized as having connotations other than merely being attributed to individual sloth and deceit.

The infallibility of rigid individualism was being eroded by 1890 with socio-economic concepts such as those broadcast by the New Liberals, Socialists and former COS allies now anxious to dilute their rigidities.[36] Some of those most actively associated with COS principles twenty years earlier now favoured solutions featuring elements of simple compassion and eased away from what were now seen as unnecessarily harsh pseudo-scientific methodologies. They joined the expanding public chorus implying that expenditure on COS investigation may have been better spent in relieving the dejected poor.

When compared with the majority of citizens, COS stalwarts remained steadfast to their original convictions. They continued to deride others for being faint-hearted and stuck unflinchingly to the belief that strength of character would always conquer material disadvantage. For them it remained immoral for better-off people to lavish charity on individuals whose poverty the COS judged to have resulted from personal weakness. Even then it must be recognized that in spite of their disaffection with COS philosophy, few of those among the middle-class majority ever contemplated the need for fundamental change in the existing socio-economic structures. The broader willingness to accept more state intervention was because it was seen as an essential element in a formula designed to retain the social status quo. It is therefore argued in Chapter 7 that in spite of the disagreements between the rigid COS and more flexibly-minded intellectuals as to the interrelationships of morals, character and environment on the poor, the two sides continued to share many social and economic fundamentals.

Provincial COSs are shown to have failed against criteria they originally would have chosen. Although their impeccable social credentials gained the COS early respect, they failed to capture the hearts, the minds or the trust of sufficient in the community. This made it impossible for COSs to rationalize provincial poor relief and provided little opportunity for them to eliminate the alleged shameful immorality of its wanton indiscrimination. COS ostracism from other charities meant that long-established procedures for the distribution of alms continued regardless of the Societies' efforts to rationalize them. After twenty years of largely unfulfilled effort the COS found it necessary to complain just as stridently about the careless profligacy of traditional charities as they had initially.

COS hopes, claims and early predictions are debated in the final chapter in the new light of their limited practical achievements. Rather perversely for the COS, that part of their activities remaining of lasting application has been the methodological assessment of individuals which was so persistently the target of bitter contemporary hostility. Investigative techniques based on COS templates fabricated to retain rigid individualistic principles eventually became essential tools of the welfare state they had fought so determinedly to suppress.

In the late twentieth century the powerful political voices advocating a return to voluntaristic organized welfare have underpinned their arguments with claims that this would be returning to the situation prevailing successfully across late Victorian England. In exposing the reality of how provincial organizing societies failed miserably in their attempts to rationalize poor relief, this volume shatters present-day claims of historical precedence.

2 The Poor Law Crusade against Outdoor Relief

The envisaged co-operation between government and organized charity initiated by G.J. Goschen in 1869 aimed at controlling relief to the poor. It was predicated on the strategy that the COS would organize voluntary disbursements while the state crusaded against Poor Law outdoor relief. The government plan had only become feasible following a prolonged process of social and legislative change started in 1834 and continuing into the late 1860s. This chapter describes the changes and examines the development of the crusade against Poor Law outdoor relief.

THE 1834 POOR LAW AMENDMENT

The 1832 Royal Commission was commanded to examine and report on the administration and operation of the Laws for the Relief of the Poor following government concern about diverse social, economic and political issues including the alleged immorality encouraged in the poor by the profligate provision of outdoor relief. The shape and tenor of the 1834 Report of the Commissioners indicates that they believed improvements in Poor Law activities would only occur when they had resolved 'the most pressing of the evils' which were 'those connected with the relief of the able-bodied'.[1] A Charity Organisation Society publication later in the century was to claim that because of the increase in poor-rates it was 'no exaggeration to say that the country was in danger of being consumed by its own children'.[2]

The aspect of outdoor relief which caused most government dismay was the action of guardians in augmenting inadequate wages, best known as the Speenhamland system. This was said to be morally destructive as it eroded the recipient's ambition for better-paid employment and encouraged idleness which would inevitably lead to the deterioration of all working people. It was also claimed that the economy suffered disequilibrium from low wages illegally supported by outdoor relief and so disturbed the natural freedom of the labour market. With these clear-cut, if factually dubious guidelines, the Poor Law Commissioners recommended that workhouses would be rationalised into a new framework, replacing the existing facilities in the 15535 parishes of

England and Wales, by distilling poor relief administration into fewer than 650 unions. These larger units were intended to achieve national conformity by improved workhouse management and standard accounting procedures. The upkeep of the unions would be on the basis of parish contributions calculated in proportion to parish relief expenses.

To achieve the 'well regulated' premises it was usually necessary for the emergent larger unions to either construct a new centrally located building within the old parish network, or to radically extend existing premises. Segregation between sexes and age groups was seen as essential to 'avoid the extension of vicious connections between inmates'. Four categories of pauper had to be housed in separate sections, namely: the aged and the really impotent, children, able-bodied females and able-bodied males.[3] Strict discipline would be applied with each family member assigned into their appropriate section of the institution.[4] The principle of 'less eligibility' would ensure that the 'offer of the house' would fairly test whether or not the supplicant was 'deserving'.

A flaw in the amended outdoor relief strategy was the obsession with the problem of profligate benefits allegedly being ladled out to the able-bodied in agricultural areas across the country. This they blamed on local maladministration fostered by misplaced benevolence and the indifference of parish officials. However, the Commissioners failed to take sufficient account of repercussions from socio-economic problems specific to urban growth or to resolve the defects in the parochial rating system with its grounding in a 'fairly static society with a reasonable balance between propertied and poor in each area'.[5] The architects of the 1834 Act were well aware that the Laws of Settlement and Removal, still essentially unscathed from 1662, would continue to inhibit workers from searching for employment. Their Report referred to the 'exposition of the evils arising from the Laws of Settlement'.[6] Difficulties were commonplace with the vexatious and costly litigation between parishes which for generations had remained practically unaffected by the 'trivial and ill-considered alterations of the law'.[7] In spite of the 1834 Commissioners preaching 'a sermon on the frauds, abuses, perjuries and falsehoods' caused by the settlement system, the opposition to reform marshalled by the landed establishment prevented worthwhile improvement being included in the Act itself.[8] The crucial weakness retained was that of the parish or the township remaining the unit for both rating and settlement with trivial legal alterations merely increasing their 'already impressive complexity'.[9]

Adam Smith had earlier called the settlement and removal legislation 'an evident violation of natural liberty and justice' because they violated the principle whereby the labourer, like other factors of production, ought to have the means of unhindered response in a free market.[10] The legislation deterred the worker from looking for employment outside his settlement parish knowing that sickness or accident could result in him being forcibly removed back to his place of settlement from which he had severed connection and where he may be no longer welcome. Magistrates were empowered to transport persons not possessing rights in that parish to their place of settlement, a procedure that could be complex, time-consuming and costly. In spite of their faults the settlement laws were occasionally a useful fallback for the poor, with the labourer viewing them as 'his guarantee of parish relief during a period of poverty'.[11]

The failure of the 1834 Act to include real improvement in the settlement laws did not diminish the government's enthusiasm for making it more difficult for the poor to get benefits outside of the workhouse. The verbal offensive against outdoor relief was initially directed against the able-bodied but by 1836 the Poor Law Commissioners were recommending pressure on other outside paupers. Guardians were encouraged to emphasize that responsibility for providing against infirmity and old age lay with the individual and with his family.[12] The Commissioners then decided that more than one-third of the aged and infirm outdoor paupers were 'partially able to work', as were many widows habitually receiving outdoor benefit. Officialdom also perceived the danger that out-relief to these disadvantaged cases could lead to a reduction in wages, just as certainly as with the able-bodied. By 'fraudulently' burdening the country with relief costs such people allegedly subjected the 'independent poor' to 'unfair competition'.[13]

But the Commissioners had to recognize that although they could pronounce on such matters, they had little chance of actually applying tighter constraints until parishes had been rationalized into the new unions each with the requisite amount of segregated accommodation.[14] In spite of this hurdle, they were convinced that once the construction and refurbishing work was eventually completed, the resulting network of unions would allow them to exert a near dictatorial influence on local affairs. Such ambitions remained largely unfulfilled. Although reforms were attempted from time to time, it was to be more than thirty years before the central Poor Law authority considered themselves strong enough to launch an effective onslaught to reduce outdoor relief using tactics which, for a while at least, were publicly acceptable. Throughout these three decades British governments encountered the dilemma of being faced by hardliners determined to follow the 'main object of the Poor Law Amendment Act' of repressing outdoor relief generally and 'not merely to the able-bodied' while others asserted equally strongly that the existing law had already gone too far in restricting outdoor relief.[15]

POOR LAW ADMINISTRATIVE CHANGES, 1834–1869

Notwithstanding their difficulties, the central Poor Law authorities never lost sight of their primary objective and by the early 1840s sufficient new unions had developed 'well regulated workhouses' to provide Commissioners with the confidence to attempt further legal change aimed at reducing outdoor relief to the able-bodied. The resulting 1844 Outdoor Relief Prohibitory Order was addressed to all rural unions and ostensibly prohibited assistance to the able-bodied poor or to their families, other than as workhouse inmates. But the rigorous veneer of the Order was not matched by its substance. Numerous escape clauses, included as a result of local pressures, gave it colander-like characteristics when guardians chose to apply them. 'Exceptions' to the Order included: cases of sudden necessity, sickness, accident, infirmity, burial of relatives, widows with children, families of the armed forces, the resident family of a non-resident head and payment of a pauper's rent.

Another eight years elapsed before there was a parallel attempt to tighten the urban rules but, for the many guardians who chose to interpret them benignly, the 1852 Outdoor Relief Regulation Order lacked even the surface stringency of its rural predecessor. It made little attempt to prevent able-bodied females getting out-relief and allowed able-bodied men to be given relief provided they were set a work-task and that at least half the dole was non-monetary.[16] Although from the early 1870s guardians were urged to interpret them more rigorously, the 1844 and 1852 Orders remained the basis of outdoor relief for the remainder of the century with an increasing proportion of unions coming under the later Order as urbanization progressed.

Faced with local realities, most guardians were not greatly impressed by the theory that applicants refused outdoor relief would be saved from idleness and would naturally translate themselves into independent thriving members of the community. Guardians usually found it more expedient to be influenced by another aspect of laissez-faire principles which encouraged them to shun bureaucratic interference. In supporting outdoor relief this guardian localism was prompted by two factors, one political and the other compassionate. First was the voting popularity gained by guardians from maintaining low poor-rates. Although the central Poor Law authorities propagated the opposite view, local opinion usually supported the idea that it was imprudent for guardians to insist on paupers being taken into the workhouse at a much higher unit cost when there was the popular and seemingly attractive economic alternative of a few shillings in out-relief. The second reason was that guardians believed out-relief caused less distress among the local community. Even when the larger, less personal, union system came into vogue it remained true that the individual circumstances of most supplicants, particularly in rural areas, were known to at least one of the guardians or relieving officers. They were conscious of the emotional pain felt by neighbours when a friend was forced to enter the workhouse, particularly as it condemned a family to segregation. Both regulatory Orders left guardians ample 'room for manoeuvre' mainly through ambiguity about the term 'able-bodied'.[17] As late as the 1860s, in attempting to specify an 'adult able-bodied pauper', Whitehall admitted that a description could not be 'made in accord with any strictly defined rule'.[18]

The Poor Law Board (PLB), which replaced the Poor Law Commission in 1847, recognized that before they could orchestrate a worthwhile new assault against outdoor relief it would first be advantageous to awaken greater interest in rating procedures and in local Poor Law expenditure. During the 1850s, parliamentary questions relating to the need for revised rating assessment procedures, chargeability areas and removal reforms were consistently stonewalled by landed interests. But gradually there was greater exposure to the social stresses caused by the darker sides of industrialization. Furthermore, an urban situation developed which had parallels with the rural open : close parish relationship in that rates in poor parishes were often higher than in better-off areas. Possibly of greatest relevance was that by 1865 the supremacy of landed interests in the Commons had been displaced with the majority of seats held by members with industrial, commercial or financial backgrounds.[19] As early as 1861 the drift of voting power away from the territorial aristocracy, and their ability to protect the sanctity of close parishes, had allowed C.P. Villiers to negotiate the important Irremovable Poor Bill through Parliament. Instead of five years it now required only three years to acquire irremovability; the union became the locality of residence instead of the parish only; and, most significantly, union common funds were created based on parish rateable value rather than on the amount of pauperism.[20] The Parochial Assessment Bill (1862), which soon followed, made accurate rating assessments possible without undue hindrance from entrenched local influences.[21] The long-term policy of making the Poor Law union the sole area of local administration was essentially completed by the 1865 Union Chargeability Act. This also reduced the irremovability residence period to one year and transferred the power of removal from the parish overseer to the union guardian. Villiers claimed that the 1834 Commissioners had always intended that the union should replace the parish as the unit for rate assessment and chargeability.[22] Further consolidation was achieved by the Poor Law Amendment Act 1867 with its district institutions funded jointly by a number of contiguous unions to care for sick, insane or infirm persons, now considered inappropriate objects for the harshness of workhouse administration.

The prolonged pressures to reduce outdoor relief, regardless of the limited legislative change prior to the 1860s, were not without some success even if undramatic. From mid-century, the number of outdoor paupers reduced nationally and is more significant when viewed against the rising population (see Figure 2.1). From being approximately 5 per cent of the population in 1850, outdoor numbers had fallen to around 4 per cent ten years later. Numbers remained roughly constant throughout the 1860s except for a surge in 1863–4 associated with the exceptional industrial distress. Workhouse inmate numbers during the two decades remained well below one per cent of the population.[23] The expenditure on inmates and outdoor paupers over the same twenty years is shown in Figure 2.2. The unit weekly outdoor dole, expressed as an average over all

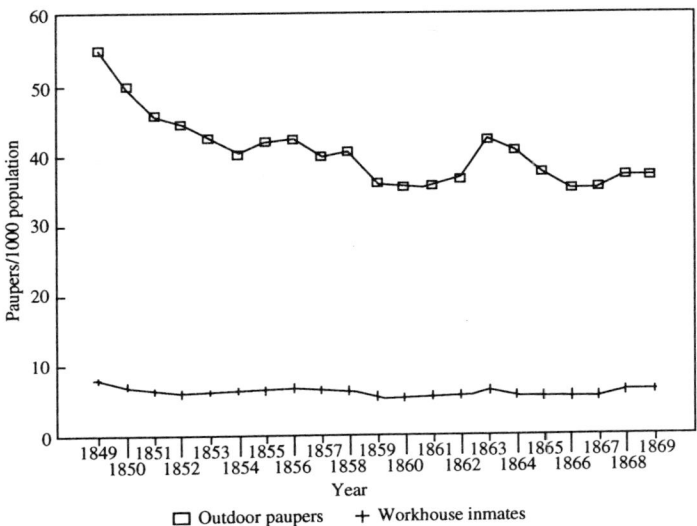

Figure 2.1 Numbers of outdoor paupers per 1000 population (England and Wales 1849–1869).

20   *Sin, Organized Charity and the Poor Law in Victorian England*

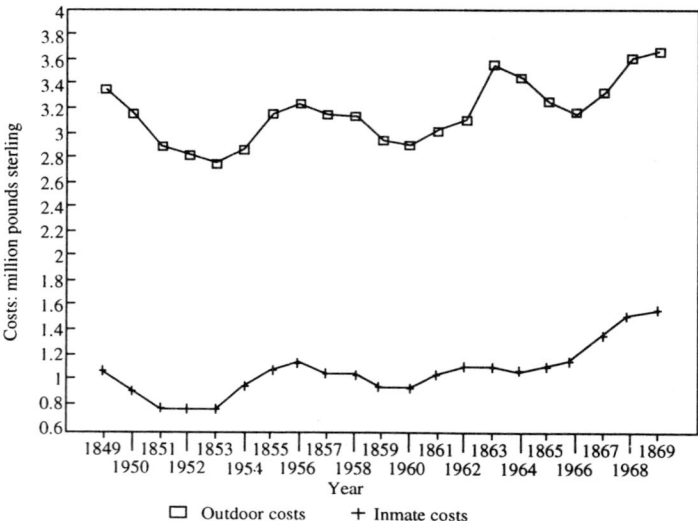

Figure 2.2   Direct expenditure on paupers (England and Wales 1849–1869).

categories, rose from around 1s.4d. per week at mid-century to nearly 1s.9d. in 1869.[24] By then the advances in removal and chargeability legislation were considered sufficient for the PLB to claim that it was now unreasonable for labour to plead for outdoor relief immediately work became scarce locally. They also repeated the concerns of the early 1830s with the allegation that 'a careless administration of out-relief was once more threatening to become a social danger' as 'for some years there had been a great and continuous increase in expenditure'.[25]

In London, troughs in economic cycles and adverse weather, brought a clamour for outdoor relief on East End Poor Law unions towards the end of the decade (see Figure 2.3).[26] The PLB claimed that London's outdoor pauperism had shown such a dramatic growth as to make it necessary to 'guard against any alarm which might arise on the part of the public'.[27] Little cognisance was given to the trade slump and the associated unemployment among East End weavers, dockers, shipbuilders and ancillary trades dependent on riverside activity.[28] Nor did the PLB mention that London's population had grown rapidly with a decadal increase of 16 per cent by 1871.

The conditions in 1869 London were seen by the PLB as being propitious for a public reminder about long-standing ideas concerning the moral, economic and social advantages of housing paupers in workhouses

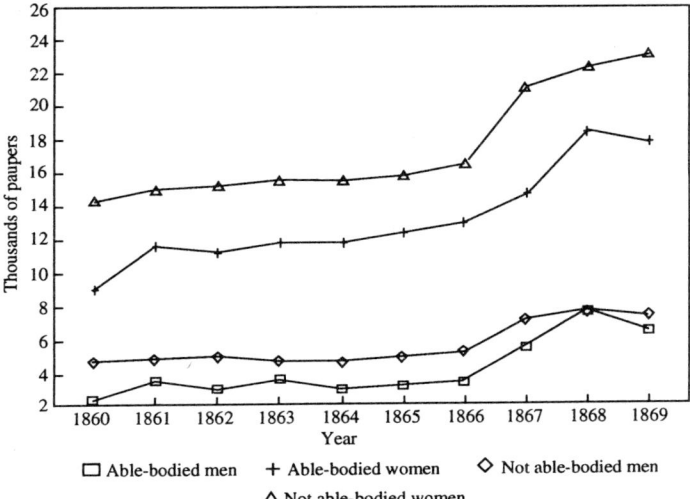

Figure 2.3 Metropolitan outdoor adults (excluding lunatics, the insane, etc.) (1860–1869).

and about the relative disadvantages of outdoor relief. It seemed logical to the PLB that they should enlist the co-operation of the Charity Organisation Society, the recently formed group supported by influential elites committed to rationalizing charity by inviting them to co-ordinate responses from official and voluntary relief sectors. G.J. Goschen claimed that this combination would provide an effective spur towards self-sufficiency for the deserving poor, with the workhouse remaining for the residuum. It was because of what the PLB saw as a dangerous trend by metropolitan guardians to increase out-relief numbers as a palliative to those without jobs that London was chosen as the logical forerunner for the national campaign in the early 1870s of what became known as the crusade against outdoor relief.

NATIONAL DEVELOPMENT OF THE CRUSADE

Poor Law historiography has underplayed the social impact of the 1870s crusade against outdoor relief. McKinnon expresses surprise that the crusade has 'received little attention' and has emphasized its importance in any attempt to understand earlier periods.[29] Williams considers that Poor

Law activities in the 1870s have been insufficiently researched and dismisses suggestions that during this period the Poor Law can sensibly be recognized as a precursor for the welfare state. He argues that during the crusade the Poor Law was 'an apparatus that intertwined repression, classification, special treatment, and surveillance'.[30]

Misleading implications have arisen from some commentators who have ventured into mentioning the Poor Law crusade. Digby suggests that the tougher attitude against outdoor relief claimants was especially directed 'against adult able-bodied males'.[31] Bruce considered that 'from the 1870s the policy was increasingly adopted to confining deterrence to the able-bodied ...'[32] But the alleged droves of robust loafers were largely illusory in that the 'shiftless, able-bodied idler always seemed on closer investigation to fade into a mass of orphans, widows, sick or aged, unemployed or exploited workers'.[33] The persistent common characteristic of official attacks over many years to focus on outdoor relief to lazy able-bodied males have little substance. In the USA as well as in Britain, there is usually a 'lack of correspondence between the actual demography of relief and reformers' images'.[34]

Before the crusade got under way, the PLB inadvertently went some way to confirming the dubious nature of official statements that many able-bodied idle-jacks were gaining benefits. They corrected impressions 'prevailing among persons not practically conversant with the system' that many of those termed 'adult able-bodied pauper' were actually capable of work. As the PLB explained 'only a small proportion of such persons' were able to 'earn their own livelihood' at the time of receiving relief because most so-called able-bodied men were genuinely '*temporary sick*'.[35] Furthermore, when the sick out-relief recipient was head of a family, their dependents were also recorded individually as able-bodied outdoor paupers.

In any case, able-bodied adult paupers involved only a small part of those receiving outdoor relief. Of the 824 600 outdoor paupers in England on 1 January 1872 only 3.6 per cent were able-bodied men, including those who were temporarily sick. In contrast, 31.2 per cent were destitute old women or were suffering permanent disability, 13.5 per cent were men similarly disadvantaged, 35.2 per cent were children, 4.4 per cent were lunatics or insane persons or idiots, 7.5 per cent were women with dependent children, 3.8 per cent were wives whose husbands were absent or in receipt of benefit and 0.7 per cent were single women.[36] Table 2.1 which lists adult able-bodied outdoor paupers shows that most men in this category received relief on account of 'sickness, accident or infirmity' with only a small minority claiming 'want of work' dole.

Table 2.1 Adult able-bodied paupers in receipt of relief in England 1 January 1872

Total in unions		Description
199	(1)	Adult males (married or single) relieved in cases of sudden and urgent necessity.
20 181	(2)	Adult males relieved in cases of their own sickness, accident, or infirmity.
7 281	(3)	Adult males relieved on account of sickness, accident or infirmity of any of the family, or a funeral.
2 132	(4)	Adult males (married or single) relieved on account of want of work or other causes.
24 148	(5)	Wife of adult male in items 1, 2, 3 or 4, resident with male.
60 274	(6)	Widows.
5 839	(7)	Single women without children.
1 516	(8)	Mothers of illegitimate children.
1 650	(9)	Wives with husband in gaol.
518	(10)	Wives of soldiers, sailors and marines.
4 996	(11)	Resident wife of non-resident male.
128 734		Total

Sum of categories (5) to (11) = 98 941 Women
Sum of categories (1) to (4) = 29 793 Men

Total outdoor Paupers 1st January 1872 = 824 600

Sources: *Accounts and Papers*, BPP 1872 (c387), LI, pp.4–5; and *Accounts and Papers*, BPP 1872, (c126-B), LI, pp.1–3.

In 1871 the PLB repeated official allegations that across the nation carelessness had crept into the local administration of outdoor relief with the perceived danger of disturbing the labour market by augmenting low wages. One of their inspectors, E.H. Wodehouse, claimed: 'I do not recollect that I met a single case in the course of the inquiry in which total destitution was relieved out of the workhouse ... in every case, therefore, the Guardians must be considered as supplementing income.'[37]

When the Local Government Board (LGB) succeeded the PLB in 1871 it became a major ministry of state supervising most local government activities. The LGB President had a position of seniority and power amongst government departments and usually enjoyed Cabinet status. It might be expected that comparative small-fry like local guardians would have been easily pressurised into adopting the enhanced LGB objections to outdoor relief. This is especially so when recognizing the tight LGB constraints over local administrators, including the power to issue binding orders and circulars extending over administrative minutiae, the control of local Poor Law officer appointments, the authority over building works, the compelling of detailed information to be forwarded regularly, the power of audit with the right to surcharge guardians personally for profligacy, the enforcement of official enquiries and, perhaps of most importance, the authority for their diligent inspectorate to attend any Poor Law meeting.[38] In any case, regardless of this strait-jacket over legal, administrative and financial procedures, it would be reasonable to expect that the LGB would naturally receive broad support from guardians who were themselves pillars of local society sharing many Smilesian attitudes about individual motivation.

The LGB crusade was triggered by their Secretary Mr H. Fleming in a circular dated 2 December 1871 which expressed the emergent board's confidence about how outdoor relief would soon be drastically reduced. Fleming called attention to the 'large increase' in outdoor relief over 'the last few years', which the LGB regarded 'with much anxiety'.[39] The fault was said not to be legislative but was entirely attributable to slack local Poor Law administration disbursing indiscriminate and demoralizing alms. He argued that the most important item in the administration of outdoor relief was the application of 'an efficient workhouse test to all able-bodied applicants for relief, whether male or female ...'[40] He emphasised the alleged dangers of providing the working-man with 'the certainty of obtaining outdoor relief in his own home, whenever he may ask for it' in that it 'extinguishes in the mind of the labourer all motive for husbanding his resources'.[41]

In spite of Fleming's moral overtones there were clear signs that economic considerations had most priority with the LGB. They believed that out-relief was the 'branch of expenditure' affording them 'the best prospect of effecting any material reduction in the burthen of pauperism'.[42] According to Fleming, the growth in cost of out-relief during the 1860s even after 'making every allowance for the increase of population, stagnation in trades, and temporary disturbances in the labour market, variations in seasons, and other causes' was so 'great as to excite apprehension' (see Table 2.2).[43] At first sight, the 20.6 per cent growth in out-relief expenditure to £3 633 051 over the decade, does justify official caution. However, Thomson claims the LGB were unnecessarily alarmist in that the national population upsurge during the 1860s, coupled with a 10 per cent retail price growth between 1863 and 1868, implies there may actually have been a unit cost reduction in real terms.[44]

Table 2.2 Outdoor relief and outdoor paupers in England and Wales 1861–70

Year end: Lady Day	Outdoor relief £	Average number of outdoor paupers	Out paupers: population %
1861	3 012 251	758 055	3.8
1862	3 155 251	784 906	3.9
1863	3 574 136	942 475	4.6
1864	3 466 392	881 217	4.3
1865	3 258 813	820 586	3.9
1866	3 196 685	783 376	3.7
1867	3 358 351	794 236	3.7
1868	3 620 284	842 600	3.9
1869	3 677 379	860 400	4.0
1870	3 633 051	876 000	4.0

Source: *1st AR, LGB, op. cit.*, p.64.

Although Fleming's circular sparking the out-relief crusade had set the scene with images of idle characterless able-bodied applicants, it also considered other applicants which were claimed to have been treated with illegal leniency and should now be 'well administered'.[45] These categories included single able-bodied women with or without illegitimate children, women deserted by their husbands for the first twelve months, able-bodied widows with one child, and widows with more than one child who should be given the offer for some children to be taken into the workhouse. Guardians were urged to follow the recommendations: the workhouse test should be strictly applied, outdoor relief should be granted with great discretion and never exceeding a three-month period, labour-yard relief to able-bodied men was to be from week to week, outdoor relief should never be granted without a relieving officer having first visited the house, compulsory maintenance of paupers should be by relations legally liable, and that recommendations by medical officers for meat or stimulants should be regarded as equivalent to orders for additional relief.[46] Fleming advised that any expenditure incurred through the appointment of additional relieving officers to 'ensure a sound system of outdoor relief involving appropriate zeal and vigour' would 'almost certainly be more than counterbalanced by a diminution in the cost of outdoor relief'.[47]

When launching their crusade against outdoor relief the LGB published data comparing the performance of unions selected with respect to the number of outdoor paupers and the expenditure per head of population. This was intended to demonstrate how some unions, such as Atcham (Salop), already had praiseworthy low out-relief costs whereas other named unions had inexcusably high expenditure. Comparative information of this type became a regular feature of LGB reports and of Poor Law Conferences which through the 1870s and 1880s published 'every form of paper adverse to outdoor relief'.[48]

The motivating moral principle driving the crusade was that while the present generation of labourers may suffer transitional personal hardship, they would eventually benefit through the miracle of self-help. This would be good for the labourer, good for his family and good for the nation at large. The LGB were 'reinforced by the conviction that the doctrine of the survival of the fittest could be successfully applied to human society'.[49] Both the statutory and organized voluntary sectors had parallel views with J.R. Pretyman who, writing in the 1870s, recognized poverty as being the 'outcome of men's self-interests, passions, vices and follies' and 'like disease and other ills to which flesh is heir' could not be 'prevented or abolished by any human contrivance' so that 'the only chance of the minimisation and mitigation of poverty lies in self-help, supplemented whenever that may fail, by benevolence'.[50]

The response to the crusade from guardians during the early years must have encouraged the LGB in terms of the numerical reduction of those on outdoor relief. They were also pleased that there was little evidence of working-class protests about the crusade of the intensity engendered earlier in the century by various attempts to constrain outdoor relief.[51] This may be simply explained by the government's crusade being timely and opportune. It is also possible that the passivity of workers, in spite of strengthened trades councils and unions, was because the social emancipation of the working class was at a stage where their leaders would not countenance misconduct incompatible 'with earning the respect of their neighbours'.[52]

Despite the relative calm, the LGB sensed that their proposals 'may not have been received without being questioned'.[53] William Fowler, Chairman of Aston union, was openly contemptuous of the LGB's tougher approach and scorned stricter boards of guardians, 'a majority of whom are philanthropists of that strange type that would, on principle, starve to death the present generation in the hope of improving the moral and social condition of the next', and believed such a principle was capable of becoming 'a terrible engine of oppression and cruelty'.[54]

George Culley, an assistant LGB inspector, provided a rare example of a senior government official expressing an awareness that there could be social, economic or demographic circumstances whereby, even in adjacent unions, large and justifiable differences could occur in outdoor pauper statistics. Culley explained how some unions had bigger proportions of the weak and elderly, while others, because of high accident rates in areas involved in dangerous industrial activities like mining, shipbuilding and chemical manufacture, often had more widows with young families.[55] Further reflections of this nature from within their own ranks were not encouraged by the LGB.[56] They preferred to believe that neither 'locality, trade, seasons, weather, or population' interfered with the 'universal applicability' of the crusade principles.[57]

In close alignment with LGB wishes Henry Longley, one of their most prestigious inspectors, recommended in 1874 further tightening of out-relief restrictions against widows, the disabled and the aged.[58] He argued that no widow should receive outdoor relief: when in receipt of a regular weekly wage, where their earnings were below the market rate, where there was reasonable belief they had not truly stated their means, where they were without a home or what the authorities might consider a satisfactory home, where there was reason to believe they were of drunken or immoral habits, where they had received out-relief for a specified period without making suitable progress towards independence or where they had refused a definite offer of employment. Nor did Longley consider that disabled people, in which he included the aged, should be offered outdoor relief where their home was such that they could not be properly cared for, where they had a bad character, where it appeared they had relatives able to contribute to their maintenance or where they had made no provision for their future wants when earning reasonable wages.[59]

Longley was solidly behind the Goschenian edict advocating close working relationships between the Poor Law and organized charity. He believed relief given of right 'must tend to encourage improvidence to a greater degree than that which, being a matter not of right, but a voluntary, precarious, and intermittent charity ...'[60] All guardians were recommended to use the technique long practised at unions like Atcham where rules were displayed publicly to deter relief applications. Whereas the 1834 Amendment Act aimed firmly, but passively, at deterring able-bodied males from applying for out-relief by offering the workhouse test, Longley's prescription emphasized the need for 'knowledge by the poor'.[61] Fundamental to Longley's philosophy was the unshakeable belief that the lower orders of society lacked the integrity and moral strength of the better-off. The same rectitude motivated the strictness at the Bradfield union where the board emphasized that 'those who are placed in a position of trust cannot be too careful to restrain the natural tendency of human nature to be liberal at the expense of others'.[62]

An LGB memorandum 'Administration of Out Relief' demonstrated the extent to which the principles of the 1871 Fleming circular had 'operated beneficially' over its first six years with a 28.6 per cent decrease in national out-relief cost from £3 663 970 to £2 616 465.[63] But the LGB's main thrust was to compare how within the national reduction there remained unacceptably massive response differences between unions with some 'correctly' interpreting the legislation while others were not. Mr J. Sclater Booth, the LGB president, considered it 'especially worthy of remark that, so far as the Inspectors have been able to ascertain', the reduction in outdoor paupers had 'been arrived at without any real hardship to the poor'.[64] He then offered the opinion that before long non-resident relief 'might be almost entirely discontinued' because it was evident that 'if the proper means were taken, no inconsiderable sums might be recovered from the relatives of paupers towards their maintenance'.[65] The advantages of relieving the remaining outdoor paupers in 'kind' rather than money was encouraged because in 'the rural districts the greater proportion was spent in the beer shops, and in the towns was expended in the gin shops'.[66]

Sclater Booth was not to know that from around 1877 the success of the crusade was to falter nationally. Although the LGB still continued with their strong support of the doctrine of deterrence there was beginning to be acceptance in the late 1870s amongst some sections of government that, particularly in manufacturing districts, economic depression could be a bona fide mitigating factor for outdoor relief applicants. Cyclical industrial downturns had seen huge surges in unemployment with accompanying worries of social disequilibrium from working-class demands for support in the absence of work. In the agricultural districts attitudes were also changing. There was now broad agreement that the poor were not inherently lazy and that Fred Bettesworth typified agricultural workers with his opinion that 'a man's never so happy, to my way o' thinkin', as when he's goin' to his day's work reglar'.[67]

The next chapter examines how 'anti-outdoor relief' unions justified their crusading actions and how these differed from the great majority of guardians who in the late 1870s refused to further tighten their constraints.

3 The Provincial Crusade: Results and Reactions

THE SELECTION OF POOR LAW UNIONS FOR ANALYSIS

Focus now centres on a number of provincial Poor Law unions which either had the reputation of applying strict anti-outdoor relief policies during the LGB crusade or where such strictures might reasonably have been expected because of the establishment of a nearby Charity Organisation Society. When viewed in the context of the national pattern and accepting the law of averages, other unions must have been unusually lenient in dispensing out-relief. The majority of unions which, after acquiescence in the early years, tended to cock a snook at the stricter out-relief doctrines were rarely featured in LGB Annual Reports or at Poor Law Conferences, other than to provide objects of derisory criticism. In contrast, to quote the Webbs, throughout the 1870s and 1880s the few 'bright and shining examples of "orthodox Poor Law policy" were made the subject of perpetual laudation; they were advertised in the publications of the LGB, and quoted endlessly by Poor Law Inspectors; they were studied at COS meetings and discussed at Poor Law Conferences, without, in the result, finding imitators among the 600 other Boards of Guardians ...'[1] The general reduction of out-relief paupers in the early years of the crusade indicates that over this period the Webbs' estimate of 600 non-conforming unions was an exaggeration. However, it became much nearer reality from the mid 1870s when around 90 per cent of Poor Law unions largely disregarded further LGB exhortations to reduce outdoor relief dramatically. This realization provides an essential backcloth for the following discussions concerning the strict unions. By the end of the century the chairman of one formerly strict Poor Law union was claiming that those following the 'guidance of the Charity Organisation Society can be actually counted on the fingers of one hand'.[2]

William Chance, the Hon. Secretary of the Poor Law Conference and one of the most unremitting propagandists of the strict LGB policies, was still campaigning in 1895 to direct guardians towards 'better administration' and listed unions which had followed an 'anti-relief policy' from the 1870s.[3] The non-metropolitan unions listed by Chance will be used as examples of those which in his words either 'practically give no relief' or administered 'outdoor relief strictly'.[4] They include the rural unions at Wallingford and at Bradfield (both in Berkshire),

Brixworth (Northants), St Neots (Huntingdon) and Atcham/Shrewsbury (Salop) together with the urban unions at Reading, Manchester and Birmingham. According to Goschen's Minute of 1869 and subsequent LGB expectations in the early 1870s, an important adjunct to the stricter interpretations of the Poor Law was that organized charity would be locally available to support deserving cases rejected by Poor Law officials as not being eligible for legal benefits. Consequently the second group of Poor Law unions examined here are located nearby provincial enthusiasts determined to apply COS concepts and whose local influence might have been expected to persuade guardians to support the LGB crusade. They include Birkenhead, Brighton, Leamington (Warwick union), Liverpool, Oxford and Southampton. Each of these localities featured in COS publications over the years as provincial examples of how the London influence was seemingly being beneficially applied in the provinces. In a few urban centres, notably Liverpool and Manchester, prior to 1870 there had already been long-term formalized attempts to structure local philanthropy which later moved towards absorbing COS ideology, as discussed in Chapters 4, 5 and 6.

Figure 3.1 shows that nationally the LGB crusade succeeded in sharply reducing the numbers of outdoor paupers from 1871 to 1877. The average of

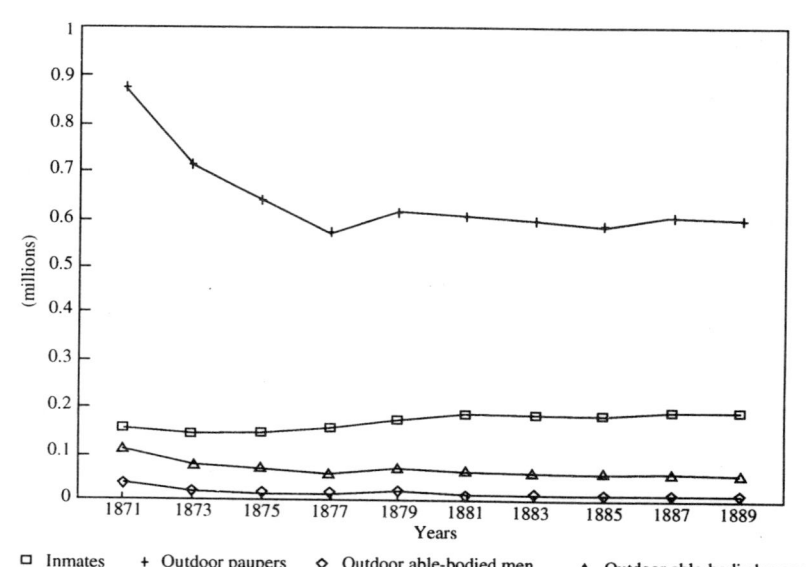

Figure 3.1 Paupers: England and Wales (average of daily counts 1870–1889).

the 1 January and 1 July daily counts of outdoor paupers in England dropped from 874 069 in 1871 to only 567 207 in 1877.[5] From that time there was a slight rebound in numbers and throughout the 1880s the number on out-relief hovered around the 600 000 mark in spite of repeated LGB exhortations demanding a tougher approach. The population of England and Wales increased from 22 701 137 in 1871 to 29 407 629 twenty years later.

As discussed in the previous chapter, even at the start of the crusade the number of adult able-bodied paupers within the totals was small and most of these were certified sick at the time they were given relief. As the LGB emphasized in 1890, 'when persons who are relieved are ordinarily able-bodied, they are classed as able-bodied paupers, although they may be in receipt of relief on account of their own sickness, accident, or infirmity'. They went on to say that 'the greater part of the adult male paupers in receipt of outdoor relief who are entered as able-bodied in the returns are relieved for one or other of these causes'.[6]

By 1877 the number of able-bodied men nationally on out-relief had dropped from nearly 30 000 at the outset of the crusade to just over 13 000. Then the number pushed back towards the 20 000 level in 1880 from when it settled to around 16 000 for the rest of the 1880s.[7] As we saw in the previous chapter many more able-bodied women received outdoor relief than men. The average daily number in 1871 of 108 368 dropped to a nadir of 59 661 in 1877 before recovering to stay in the 60 000s throughout the 1880s. As can be deduced from Table 2.1, the greatest numerical reduction amongst those categorized as adult able-bodied females were mothers who had lost their husbands through either death, desertion, gaol or military service and who prior to the crusade would have expected to have been relieved without the need to enter the workhouse.

The number of disadvantaged paupers hit by the crusade was substantially greater than those who were able-bodied. The daily average number of men relieved outdoors who were not able-bodied in 1871 was 114 847 and this was squeezed down to 74 691 by 1877.[8] The fall in the number of physically disadvantaged women was even greater. In 1871, there were 262 800 women receiving outdoor relief on the average day in England who were either old, disabled or chronically sick. By 1877 the number had been reduced by 69 026. From then, the numbers of not able-bodied for both sexes remained reasonably constant and were rather less directly affected by the economic fluctuations of the late 1870s and 1880s than were the able-bodied groups. It will of course be recognized that although outdoor pauper numbers remained little changed in the 1880s, when considered against the decadal population surge of 13 per cent there had been a decline in the ratio of outdoor paupers to population.

ANTI-OUTDOOR RELIEF UNIONS AND THEIR SPECIFIC RULES

Writing in 1895, William Chance shared the general COS disappointment that Britain remained full of inefficiently administered Poor Law unions. Among the 'few brilliant exceptions' was the Atcham union in Shropshire where strict reforms had been in vogue since 1834.[9] By 1858 Atcham guardians had reduced outdoor pauper numbers to equal that of workhouse inmates with the proportion of paupers in total to population less than one-third the national average. Atcham guardians were held in such esteem by the central Poor Law authorities that one of the LGB's first decisions was to incorporate into Atcham the more heavily populated contiguous Shrewsbury union which itself already practised a fairly rigorous out-relief policy. The LGB were soon able to congratulate themselves on the amalgamation and a further fall in pauper numbers which was said to be 'striking' and wholly attributable to the 'more careful system of administration'.[10]

The Atcham rules meant giving no outdoor relief to (a) those renting more than one half an acre of land, (b) orphan children, (c) non-residents, (d) those without work, (e) those in dirty cottages, (f) those paying annual cottage rents of £4 10s. or more, and (g) no clothing was included as part of out-relief 'except to children going in service'. For funerals, the Atcham union provided 'everything or nothing' in that they refused to supply a coffin and then 'allowed the relatives to do the rest'.[11] The LGB were sufficiently constrained about reactionary criticism as to report that a Mr Baker, one of the Atcham relieving officers, had assured them that although the guardians had 'carried out the Law with strictness they have given the most considerate attention to the claims of the poor'.[12]

The LGB also lavished praise on the Brixworth union. This is another instance, exemplified elsewhere by individuals such as Thomas Chalmers, Edward Denison, Octavia Hill and Samuel Barnett, of how exceptional vigilance, determination and energy by a limited number of people appears to achieve extraordinary results when committed to an ideological concept typified by that of the COS. It was Albert Pell MP and the Revd. W. Bury who dominated reformers at Brixworth right through to the 1890s.

The Brixworth guardians in January 1873 appointed an investigatory committee, under Pell's chairmanship, to devise proposals for limiting the union's out-relief burden. The Pell committee focused immediately on the 'not able-bodied' where 'as much as anywhere ... imposition and abuses prevail'.[13] The 'partially disabled' were said to often develop idleness so that in future only 'deprivation of limbs, or eyesight, or extreme old age' would qualify for outdoor relief and then for a limited period. Pell reminded guardians elsewhere that they were not authorized dispensers of philanthropy and suggested they would be well advised to co-operate with organized local charity.[14]

Brixworth guardians saw the need to inculcate the working classes about their responsibilities towards even poorer relatives. They attempted to mitigate any impression that their banning of various female categories who traditionally had benefited from outdoor relief was hard-hearted by emphasizing their willingness to take excess children into the workhouse. Conscious that this itself may seem a 'harsh proceeding' in that it divided a family, the Brixworth board gained comfort by pointing out that such methods had been used elsewhere with 'marked success'. They explained that by their proposals 'the woman is set free for work' with the knowledge that her children taken into the workhouse would be 'better fed, better disciplined, and better and (to the ratepayer) more cheaply taught'.[15] One child was usually left with the mother to support 'lest she forget her dual role' with no attempt to provide day-care facilities.[16] Another nuance to Brixworth stringencies was their incorporation of the full value of benefit club allowances when assessing outdoor relief with the aim of motivating increased club subscription rates so that eventually they would provide self-supporting payments to sick members. Brixworth's stricter approach allegedly encouraged the 'thrifty and industrious' while informing the poor who 'would not save or who had lived notoriously vicious lives' that they would be offered nothing but the workhouse.[17] Ratepayers would not be the only beneficiaries of stricter out-relief policies as apparently the poor would also eventually gain by being forced to recognize the value of 'providence, truthfulness, industry and independence'.[18]

Slackness in medical relief provision also concerned the Brixworth board because it 'provided a fruitful source of pauperism' by circumventing the system, and to overcome this they recommended an amalgamation of existing medical clubs.[19] They then pressurized applicants into becoming club members by abolishing outside Poor Law medical support except on a loan basis. In support of this plan, the Revd. Bury instanced the additional Brixworth expenses caused during 1873–4 from 'fevers and epidemics' which he predicted could possibly leave 'a residuum of pauperism as a lasting burden upon the whole Union'.[20] He believed that the poor could be made to recognize the evils of pauperism and at the same time improve their awareness of sanitation, by requiring them to contribute to the poor rate. Bury did not mention that the increased sickness among the Brixworth poor in 1873–4 may conceivably have been related to the recent withdrawal of traditional outdoor relief from those already struggling on life's economic margins.

Brixworth's 'complete and able report' on their stricter measures was 'received with much satisfaction' by the LGB.[21] The high Brixworth ratio of outdoor to indoor paupers of 12 : 1 in January 1873 dropped in twelve months to 8 : 1. Bury thought it especially praiseworthy that the change had occurred in spite of a local trade decline and believed the Brixworth guardians should be exonerated from 'any suspicion of harshness'.[22] He did accept that there may have 'been a certain amount of suffering, often endured in silence' but blamed this anguish on the profligacy of earlier guardians and their failure to encourage providence among the poor.[23]

Much the same attrition of outdoor relief occurred at other strict unions with differences of detail affected by local factors and guardians' whims. Bradfield Poor Law board in 1872 concentrated on making most of their small amount of out-relief on a loan basis. This included: midwifery orders, sickness relief to single able-bodied women with illegitimate children, and relief to females deserted by their husbands.[24] When the effects of the crusade began to wane in 1877 a fresh dose of reforming zeal was introduced at Bradfield by Mr T. Bland-Garland.[25] He thought it 'obvious that medical relief was one of the most fertile causes of pauperism' and persuaded his board colleagues to extend the loan principle to general medical attention.[26] The result was that whereas in the mid 1870s annual medical relief orders at Bradfield union had exceeded 700, within a few years the applications had 'nearly ceased'.[27] Bradfield guardians also spared no trouble in extracting contributions from relatives towards the maintenance of paupers. The Revd. C.D. Francis at nearby Banbury union concurred that outdoor relief tended 'to undermine that sense of duty we owe to parents, which nature and religion has planted within us'.[28]

Another twist of the crusading tourniquet at Bradfield was the late 1870s decision to provide no out-relief for new applicants. Within a few years, the few outdoor paupers still on their books were mainly aged 70 years or more. Easily their youngest outside pauper was Sarah Knight, aged 34, who had been a charge on the rates for 22 years.[29] The rejection of new out-relief supplicants fell especially hard on widows with dependent children. Of course, as Bradfield guardians pointed out, workhouse accommodation was available if they were really destitute. When others argued that the horror of stigmatization prevented acceptance of the workhouse offer, Bland-Garland claimed *'the cruelty of driving the poor into the house cannot be said to exist when they do not go into it'*.[30] Bradfield guardians reported towards the end of the 1880s that 'of the 48 widows with 182 children who have since applied for relief, no widows and only 8 children are in the workhouse'.[31] He refuted allegations that the measures were draconian and explained how the widely held belief amongst the poor whereby widows would receive out-relief had 'contributed very largely to pauperism' by leading to 'recklessly improvident marriages'.[32]

For those guardians wishing to tighten outdoor relief in urban areas, the stringent procedures included in the rules at Manchester became a model. Formally adopted in 1875 after some years of experiment, they were copied not only by Lancashire unions but also as far afield as Brighton, Carmarthen and Ruthin.[33] As in rural areas females without husbands became a main focus as did poor people residing with relatives where the combined family income was considered sufficient to support the applicant, whether or not such relatives were legally liable.

When Birmingham guardians first adopted a stricter out-relief in 1871, their outdoor : indoor pauper ratio of 3.9 : 1 was high compared with other industrial cities. Although tougher attitudes sharply reduced out-relief numbers, the 1878 slump in trade compounded by severe weather forced guardians to take special action as the poor clamoured for relief. Guardians then provided emergency work facilities for those outdoor relief applicants satisfying a labour test.[34] A large labour shed for men, oakum work rooms for women and a refurbished disused factory were among the temporary expedients. The severe discipline resembled the infamous Poor Law institutions at Poplar and Kensington.[35]

By 1880 the number on outdoor relief at Birmingham climbed to 9354 which was some 1500 more than at the outset of the crusade. Warehouses were acquired to store furniture owned by the unemployed who were forced into the workhouse until they were able to re-establish their home.[36] The board's insistence that the families of the temporarily unemployed should be declared inmates seemed very reasonable to the Birmingham COS but from the wider public it caused 'an outcry against the Guardians and Relieving Officers'.[37]

As trade improved from mid 1882, Birmingham out-relief numbers again renewed their decline through the rest of the decade under persistent guardian pressure. When in February 1886 the guardians were asked at the instigation of Joseph Chamberlain whether the numbers applying for outdoor relief were a true indication of possible distress among workpeople, they were able to reply truthfully that numbers had actually decreased. They did qualify their response by mentioning an awareness of a 'considerable amount of distress amongst the artisan classes generally, but as they will not apply to the parish a fund has been opened by a committee of citizens, headed by the mayor, to assist them ...'[38]

There were also other isolated, less publicized, reforming boards committed to reducing outdoor relief. Take the example of Reigate union which was proud to have adopted its own strict 'definite Rules ... in administering out-relief' even prior to the Fleming circular.[39] Reigate's intentions were featured at the inaugural Surrey Poor Law Conference and appeared to gain support for a tougher approach from guardians in attendance. But this broader enthusiasm among delegates seems to have been grounded on a temporary group bonding factor helped by a convivial luncheon at a nearby hotel 'prepared in the style which has rendered' the proprietor 'famous'.[40] On sober reflection few Surrey unions actually adopted a commensurately tough policy. Indeed the fact that 'many Boards of Guardians' across the country strongly 'objected to be bound by the rules' and preferred to deal with every case 'on its own merits' was a source of persistent exasperation for the LGB, their surrogates, and their reforming COS supporters.[41]

RESULTS OF THE CRUSADE IN ANTI-OUTDOOR RELIEF UNIONS

We turn now from the rules to the material details of how the crusade actually affected the numbers of paupers relieved at the various anti-outdoor relief unions. Figure 3.2 shows as an example the number of outdoor paupers and the number of workhouse inmates in the Brixworth Poor Law union between 1870 and 1890. It typifies the distinguishing characteristic of the rural 'anti-outdoor relief' unions, namely their persistence to reduce outdoor numbers through to the 1880s. Even then, in spite of their fervour, unions of this type were occasionally obliged to temporarily reverse the policy when faced with destitute families determined to starve rather than become stigmatized as workhouse inmates. These pressures from below are discussed later together with indications that some 'strict' guardians deviously camouflaged the social need for them to backtrack on their rigorous policies.

The LGB and their COS supporters were quite clear that in the strict rural unions the reductions in outdoor pauper numbers were dictated more by attitudes and decisions of local Poor Law officials than by economic, social or environmental factors. Mr R.I. Dansey used Bradfield, Brixworth and St Neots as admirable examples of how in strict unions outdoor pauper numbers had been minimized. He contrasted the performance of more traditionally administered unions such as those at Hungerford, Woodstock, St Ives and Nantwich with similar socio-economic conditions but where the numbers on outdoor relief had remained much greater. Dansey argued that if Nantwich guardians were permitted to use their 'lax' methods at

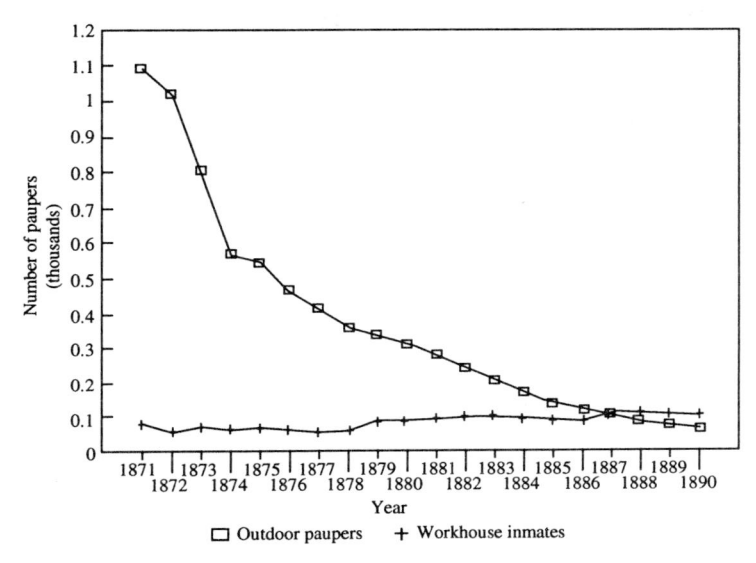

Figure 3.2 Brixworth Poor Law union (average of 1 January and 1 July day counts 1870–1890).

Bradfield they would 'transform about 506 independent persons into 506 paupers, and, vice versa, if the Bradfield Board take over at Nantwich they would, by acting on fixed principles, reduce the number of outdoor paupers by about 1,670'.[42] He relished Pell's announcement that 'the wine, the brandy, the gin, the stout, the ale, the cod-liver oil, the quinine, the black dose, the mutton chop, the beef tea and the medical extras chargeable on the rates' traditionally provided by the Brixworth union up to the early 1870s were all 'curiosities of history, but not the concern of 1890'.[43]

Figure 3.3 shows for Brixworth the numerical trends for various pauper categories receiving out-relief disregarding those who were mentally disadvantaged. In 1871 less than 8 per cent of Brixworth outdoor paupers were able-bodied men and in common with other unions most of these were suffering temporary sickness certificated by a medical practitioner approved by the Poor Law authorities. Just over 15 per cent of Brixworth outdoor paupers during 1871 were classified as able-bodied females many of whom were widows with dependent children. By the late 1870s no able-bodied man at Brixworth benefited from out-relief no matter what their need and out-relief for able-bodied women was also well on the way to being eradicated. Figure 3.3 shows quite clearly that the vast majority of those receiving Brixworth out-relief at the outset of the crusade were not able-bodied.

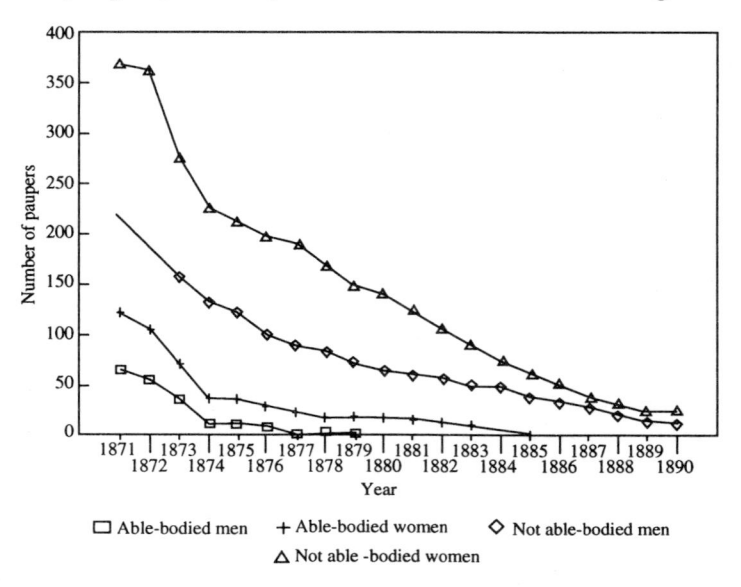

Figure 3.3 Brixworth outdoor paupers (average of 1 January and 1 July day counts 1870–1890).

The Revd. Dr J.C. Cox who succeeded to the Revd. W. Bury at Brixworth exposed how his predecessor had for years been determined to go to extraordinary lengths 'not to admit the necessity of out-relief from a State-provided fund'.[44] Cox explained that when finding themselves 'face to face with a determination, in not a few cases, to die rather than enter the Workhouse', Bury and three collaborators had devised 'The Private Fund'. From this fund surreptitious 'pittances were doled out' to 'prevent the scandal of their continuous application and continuous rejection' by those responsible for the provision of Poor Law outdoor relief at Brixworth.[45]

Within five years of the crusade's launch at the newly combined unions of Atcham and Shrewsbury out-relief had approached the previous independent Atcham situation with an outdoor : indoor pauper ratio of unity. By 1880 there were about twice as many workhouse inmates as there were outdoor paupers. As at other strict unions it was those who were disadvantaged in some way while remaining of sound mind who mainly absorbed the remorseless pressure. At both Bradfield and at St Neots, the number of outdoor paupers was reduced during the 1880s to a level similar to that of workhouse inmates and although Wallingford guardians did not attain quite the same level of success, they attracted LGB praise for what was seen as a commendable effort.

Turning now from the strict rural unions, we will consider some of their urban peers which were also in the minority. Reading was one such strict union where a new workhouse completed in 1867 to accommodate 250 inmates was already overflowing within a few years. During the crusading 1870s and 1880s, sufficient Reading supplicants were forced to accept 'the offer of the house' as to require further workhouse extensions to accommodate a total of 400 inmates. On the other hand, there was a steady reduction in the number of outdoor paupers through the 1870s. The lack of local jobs then led to an upward trend before being again pushed downwards by renewed pressure from guardians assisted by a more buoyant local economy. By 1890 the Reading indoor : outdoor pauper ratio was seen by the LGB as a commendable unity.

Figure 3.4 illustrates that Manchester guardians were already reducing out-relief numbers before formally implementing their widely quoted rules in 1875. Most Manchester outdoor paupers at the beginning of the crusade were women but within seven years their numbers had nearly been reduced to those of men which themselves had fallen considerably. Figures 3.5 and 3.6 indicate that at times of exceptional distress as in the late 1870s and again in 1886–7 the numbers of able-bodied men and women receiving out-relief at Manchester leapt sharply, in common with other industrially based unions. In contrast, the not able-bodied numbers were pushed ever downwards. Alexander McDougall Jnr of the

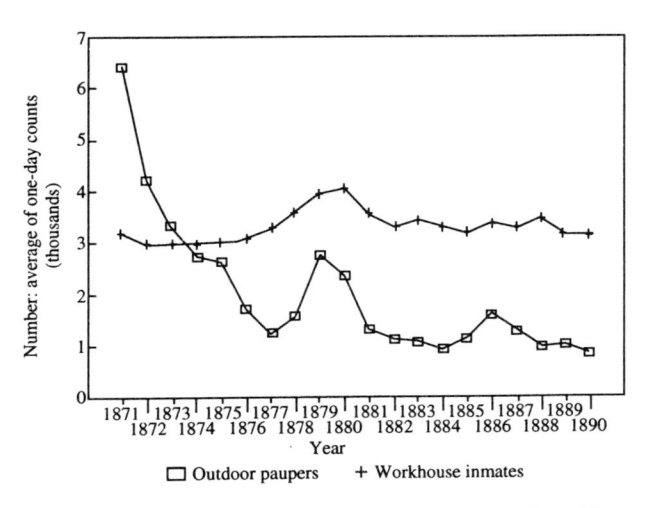

Figure 3.4 Manchester Poor Law union: outdoor paupers and workhouse inmates (1870–1890).

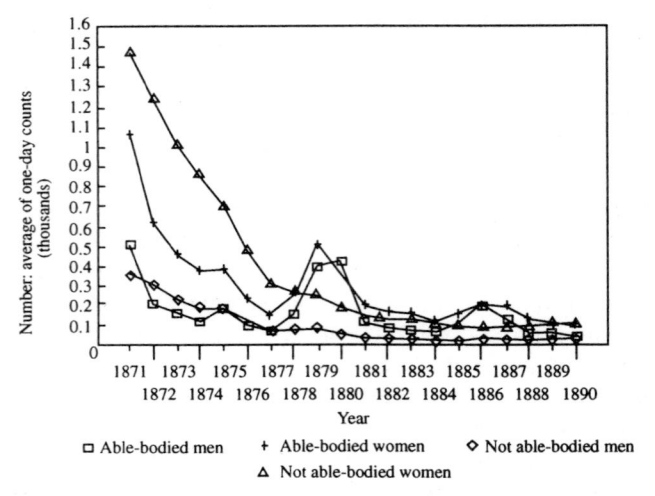

Figure 3.5 Manchester Poor Law union: adults on outdoor relief (1870–1890).

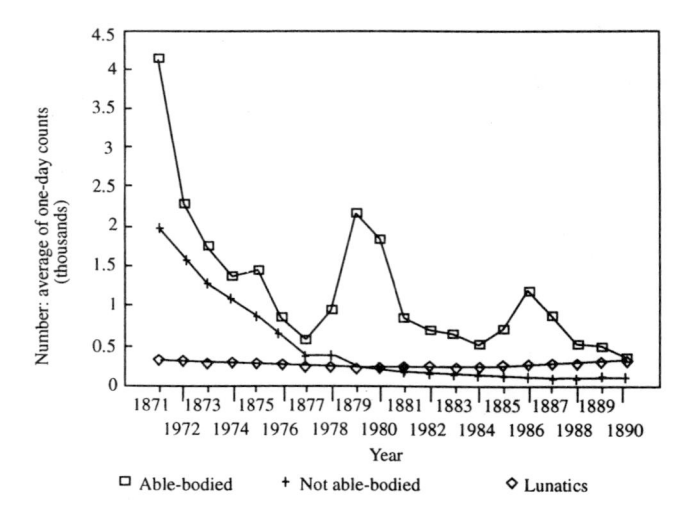

Figure 3.6 Manchester Poor Law union: out-relief – adults and children (1870–1890).

Manchester Poor Law board claimed that '51.24 per cent' of pauperism was 'brought about by causes directly arising from drinking habits'.[46]

A characteristic shared by Manchester with most unions, was that throughout the two decades 1870-90, the numbers categorized as lunatics, insane persons and idiots increased as rationalized institutions were developed for mentally disadvantaged people. These appeared in LGB statistics as 'outside' paupers which meant that at Manchester where the mentally deficient were less than 5 per cent of outdoor paupers on 1 July 1870, the situation twenty years later was that more than 41 per cent were in this category. Even then the total number on out-relief at Manchester was small with only about 16 per cent of paupers relieved outdoors by the end of 1890.[47] Both the contiguous unions, at Chorlton and Salford, were distinctly more responsive than Manchester with their outdoor benefits relieving 62.5 per cent and 49.5 per cent respectively in this way.

The success of the Birmingham's belated mini-crusade during the 1880s was dramatic with sharp reductions in numbers at a time when Whitehall reformers were finding it extremely difficult to make further inroads into national out-relief totals. From an outdoor : indoor ratio well in excess of 2 : 1 in 1882 the Birmingham out-relief was so squeezed by 1890 that there were around 30 per cent more workhouse inmates than outdoor paupers.

The strictness of the Birmingham board in the 1880s possibly had repercussions locally and Mr F.D. Longe, the LGB West Midlands inspector, reported in 1890 that unions surrounding Birmingham had a high rate of pauperism. He urged neighbouring guardians to firm their principles and did not raise the possibility that their higher numbers might have had some consequence to the strict Birmingham policy. Longe attributed Birmingham's low figures to observance of strict by-laws and their employment of a 'superintendent of relief' who performed 'a searching investigation of the condition and circumstances of all applicants, and a careful supervision of persons receiving relief'.[48]

UNIONS ADJACENT TO PROVINCIAL CENTRES WITH A SOCIETY PRACTISING METHODOLOGICAL CHARITY

The Poor Law unions examined in this group, unlike the celebrated strict unions, did not necessarily qualify for felicitous mention in LGB reports but are included because geographically each was in the vicinity of a Charity Organisation Society having the expectations that they would spur guardians to follow Goschenian precepts. Figure 3.7 is an example of unions of this type and shows the number of paupers at Birkenhead between 1870 and 1890. This accorded reasonably well with the general picture in the 1870s in that the numerical downturn of outdoor paupers ceased around 1877 but recovery in out-relief numbers at Birkenhead was steeper than most. By the late 1880s those on outdoor benefits at Birkenhead, as at Brighton, reached

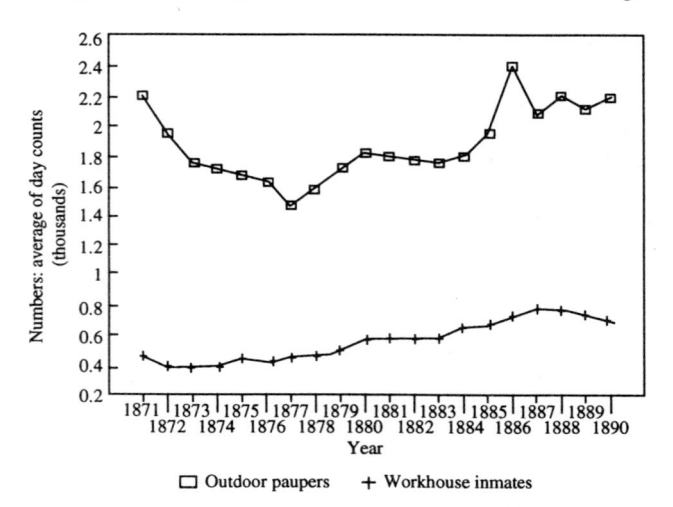

Figure 3.7 Birkenhead Poor Law union: outdoor paupers and workhouse inmates (1870–1890).

the levels pertaining at the start of the crusade. At Liverpool, helped by a parish population decline, Poor Law out-relief numbers dropped from a massive 11 601 on 1 January 1871 to 3233 at the start of 1877. There was then a tendency, in line with many unions across the country, to display only a modest numerical increase through the 1880s.

At Birkenhead outdoor relief was made available to able-bodied men during the winter in the form of an order for the labour yard where a man could 'earn 1s.6d. per day' although 'in the case of a married man with a family' additional relief was sometimes provided. Birkenhead guardians' policy was to provide for the sick and elderly, 'respectable in character, and able from such relief and from other sources, to maintain themselves at home'.[49] This approach ran counter to Goschenian intentions in openly recognizing together with guardians nationwide that their dole was a partial relief.

The Brighton board achieved a sharp drop in outdoor pauper numbers during the 1870s by adopting similar rules to Manchester. The peak of 4503 Brighton out-relief paupers on 1 January 1871 was reduced to below 2000 by the end of the decade prior to a pronounced upward trend some years later. In 1886, guardians at Brighton became more aware of 'distress of an exceptional character amongst persons of the working class'.[50] Although traditionally Brighton guardians had refused to accept lack of work as a legitimate out-relief claim, the scale of the problem was such that they found themselves with little alternative but to accede to the demanding clamour of hungry workers by devising a deterrent test-house system to blunt the upward surge in out-relief applications. This replaced the procedure of employing able-bodied men for a few days on land adjoining the Brighton workhouse in exchange for a week's outdoor relief. Under the new system, a temporary building enabled five days' work to be extracted at low wages regardless of the weather and proved 'most satisfactory in getting rid of loafers'.[51]

In 1886 the Liverpool guardians reported 'an exceptional lack of employment amongst the wage-earning classes' which were 'experiencing a time of very severe pressure'.[52] Parish officers reported clear signs of diminishing living standards with a decline in the appearance of houses occupied by working people who were not habitual poor-relief applicants. Many now lived in rooms where formerly they had occupied a house. Even then Liverpool guardians did not appreciate the success of their own deterrent devices in arousing detestation of the Poor Law and were puzzled as to why the exceptional privation reported by their own officers had not created a bigger surge in out-relief applicants.[53] Unskilled dock labourers hired, when they were lucky, by the day or part-day suffered particularly harshly. Liverpool guardians blamed the higher pay rate won recently by the dockers following a protracted strike as being at the root of the problem because it had attracted labourers from elsewhere than Merseyside. The guardians' advice to the Liverpool dockers was that they should accept a lower pay scale so as to make the work less attractive to distant workers.

At Southampton the number receiving outdoor relief was halved during the first five years of the crusade. Even this did not satisfy Dr Richard W.W. Griffin who, as a founder member of the Southampton COS, criticized the 'flagrant and irresponsible abuse by the relieving officers' of out-relief which had created a local 'system of pauper breeding' because of Southampton guardians being 'too uninformed, too political, too corruptible, too temporary, and above all, too lenient'.[54] It must have been frustrating for Southampton COS to find that Griffin's vitriol did not reduce Poor Law out-relief numbers and from the mid 1870s, when the Southampton COS was formed, local out-relief numbers steadily increased. Reluctance of unemployed workers to apply for Poor Law assistance became apparent in 1886 when the clerk to the Southampton board C. Crowther Smith informed the LGB there was 'distress of an exceptional character amongst the working classes who have not applied for relief to the extent of some hundreds, their occupations being those of seamen, mechanics, and labourers'.[55]

The Oxford Incorporated Parishes union was greatly influenced by the Oxford COS and university colleges. It was somewhat unusual among urban unions in continuing to reduce out-relief through the 1880s and contrasted with the other Oxford workhouse at Headington which was markedly more lenient.[56] The paucity of out-relief from the Incorporated Parishes union prompted A.W. Hall, a local Conservative MP, to take 'a hostile action ...' to 'the gentlemen who have been organising the relief, principally members of the University'.[57] Opposition to the restrictions became so intense as to prompt two Oxford aldermen to unearth 'an obsolete statute' with which they aimed to provide outdoor relief to 'paupers at their homes, independently of the Guardians'.[58] Expenditure on the salaries of Oxford union relieving officers and associated staff, largely employed to squeeze outdoor relief, was almost four times the cost incurred per head of population at the nearby Headington union.[59]

DISCUSSION ON THE MIXED RESPONSES TO THE CRUSADE

When devising their crusade against outdoor relief the government were determined to apply the concept of the 1834 amendment whereby workhouse incarceration would be the only statutory solace available to the able-bodied. Even then, the workhouse offer would be made in a way which said to the poor 'Yes, you have a right. Come and use it if you dare.'[60] Any awakening of an individual's consciousness about the legality of their Poor Law claim would be coupled with the implanted dread of stigmatization. The authorities knew that acceptance of in-house benefits would cut through any gossamer-thread of self-respect to which the applicant had been taught to cling.

The 1870s crusade forcefully attacked the retained practice of granting the poor a few shillings in outdoor relief so that they may retain the dignity of existing in their own home. Nevertheless, the official strategy proceeded by stealth in that it involved no legislative initiatives. The LGB merely repeated, year by year, homilies on the evils and demoralizing influence of outdoor relief. In spite of relentless pressure throughout the 1880s for increased guardian recognition of the alleged financial and moral advantages of 'correctly' interpreting outdoor relief legislation, the LGB were generally not able to improve on their successes of the early 1870s. Most guardians began to believe that if local administration of the Poor Laws had indeed become slack in the 1860s, then five or six years of crusading reforms had tightened them sufficiently. The national consensus was that an irreducible level had been achieved below which further bullying by Whitehall and its surrogates had little effect.

There was also a realization among guardians that LGB claims about a squeeze on outdoor relief automatically reducing poor rates was misleadingly simplistic. Even the most stringent crusading unions often failed to reduce unit Poor Law costs to the level attained at more relaxed unions. For example, the relief expenditure per head of population in 1890–91 was 4s.1d. at Bradfield, 4s.4d. at Atcham and 4s.7d. at Brixworth union. In contrast, costs at Wigan and Wakefield were 2s.10d. and 3s.7d. respectively, with each union relieving more than ten outdoor paupers to each workhouse inmate.[61]

When in the late 1870s the general impact of the crusade waned, the vociferous reforming minority appealed for tighter legislation to force firmer measures on reactionary wets. Courtenay Boyle, Eastern District LGB inspector, considered that 'unsound administration will not be put to an end unless the legislature or the central authority interfere'.[62] Although the Local Government Board welcomed the reforming enthusiasm, they were also aware of the accompanying potential social dangers in that tougher legislation could well be counter-productive by engendering more cohesive reaction amongst what were still disparate passive objectors.

On 12 May 1877, LGB secretary John Lambert responded to a recent Poor Law Conference recommendation that practices already being applied at strict unions should be enshrined in law. The conference proposed that: liability for pauper maintenance should extend to grandsons, relief should be recoverable at the discretion of the guardians, medical attention should be by loan, and the 1844 Prohibitory Order should be tightened to disallow out-relief to widows during the first six months after their husband's death.[63] Lambert's reply was sympathetic and assured the conference that the LGB president was 'fully in accord with them in the desire to place the administration of outdoor relief upon a sound and proper footing ...' but offered nothing tangible beyond promising a national circular promoting 'saving habits amongst the working classes'.[64] At the next Poor Law Conference, Albert Pell expressed 'uneasiness and surprise' that even the promised LGB memorandum on working-class thrift had not materialized.[65] More than a decade later and following repeated reformist demands to strengthen the outdoor Orders, Baldwyn Fleming revealed something of government's deep-seated fears about being conscious of the danger that 'a general order prohibiting out-relief would create so much opposition, and at first so much hardship, that probably a repulsion of public feeling would very rightly set in ...'[66]

The severe winter of 1879 coupled with a downturn in trade pushed hungry marginal paupers over a wide area to abandon their pride and national numbers on out-relief drifted upwards. Difficulty was encountered by the LGB in attempting to constrain local deviations from the 'correct' legal interpretation. For example, they were dismayed when Aston (West Midlands) guardians departed 'from the principles of the Out-Door Relief Order' and LGB inspector Henley reported that it was only after direct pressure from Whitehall that the Aston board 'were induced to return to their usual mode of administering relief'.[67] Even then, the 1879 distress found some workhouses 'already fully occupied' with guardians compelled to give outdoor relief under the Labour Test Order.[68] At Wolverhampton, where guardians were quite strict, labour yard applications increased so rapidly as to prompt the provision of special temporary out-relief to infirm inmates so as to make sufficient workhouse space for the hordes of applicants to be meaningfully challenged with the deterrent house test.

Whereas the LGB preached consistently about public assistance given outside the workhouse eroding the dignity of the individual and weakening the independent spirit, they did not ascertain the actual effects of their restrictions on those they rejected. They did not determine whether their refusal to provide out-relief doles, as in more tolerant days, may have forced applicants, who were horrified at the thought of becoming workhouse inmates, into clinging to an existence that compounded their humiliation, degradation, squalor and ill-health. Such situations were later exposed as commonplace by Booth, Rowntree and others. In the early twentieth century, Miss G. Harlock enquired on behalf of the Royal Commission on the Poor Laws into the case-histories of applicants fairly recently refused out-relief. She concluded that 'in no case was the support of relatives increased through the refusal of out-relief. In practically all the cases, relatives were so poor themselves, that they were not in a position to give systematic assistance.'[69] In Harlock's opinion, 'if such additional help had been given it must have been at the cost of physical efficiency of the younger generation.'[70]

In an attempt to win wider public support the anti-outdoor relief faction claimed that the concept was economically unfair to the respectable working class. The Revd. C.D. Francis considered it extremely unjust that 'as soon as a man by his industry raises himself in the social scale, ... he is immediately called upon to pay towards the support of his careless and improvident fellow workmen.'[71] It is really conjecture as to whether most ratepayers were opposed to out-relief in that the alternative not only seemed costly but involved the stigmatized workhouse incarceration of poorer neighbours.[72] At Bradfield, for example, voters petitioned the local Poor Law board requesting that outside relief be provided to a Thomas Rummey but guardians found it 'impossible to comply with the request'

Provincial Crusade: Results and Reactions

because 'no greater mistake is made amongst those who have not studied Out-Relief than the belief that it is cheaper'.[73] They claimed that 'if twenty applicants are offered relief in the workhouse, nineteen at least will refuse it, and will manage without any relief at all.'[74]

A theory of elites, which the LGB shared with the COS, was fundamental to the crusade concept. It assumed that people of a higher social and financial status were naturally also morally, spiritually and intellectually superior. This strengthened their certainty about relief being best given within the workhouse in that recipients could then benefit from a regime of moral correction. It was also argued that any outdoor dole that was provided should itself be fully adequate to meet the pauper's needs and not be just one amongst a number of accumulated means of support. The unit inadequacy of Poor Law out-relief was repeatedly claimed by the LGB and echoed loudly by the COS as a basic evil. Chapter 6 provides clear evidence that the frequently repeated COS implications about how in comparison they always provided appropriate levels of support sufficient to encourage eventual self-sufficiency were mainly illusory.

The LGB refused to consider that individuals in unskilled or casual jobs often did little better than exist from day to day on the margins of subsistence. They were loath to recognize that employment conditions were frequently such that even thrifty workers could easily find themselves in circumstances related to accident, illness or infirmity which so stretched their limited means as to rapidly make them no longer adequate. Courtenay Boyle, of the LGB, expressed annoyance that outdoor relief was still being provided overgenerously by guardians in many of the unions he inspected in spite of some being agricultural, some manufacturing and others heavily involved in the fishing industry. He found it 'contradictory' that although these unions covered markedly different economic activities, each had provided him with identical excuses as to why men in their particular area found it difficult to manage without being supplied with outdoor relief.[75]

For the guardian and relieving officer, operating at the sharp end of the Poor Law hierarchy and with personal knowledge of individual cases, there was often intimate awareness about the domestic distress of poorer neighbours. In any case, contrary to LGB claims, local Poor Law boards usually found it economically sensible to supply a few shillings in outside doles. Reactionary guardians also argued that there were moral and economic benefits in providing out-relief to some impecunious elements in that it encouraged them to use their initiative while salvaging a morsel of pride by augmenting their dole through odd-jobbing or by carrying out badly paid tasks.

From the mid 1870s most local guardians operated tactics akin to dumb insolence in their responses to Whitehall directives. While concurring enthusiastically enough with the principle that profligate outdoor relief was bad, they drew back from LGB interpretations involving what they saw as the abandonment of needy applicants to the vicissitudes of charity which by its nature was undependable. Local guardians religiously completed and returned the detailed administrative paperwork as statutorily required while remaining quietly obdurate about further out-relief reduction. As a result, in spite of persistent central pressures throughout two decades, there remained over England as a whole around three times as many paupers receiving outdoor relief in 1890 than there were inmates.

Where the LGB Whitehall perspective often differed from local experience was the former's conviction that the poor preferred outdoor relief to the honourable sweat of work. The possibility that the poor themselves may suffer emotional stress when threatened with workhouse incarceration was brushed aside by the LGB as carrying the danger of creating misplaced compassion among local administrators. Henry Longley, an LGB high-flyer, thought the frequently used phrase, 'the breaking up of the Home' was for the 'most part imaginary' with its assumption, 'in many cases erroneously', that the applicant had a home 'such that its loss will be otherwise than to the ultimate benefit to himself and his family'.[76] Longley believed that the decision as to whether the applicant's home was to be worth saving should not rest with the individual. He was convinced that even when 'the question of breaking up a home ... is fairly raised' the advantages of indoor relief remained because despite the 'inconvenience and hardship to the individual, great and undeserved as it may be in the particular case', there was more importantly the 'general good which accrues from the discouragement to improvident habits offered by a deterrent form of relief ...'[77] Baldwyn Fleming was equally contemptuous of comments implying that 'applicants would rather die than go into the workhouse' because his experience had proved, to his complete satisfaction, that such claims from poor people had nothing to do with 'their independent spirit', but indicated their objection to 'the receipt of relief in a form which is unacceptable to themselves'.[78] In answer to questions raised about the disturbing number of deaths by starvation in London, an LGB investigation claimed that 'in one case only out of ninety-seven deaths ... had an order for the workhouse, exclusive of other relief, been previously refused by the deceased'.[79] They then added, 'it is fair, however, to say that these records were at this particular time somewhat imperfectly kept.'[80]

Provincial Crusade: Results and Reactions 49

William Chance argued that the 'so-called' stigma of pauperism and suggestions that it was inhuman to clothe inmates in a special uniform were erroneous sentimentality. 'It must not be forgotten', he insisted, 'that the application of the workhouse test is intended to act as a deterrent' and that by this 'test *alone* can real destitution be discovered and fraud, imposition and lying defeated.'[81] The impact of reformers like Joseph Chamberlain on LGB diehards was to eventually force attitudinal readjustment and some abatement of the unfettered barrage against outdoor relief. J.S. Davy described how the year 1890 formed 'a sort of epoch in Poor Law administration'.[82] Treble identified the same year as being when 'discontinuities in social thought' occurred with an increased willingness to acknowledge the 'multi-causal nature of unemployment' and that hardship 'could be attributed to exogenous variables at work in the national and regional economies'.[83]

The gradual influence on public opinion of popular interpretations of philosophies such as those adopted by the New Liberals and various socialist strands had guided the state through two decades towards more socially conscious policies in the 1890s. The LGB became more aware that as a government department they had a broader remit than merely regimenting the poor. More enlightened LGB elements eventually argued that whereas deterrent workhouses may be appropriate for an unprincipled residuum, there was need for a greater government involvement towards developing more sympathetic responses at district and county level for the chronically sick, the insane and for children.

But even in the twentieth century there were still LGB conservatives, in concert with COS ideals, who looked back nostalgically to the crusade successes of the early 1870s. The majority report of the 1905–9 Royal Commission on the Poor Laws, influenced by COS members such as Charles Loch, Helen Bosanquet and Octavia Hill, attributed the early success of the crusade to the persistent efforts of the central authorities to 'expose the evil consequent on a careless administration of out-relief and to induce the Guardians to adopt a stricter policy'.[84] While accepting that the years 1871 to 1877 had been 'a time of great economic prosperity', the COS contingent were adamant that 'prosperity by itself had little or no tendency to reduce pauperism where administration remained careless'.[85]

In Chapter 4 we move in emphasis from statutory relief to the voluntary sector with explanation of how the procedural rationalisation advocated by Goschen and his successors was attempted by provincial would-be organizers of charity and how they were obstructed by traditional agencies whose response to scientific charity moved from initial disinterest to eventual disfavour.

4 Victorian Ideology, Early Attempts to Organize Charity, and the Beginnings of the Charity Organisation Society

By the early 1870s the national facade of British global omnipotence was shielding insidious socio-economic factors. The influence of rapid population growth, industrialization, expanding conurbations and overseas threats to Britain's manufacturing dominance were, in their different ways, to herald the need for more positive state involvement. Increasingly there became an acceptance that the well-being of the individual and of the nation depended on a greater fulfilment of the ideal whereby all citizens would benefit from reduction in the scourges of ill-health, ignorance and poverty.

Even then, state intervention was far from cataclysmic but gradually accelerated as the condition of the poor exposed the inadequacy of the 'dilatory and flimsy' character of earlier attempts at social improvement.[1] Chadwick's 'sanitary idea' earlier in the century had been a torch for the necessary betterment but legislative and practical progress had been minimal.[2] Mortality was still indecently high at around 22 per 1000. The need to improve the living standards of the poor became part of the platforms of both political parties with both Gladstone and Disraeli each inaugurating important Public Health Acts. By the end of the century local government changes were to gradually bring widespread improvements in water supply, sanitation, food quality, housing standards and urban infrastructures.

But state advance was slow and the Victorians continued to view the giving of charity as commendable. It provided esoteric benefits for the donor as well as material relief to the recipient. At the same time, there was an uneasy feeling around 1870 amongst would-be reformers of charity that many supplicants for assistance were imposters. Thousands of cunning wastrels were allegedly succeeding in extracting a comfortable living by duping numerous incautious naive charitable agencies each carelessly unaware of the others sinful indiscriminate generosity. Reformers drew strength from their conviction that the haphazard nature of traditional charity was also manifestly unfair because of its failure to provide adequate support for the deserving poor. They were also confident that by rationalizing the voluntary sector they would stem and even reverse the trend towards more collectivist poor relief.

Anecdotes about how the innocent were being hoodwinked were embellished by those keen to organize the traditional eleemosynary scene. They knew that people dislike being cheated and made to seem foolish, especially by their social inferiors. In such circumstances, it might be expected that when reforming groups of responsible citizens in the provinces launched local Charity Organisation Societies with the avowed aim of protecting traditional charities from the deceits of devious miscreants they would receive enthusiastic middle-class support. Surprisingly for the would-be reformers, a very different response was usually encountered.

REFORMING IDEAS, THE PERSISTENCE OF OUTDOOR RELIEF AND THE FORMATION OF THE COS

Those intending to organize charity had been buttressed by positivist claims in the 1860s that modern science had provided additional proof, should further proof be needed, that the Smilesian concepts about the ascendancy of the individual were inviolably correct as portrayed through the paramount ideas of self-help, character, thrift, work and duty. Latter-day classical economists like Herbert Spencer had found it easy to compound Malthus's doom-ridden biological determinism with Darwin's contemporary more sophisticated *The Origin of Species*. Darwin was seen to have confirmed scientifically that earthly success depended on individual strength of character. Equally, moral degradation of individuals and the nation would follow from paternalistic attitudes which softened personal resolve by confusing 'sympathy with justice'.[3]

Would-be reformers of charity invoked scientific evolutionist concepts in arguing that the mechanics of social change were generated endogenously and that attitudinal readjustment was needed about the make-up of society. 'Structural differentiation' involving complex organic complementary divisions in society were said to be essential to translate the existing 'incoherent homogeneity' to 'coherent heterogeneity'.[4] Society was seen to be naturally hierarchical, with the superiority and inferiority of individuals closely related to whether they occupied an upper or lower station in the community. Potential difficulties arising from modernisation processes were not expected to cause undue social friction. Individual endeavour would seemingly be mobilized at every social level through the inherent ability of the middle-classes to initiate a smooth transition to a nationwide bourgeois nirvana.

It was believed that improvements having real practical value depended upon the development of a sense of responsibility throughout society. The immorality and ignorance allegedly so prevalent among the poor had prevented them from adopting the positive attitude needed to attain their own economic salvation unaided. The moral duty of those in the higher stations of society was therefore to nurture the necessary character improvement of those below them. In this task they had to guard against the possibility of themselves weakening to what would be their own misplaced sentimentalism. Spencer warned them that 'sympathy with one in suffering suppresses, for the time being, remembrance of his transgressions' and that incorrectly such people 'are assumed to be all worthy souls, grievously wronged; with none of them ... thought of as bearing the penalties of their own misdeeds ...'[5] He ridiculed the suggestion of socialists and 'those so called Liberals who are preparing the way for them' that if given a reasonable standard of living even the most pathetic cases could translate into useful citizens. According to Spencer there was 'no political alchemy by which you can get golden conduct out of leaded instincts'.[6]

Poverty was still viewed by most of the 1860s middle class as a social condition which they could personally alleviate by their direct action. It was fashionable for a comfortably placed person to allow their conscience to be stirred towards instructing social inferiors about how through hard work they too may gain bourgeois respectability. In London alone 279 charities had been founded in the first half of the century before a further 144 came to life during the next decade.[7] Charity was a broadly based phenomenon sponsored by religious denominations as well as by secular societies and guilds. Some directed their alms to the immediate needs of the poor while philanthropists indulged in the added attraction in more overt beneficence through the building of hospitals, asylums, schools, institutes, parks, libraries, orphanages and other public amenities.

Few quarrelled with existing Poor Law legislation making it mandatory for the state to support the truly destitute. Equally, most middle class in the 1860s considered it reasonable that those who did need support should be labelled as paupers so that their social inferiority was recognized. Such an attitude had prevailed since the 1834 Poor Law Amendment which had ensured that the claims of the poor were treated, 'not as an integral part of the rights of the citizen, but as an alternative to them; its primary purpose not being to relieve the needy but to deter them from asking'.[8]

But the persistent habit of Poor Law guardians to favour outdoor relief with its relatively low unit cost had long frustrated the 1834

Commissioners' intention that assistance other than by submitting to being a workhouse inmate should be greatly reduced. The Hon. and Revd. Adelbert Anson condemned out-relief as 'a gigantic mistake, open to the gravest abuses, undermining men's ideas of independence and increasing instead of diminishing poverty' so that 'in countries where there was no Poor Law there was not one-hundredth part of the miserable charity which was to be seen in England'.[9] According to J.R. Pretyman outdoor paupers became part of the 'debased condition' where 'illegitimate offspring abounded, idleness flourished, drinking prevailed' with the result that 'prudence for men's own selves, their wives and their families, and the care of their indigent parents, became virtues almost obsolete among the wages-earning classes'.[10]

Under the more rigorous interpretation of the Poor Laws associated with the 1870s crusade against outdoor relief discussed in previous chapters, many applicants who traditionally had expected to receive outdoor assistance were offered nothing but the chance of being a workhouse inmate. In practice there was a very real obstacle to incarcerating many of those currently benefiting from out-relief in that there was little spare workhouse space available, particularly taking account of segregation requirements. To reassure doubting guardians that they were unlikely to be caught napping in this logistical difficulty the Local Government Board (LGB) used the deterrent economic model of LGB inspector Mr E.H. Wodehouse. This recognized that the poor had been schooled for generations into averting the stigmatization of becoming a workhouse inmate and to avoid this ultimate humiliation, virtually regardless of their circumstances, nine out of ten supplicants would decline the 'offer of the house'.[11]

When launching their out-relief crusade the government had envisaged that as numbers diminished so organised charity would move centre-stage to provide help for 'deserving' cases. Indeed shortly before G.J. Goschen primed the crusade with his 1869 Minute the first Charity Organisation Society had been established to systemize the plethora of traditional charities. In attempting to explain the problems of contemporary almsgiving Sir Charles Trevelyan claimed that every religious sect 'distrusts, more or less, the method of the rest, and all distrust the political economists'.[12] In harmony with Goschen, the COS argued that the logical solution was for all relief disbursements to be rationalized scientifically.

Charity 'unwisely administered' was said by the COS to be 'capable of doing incalculable harm' by seducing 'the individual from the wise and natural toilsomeness of life'.[13] Good-for-nothing people must be rewarded for their moral failure by workhouse incarceration and its deterrent discipline. Factors such as unemployment, under-employment, casual work and the effects on earnings of trade-cycle troughs were not considered to have such great significance. Drunkenness, debauchery and immorality were seen as the major contributors to an applicant's plight. The Revd. Llewellyn Davies maintained that it was only after unworthy characters had been excluded from society and 'the present chaotic alms' had been 'sensibly organised' that voluntary charity might hope to provide for those suffering from the 'visitation of illness, and for those who are permanently disabled and without relatives to support them'.[14]

The COS agreed with the central Poor Law authorities that outdoor relief nourished dependency, sapped initiative and was a cruel deterrent preventing the poor from bettering themselves by causing disequilibrium in the 'natural' economic market balancing work and wages.[15] Unlike traditional charities, it was not the COS's purpose to ameliorate stringencies associated with Poor Law legislation but instead to remove potential obstacles to their effective implementation.

In London the emergent Society quickly set out to establish a district committee nearby each Poor Law union. Committees operated through a local COS charity office where an applicant's personal details were recorded prior to rigorous investigation and eventual committee decision on appropriate action. The COS were confident initially that those they judged to be on the 'recoverable verge of pauperism' would with appropriate spurring quickly make a transition to relative respectability.[16] Organized charity would provide opportunity for controlled disbursements by 'combining the intelligence of the scientist with the humanity of the Samaritan'.[17]

COS members never doubted their intrinsic superiority over the lower classes with the inherent power and instrumentalities to direct and control 'the material means of subsistence among the lower elements'.[18] They would soon establish an innate 'elite position' as well as 'elite control' with their determination to form 'a cohesive force presenting a common front to other forces in society'.[19] They expected widespread and speedy recognition of the COS criterion for the giving of alms whereby the objective consequences to the recipient must take precedence over the subjective gratification of the donor.[20] Charitable gifts which had seemed such innocent Christian acts of goodwill to those lacking socio-scientific knowledge were now exposed as immoral, irresponsible and economically disadvantageous to both the giver and the receiver.[21]

During the early years of the COS they had high hopes that with the co-operation of local Poor Law officials outdoor relief would soon be whittled away and with it much of the social obscenity of pauperism.[22] Politically, economically, socially and morally the COS were so strongly equipped as to seem certain of quickly capturing the high ground in charitable circles and gaining something akin to what Gramsci has termed in the political context 'ideological hegemony'.[23] The emergent COS confidently expected that they would soon become the hub of a network of closely knit countrywide relationships between locally organized charitable groups and Poor Law representatives.

According to the COS the depersonalization of the gift inherent in state intervention destroyed the joy of giving and demoralized the recipient. Poor Law relief lacked the 'redeeming influence of personal kindness' because the recipient came to regard it as 'largesse to which he has a right'.[24] In contradistinction the granting of scientifically measured charity to a deserving person was not seen as stigmatic and should always be accompanied by constructive comments emphasizing the recipient's duty to quickly become self-supporting. A gift given to a deserving applicant should be viewed as the least token of the donor's sympathy as 'devotion, intelligence, and common sense' must predominate so as to 'influence and elevate character' in the recipient.[25] The COS were confident that encouraged by tightly controlled voluntary assistance the 'honest and manly independence of self-help' would replace in the recipient 'both the abject dependence on the law-enforced help of others and the false and defiant independence based on the knowledge that such help can always be demanded ...'[26]

In fashioning their ideas the COS were well aware that even though the Poor Law dole carried state-fabricated and class-manipulated stigmatization it did provide the poor with the legal right to be saved from starvation. Potential troublemakers were therefore provided with an inherent security not present in voluntary aid. To obtain the less certain COS help the applicant needed to be deferential as well as deserving. COS intelligentsia calculated that by manoeuvring a needy person into the position of being a supplicant for their uncertain gift they were powerfully placed to inculcate ideas into a grateful underling.

EARLY ATTEMPTS TO ORGANIZE CHARITY

Concepts like investigation, individual selection and encouragement of providence were not novel. What the COS attempted in addition was to combine aspects of previous formalizing attempts with their own methodology of 'organising' other charities. Earlier nineteenth-century social experiments designed to develop self-reliance were claimed by the COS to have resulted in even the poorest elements achieving respectability after careful investigation into their personal circumstances had prompted appropriate middle-class advice and support.

Brighton was the venue of an early provincial venture combining the principles of self-help, charity and anti-mendicity. Clergy and congregations of goodwill backed by influential patrons formed the Brighthelmston Provident Institution in 1820 to encourage thrift and self-sufficiency among the labouring classes while securing them a 'supply of Food, Fuel, and Clothing during the Winter Season'.[27] By 1825 it had flowered into the Brighton Provident and District Society (P and DS) and in 1831 there were 86 volunteers visiting the poor in six Brighton districts. During that year, 2206 working families together deposited £2184 12s.3d. for safe-keeping. The Society provided support valued at £162 11s.2d in money, bread and groceries to the Brighton poor. They also relieved 607 mendicants, rejected 416 and 'punished 20'.[28] The P and DS urged residents and visitors 'to withhold all promiscuous charity'.[29] They claimed that through district-visiting involving '*voluntary* attention to the poor ... and by employing the influence of station and of personal intercourse, far more is done to prevent distress ... than has ever been done by any other process of amelioration and discipline'.[30]

The early Brighton Society encouraged thrift by guaranteeing an added 'premium' of 12.5 per cent on deposits, provided the accumulated sum was not touched until 'the winter months'.[31] Generous 'rewards' of this type were also offered by similar contemporary reforming societies elsewhere in the belief that 'nothing will so powerfully excite a spirit of virtuous emulation among the poor, as the bestowing of certain marks of distinction by the rich ...'[32] To help raise the revenue required for the premiums and administrative costs the Brighton P and DS organized social functions including, a 'Ball for the relief of the poor', a lecture on the 'Ascent and Descent of Mount Blanc' and a 'Fancy Work and Clothing Fair'. These events augmented conventional subscriptions and donations which in 1831 included £60 from the society's patrons 'their most Gracious Majesties'.[33]

Other early provincial societies included the Liverpool Provident District Society (PDS) founded in 1833 and later a constituent of the Central Relief Society (CRS) which succeeded it in an 1863 merger. In its early days the PDS offered a 5 per cent premium on small deposits intended for 'winter stores, clothing, fuel, rent, and the purchase of bibles and other useful objects'.[34] The society had itself been inspired by the earlier systems of 'minute personal inspection' promoted by Mr Walker in the Township of Stretford Manchester from 1817 and by the Messrs Ashton's efforts from 1801 in the Township of Hyde.[35] The Liverpool PDS claimed to be the model for district visiting societies soon copied in London and Manchester.[36] More than half of the sixty strong PDS committee in the 1830s were clergymen. They shared district visiting with ladies who found 'great pleasure' in the societies' work. Deposits collected from the Liverpool poor in 1833 by 462 visitors totalled £10 396.[37] Thirty years later the value of collections had been more than maintained but the number of voluntary visitors had dropped to around 265.[38] Although the relief branch was 'confessedly subordinate to the deposit system' the Liverpool PDS distributed relief in the year 1832–3 valued at £1959 and shared between 5987 deserving families.[39] During the 1862 depression the PDS relieved 34 426 families in the first few months of the year so that their office-space became 'totally inadequate' for the accommodation of 'throngs of poverty-stricken men and women ...'[40] One of the best known provincial institutions using some of the systemized structures later favoured by the COS was the Manchester and Salford District Provident Society (DPS) also founded in 1833 when the 'condition of the poor' excited the 'anxious solicitude' of a 'general meeting of persons'. They resolved that 'many of the evils' which affected the poor 'might be alleviated or removed by a judicious management of the resources within their own power' helped by 'a more active manifestation of the sympathy of the wealthier classes, and the advantages of their advice'.[41] From the earliest days there was 'registration and careful records of all cases' with the Unitarians 'particularly involved' and Mrs Gaskell a home visitor.[42] In 1845 the DPS abandoned their practice of providing a 5 per cent premium and the amount deposited fell from £5158 that year to £2088 in 1848.

Other precursor societies which developed into Charity Organisation Societies in the 1870s tended to focus most on the repression of mendicity. They include the one at Oxford founded in 1827 by Archbishop Whatley which itself was a re-birth of the 'Society for the Relief of Distressed Travellers and Others' started in 1814.[43] In later years the Oxford Charity Organisation Committee 'coalesced' with the Anti-Mendicity Society to become known in 1873 as the Oxford Anti-Mendicity and Charity Organisation Association (COS).

One of the antecedent organizations for the London COS was the Society for the Relief of Distress founded in 1860. Its almoners included Edward Denison, a member of the landed gentry who became an MP in his twenties and died young from tuberculosis. Denison's favourable reputation was built on his determination to live in the East End for eight months to prove the benefits of personal involvement in teaching the poor to be 'frugal and thrifty'.[44] Denison 'again and again' emphasized the need for a 'rigid and universal administration of the Poor Laws' to ensure that outdoor relief would not be given without a labour test and with every discouragement given to interference from haphazard charity because the 'true cure for pauperism lies ... in the growth of thrift among the poor'.[45] He had no doubts that even casually employed dock labourers should be capable of saving sufficient to cater for all reasonable emergencies.[46] Denison's premature death in 1870 led to his self-sacrifice becoming a yardstick which COS members might hope to equal.

Although there were these earlier English provincial attempts to organize voluntary visiting to encourage thriftiness, provide relief and repress mendicity, it was mainly to two experiments elsewhere that the COS turned to justify the soundness of their methods. One was the miraculous transformation in the condition of the poor allegedly achieved in a Scottish parish by the inspiration and energies of Thomas Chalmers, a clergyman and moral philosopher. The other was the structured system of social control as practised at Elberfeld in northern Germany where the community was said to have voluntarily become involved in caring for the poor with extraordinarily beneficial results.[47] There is convincing evidence, however, that neither of these ideological bedrocks were quite what the COS and their acolytes made them appear.

Take first the example of the Revd. Dr Thomas Chalmers, renowned amongst social pioneers for his formula to provide measured charitable relief only through a network of voluntary visitors and who was said to have rejuvenated the spirits of the poor in St John's parish Glasgow in the early 1820s.[48] Chalmers's memory was referred to in awe by the COS and for some members he became a 'spiritual ancestor'.[49]

Chalmers's supporters were 'stunned' when he resigned the living in 1823 after the scheme had been operating for only three years. Brown suggests that although his departure was supposedly influenced by exhaustion and illness 'perhaps the most important reason' was weariness about 'the continuing attacks upon his poor-relief programme from the Glasgow press'.[50] Chalmers's 'brutal optimism' was not universally approved by contemporaries.[51] Checkland has challenged the genuineness of Chalmers's claims and detected his 'curious accounting' procedures used in their fabrication.[52] Furgol has been even more damning with her criticism that Chalmers's 'practical experiment in poor relief in St. John's failed unequivocally as did its imitators' so that the 'ideal small community he envisaged' and which has so often been extolled never actually materialized.[53] Furgol argues that Chalmers's refusal to 'even consider that he might be mistaken led him to ignore any unsatisfactory evidence' so that he 'manipulated statistics' to 'prove' his theories.[54]

Overseas, structured relief to the poor developed famously at Elberfeld in the Rhineland.[55] The Elberfeld activities involved almoners distributed around the community with each 'volunteer' recruited by threatened loss of franchise rights and expected to take personal responsibility for the well-being of specific poor families.[56] Because Elberfeld appeared to combine the official and voluntary relief sectors in working harmony the experiment was constantly extolled in COS literature and endlessly made the subject of debate at Poor Law and COS Conferences. The 'Elberfeld system' was consequently launched in various conurbations including Liverpool, Bradford, Sheffield and Leeds but after initial flourishes each attempt collapsed through weak support.

William Rathbone the founding father of the Liverpool CRS was convinced that Elberfeld supplied the answers to British social problems. In 1871 he persuaded his Unitarian school-friend James Stansfeld, the new LGB President, to despatch Mr Andrew Doyle to report on Elberfeld.[57] Seventeen years later Rathbone again harassed the LGB to send Mr Davy, another of their inspectors, to report further on developments in Germany in association with Charles Loch of the London COS and Mr Hanewinkel of the Liverpool CRS.

Rathbone believed that Elberfeld was structured on genuine voluntary activity requiring a higher level of personal involvement than he could envisage in the English Poor Law system but the validity of his assumptions are dubious. Regarding the voluntary nature of the work, Col Granville Browne reported that at Elberfeld 'the duties of overseers and visitors are compulsory and unpaid'.[58] The reported sympathetic personal relationships between rich and poor were ridiculed by William Chance who pointed out that the conditions of obtaining relief at Elberfeld were 'harsh and oppressively rigorous'.[59] But these later visitors to Elberfeld should not have been surprised because a not dissimilar picture had been painted back in 1871 by Andrew Doyle. He had reported that 'the applicant for relief is subjected to an examination so close and searching, so absolutely inquisitorial, that no man who could possibly escape from it would submit to it'.[60]

THE FORMATION AND DEVELOPMENT OF THE LONDON CHARITY ORGANISATION SOCIETY

There have been numerous descriptions by contemporaries and by later commentators of the activities of the Charity Organisation Society in

London.[61] The 54 strong inaugural council of the COS which met in 1869 under the presidency of the Bishop of London and the chairmanship of Lord Lichfield included influential elites from the aristocracy, religion, parliament, banking, the professions, intellectuals and the armed forces. The council grew in number year by year as prominent members of society were persuaded to allow their name to be used so that by 1890 it had over one hundred members. Another powerful hierarchical layer was created early in the 1870s with the appointment of 24 vice-presidents including dukes, earls, marquises and viscounts as well as eminent public figures such as John Ruskin and George Goschen. By 1874 Queen Victoria had been enlisted as the society's patron. In the Webbs' words, the COS became 'the most exclusive of sects'.[62]

A weekly publication, the *Charity Organisation Reporter* (*COR*), was the vehicle through which the opinions of prominent activists were circulated nationally.[63] It was also intended that *COR* would provide practical guidance to the burgeoning number of provincial organizing societies which it was expected would soon be applying their methodology across the country. COS principles were claimed to improve the condition of the poor by dealing with the causes of pauperism rather than its effects. They intended to systematically co-operate with all relief agencies, carefully investigate and consider each case, provide effectual assistance to all that were deserving, promote providence and self-reliance, and repress mendicity and imposture.[64]

Within two years the COS had established district offices throughout London but this energetic outburst was not sufficient to guarantee success. Lack of co-operation from traditional charities appeared as soon as the emergent COS attempted to persuade them to fund their investigative methodology. In the 1860s Thomas Hawksley had forecast that most London charities would happily donate one per cent of their annual disbursements to the COS 'system of charity police' and that this would immediately produce £40 000 annually.[65]

The assumption that COS administrative finance would be generated exogenously was fundamental to their early strategy of setting up district offices but when this failed they were able to assemble alternative financial muscle from within their own well-endowed ranks.[66] Most charitable bodies were offended by COS ideas. They were not prepared to abrogate their own responsibilities to the poor and authorize the newly formed group to make basic decisions which for many years they had been handling to their own and to public satisfaction. COS intentions to collectivize charitable distributions seemed to many as incompatible with their individualistic principles. They detected distinct parallels between

Beginnings of the Charity Organisation Society

guardians raising local revenue through rates for redistribution to the poor and the COS's plan to collectively allocate charitable funds.

It was the unflinching COS confidence about the correctness of their methodological approach which distinguished them from other charities. They were ceaselessly critical of charitable bodies they dubbed as amateurs patronizing the poor. They could not visualize that their own procedures were also patronizing in spite of their basic premise that superior social status gave the natural right to categorise the impecunious into the worthy and the unworthy. Undoubtedly COS investigations were to expose 'some very ripe frauds' but they generally became seen as 'a sharp, suspicious method of enquiry which seemed better suited to a prosecution than a friend in need'.[67]

The London COS soon had to accept that their incisive responses raised apprehension and dismay among the needy. COS attempts to reassure the working man of their helpful intentions included making him aware that 'those who were born to easier circumstances sympathise with the severe toil and self-denial which his lot imposes on him'.[68] They accepted that unpredictable emergencies might occur occasionally to deter even the best regulated families. The COS told the poor that on such rare occasions they would be 'standing beside ... ready and even eager' to help 'by doing their best' to at least 'mitigate the suffering which it may be beyond their power to remove'.[69]

The COS were never short of resilient publicists anxious to explain that as a path-finding organization prepared to condemn and correct social weaknesses like sloth and immorality they must expect to meet opposition. A formidable group of activists disseminated the COS cause from London. Octavia Hill, Charles Loch, the Barnetts and the Bosanquets were among those dominating much of the public discussion on social issues in the 1870s and the 1880s. The personal charisma and energy generated by these moral reformers have been described by their biographers and in the various histories of the London COS.[70] It is sufficient here to emphasize their shared characteristics of certainty of purpose and a fearless determination to adhere to their principles however unpopular and harshly bizarre they sometimes appeared to others. It is noteworthy that a strong thread of Unitarianism stretched through the London COS to organizing societies in large provincial cities like Birmingham, Liverpool and Manchester.[71]

COS opinions were sought and respected contemporaneously by governments, Royal Commissions, learned institutions and the public at large. Today their contribution on a range of social welfare matters involving organizational processes and techniques are still universally acknowledged. There were areas of social concern where COS activities were not easy targets for unfriendly criticism. COS special committees addressed problems such as the training of the blind, the needs of the deaf and dumb, the special requirements of epileptic children and the education of the mentally disturbed.[72] Many a 'blind, deaf and epileptic poor person' was glad of the COS's 'concern and activity'.[73] They also 'directed attention to the needs of crippled children' aimed at encouraging proper care and 'the right use of instruments' and instigated the establishment in 1888 of the Invalid Children's Aid Association.[74] Always fundamental to the COS attempts to remove 'hindrances' from the handicapped poor was the perceived need to equip them to participate as individuals in being rational, calculating, disparate, competing atoms in society driven by interest or by economic need.[75]

Organizations like the Salvation Army were anathemas to the COS. They were seen as 'hopelessly sentimental' with their 'open-handed and undiscriminating charity' cutting 'at the root of all teachings and endeavours of twenty years'.[76] When Salvation Army plans for farm and workshop colonies were receiving public encouragement around 1890 the COS council raised 'very grave objections' to '"General" Booth's Social scheme'.[77]

Probably the most powerful opposition to the COS came from the Evangelicals who in the 1860s were already a well-established force among Victorian charities. Nevertheless, in spite of being unimpressed by COS ideas they rejoiced with most other influential factions of British society in the shared belief that there was little wrong with the nation's underlying socio-economic framework. There was comfort in accepting that a person's wealth and social standing was a good measure of their moral value and it was reassuring to convince themselves that the living standards of the poor would gradually improve when helped by the moral guidance of social superiors. In Harrison's words 'philanthropy helped to validate existing social institutions by high-lighting the generosity of the rich and the inadequacies of the poor'.[78] Dissension between the COS and Evangelicals centred on the crucial detail of how and to whom charitable support should be administered. There was also the Evangelicals' belief in 'salvation by faith through the atoning death of Christ' which introduced a more overtly compassionate moral code than did 'scientific' principles.[79] These differences widened with persistent COS criticism of the careless profligacy of Evangelical charities and hardly fostered sympathetic rapport let alone the chance of developing working harmony.

Nowhere was Evangelical opposition to the COS more clearly demonstrated than in the public fracas over Dr Thomas Barnardo whom

Beginnings of the Charity Organisation Society

they supported after his condemnation by the COS for alleged administrative misdemeanours.[80] The Barnardo Evangelical Trustees in 1877 challenged the COS through an arbitration tribunal and skilfully outmanoeuvred them on an issue so publicly intense that the 'very highest authorities in the country' awaited the outcome of the case.[81]

Even the staunchest COS supporters recognized by 1890 that the tide of intellectual, institutional and public opinion was moving away from them. It had become fashionable to accept that the impression of mankind comprising self-consciously rational beings freely selecting their future from among properly weighed alternatives 'could be dismissed as an antiquated illusion'.[82] No pessimistic soothsayer was needed by 1890 for the more realistic elements of the COS to recognize a certain bleakness about the future with their well-intentioned ideas increasingly labelled as outdated.[83] How different socio-economic ideas gained ground among the middle classes in the 1880s and affected the provincial Charity Organisation Societies is discussed in Chapter 7. Meanwhile the next two chapters focus on the responses encountered in the provinces when local groups attempted to apply COS principles.

5 The Emergence of Provincial Charity Organisation Societies and Responses, 1870–1890

THE DEVELOPMENT OF PROVINCIAL CHARITY ORGANISATION SOCIETIES

We have already seen how the London COS was formed with the backing of influential elites. In the provinces the preponderance of COS activists were senior members of the ancient professions or were successful businessmen with the occasional presence of local gentry usually as decorative appendages. Prominent among the professionals were senior Church of England clerics, medical practitioners, lawyers, academics and military men, some retired and others still professionally active. Their attitudes were typical of nineteenth-century professionals who lived by 'persuasion and propaganda' with emphasis on 'social efficiency and the avoidance of waste' directed towards organizing the distribution of rewards according to 'personal merit, professionally defined'.[1]

Provincial businessmen attracted to the COS tended to be involved in commerce and banking or were sufficiently endowed by industrial profit to merit respect in a society keenly influenced by material possessions. Although most active provincial COS members were from comfortably-off parents there had usually not been sufficient wealth for them to maintain their social status entirely from inheritance. They found it easy to convince themselves, aided by their absorption in self-help ideology, that they had seen sufficient of hard work to be dismayed by the lack of character among the poor whose failure they believed was induced by idleness, improvidence and intemperance. The concept of organizing charity crossed party political divides with MPs from both parties giving their names to COS Committees.

As a social group, whether male or female, provincial COS members had little natural economic association with the day-to-day lives of the lower classes. Contacts were usually limited to servants and the occasional pestering beggar. According to COS theory, regular interviews with a poor family by one of their caring visitors would do all that was necessary to bridge the social chasm. In practice the inadequate number of visitors mustered by provincial COSs all too often resulted in more fleeting contacts with the poor than had been theorized.

Emergence of the Provincial Societies

Nine provincial Societies, each attempting to organize local charity, provide the main foci for the remainder of this volume. They were located at Birkenhead, Birmingham, Brighton, Leamington, Liverpool, Manchester, Oxford, Reading and Southampton. These Societies are not untypical when compared with other provincial Societies. Indeed because most of them became affiliates of London they were viewed as having applied the central ideology reasonably successfully. The following synopses of the main socio-economic influences at each location are provided as background before discussion concentrates on the responses provincial COSs received from other local relief agencies. The attitude adopted by the London COS to the efforts of their provincial cousins is also examined.

It will be noted that none of the foregoing Societies are matched geographically with any of the strict Poor Law unions in agricultural areas described in previous chapters. This is because after the crusade against outdoor relief had got underway it was discovered that rural localities were not keen to attempt COS formations. As a consequence in localities such as Wallingford, Bradfield, Brixworth and St Neots the poor had no possibility of even being considered as 'deserving' of organized charitable support which had been a selling-point when the crusade was launched.[2] Furthermore even in the county town of Shrewsbury which became subject to the anti-outdoor relief Atcham formula, little evidence of local COS activities is to hand.

What becomes apparent about provincial COSs is that although they professed commitment to the never-changing principles regularly propagated from London, in practice they displayed considerable diversity in the detailed interpretation of how the common philosophy should be applied. In 1891 Sophia Lonsdale in a letter to the *Charity Organisation Review* exposed what she saw as the wide divergences existing in provincial COSs. She described a scenario of how during the previous twenty years the decision by enthusiasts to form a COS in a provincial centre had resulted in the creation of an organization which the central council 'would not recognise as its child, nor even as its second cousin several times removed'.[3] Her description of how the typical provincial COS had been formed and had failed to function effectively supports the idea that after a flood of provincial enthusiasm in the 1870s the movement lost momentum when faced with unexpected difficulties.

Lonsdale described how typically a small group of people in a provincial centre armed with pamphlets from London COS summoned a meeting at which the mayor presided. Local clergy attended '(more or less in battle array, for they have an uncomfortable suspicion that some of their favourite modes of relief are in danger), and a very few laymen, and a great many good ladies, and the result is a Charity Organisation Society' which after a number of years caused the town 'to be a good deal worse' than when it had been formed. She claimed that disillusioned locals blamed the lack of success on the COS because in their opinion it 'didn't answer at all' the need to structure the distribution of charity in a responsible way. But what was even worse in Lonsdale's opinion was that some provincial COSs continued to flourish in total contravention of their supposed principles by providing 'soup, free dinners, doles to men out of work etc., etc.,' so that they cause 'more distress than they relieve' and do 'irreparable harm'.[4] Lonsdale's portrayal of provincial COSs had elements of caricature, but the underlying pertinence of her ridicule was valid.

As discussed in the previous chapter some provincial COSs developed from societies already functioning in their locality and which had attempted various formats to encourage thrift and to rationalize charitable provision. Amongst the most prominent were those at Liverpool and Manchester. These localities are considered first in the following summaries of how and why provincial COSs were formed. The Liverpool Central Relief Society (CRS) was founded in 1863 and the Manchester and Salford District Provident Society (DPS) in 1833. Both, if with somewhat different emphases, were well-motivated attempts to structure, regulate and co-ordinate philanthropic activities so as to inculcate the poor with self-help principles. Each society eventually absorbed the words 'charity organisation' into their title.

Liverpool

The principal occupation of nineteenth-century Liverpool and the foundation of its prosperity was the handling of goods between ship, warehouse and railway. Work was mainly performed by casual unskilled labour with demand 'coming largely in sudden rushes' needing to be done at high pressure 'in order to save interest on costly ships, dock-space and warehouse-space'.[5] This was precisely the type of employment which London COS Secretary C.S. Loch had in mind when later stating that 'out of intermittent labour spring our gravest woes' in that it produced a 'labourer of intermittent energy; the off-days become habitual; with indolence comes intemperance; with uncertainty of employment comes recklessness about the future ...'[6] In addition to dockworkers and seafarers, Liverpool also had a disproportionately large number of clerks which though they included some 'level-headed men' were mainly 'ill-paid and largely recruited from among the half-hearted, the listless, the unimaginative and the dull'. Muir considered that some of these shortcomings were counterbalanced by Liverpool's good fortune in having a 'small directing class of merchants and ship-owners who tended to be alert, open-minded, hospitable to big ideas, accustomed to and tolerant of the widest divergence of view'.[7] A less flattering description of them is provided by Owen who refers to a 'merchant aristocracy' generally distancing themselves from workers with an 'indifference slightly tempered by philanthropy'.[8]

William Rathbone who inspired the development of the local CRS was prominent in the Liverpool directing class. He was the eldest son of a wealthy mercantile family who for generations had influenced Merseyside life both in business and charity. Simey describes him as having 'abounding, exuberant, extraordinarily tenacious vitality' and through his mother's involvement in 'unostentatiously performed, laborious, self-sacrificing projects had become sympathetically conscious of the great residuum'.[9] He thought it essential training for life that all young men should develop habits of 'saving and giving'.[10]

Rathbone shared the passion of the later COS for thoroughly investigating the background of applicants for charitable assistance to assess whether, or not, they were deserving. The 'combination of organised machinery with individual responsibility and freedom of action' which had 'proved so successful in private enterprise' would, according to Rathbone, also prove successful in public work.[11] But sentiment was to be excluded from the social contract to make way for duty and obligation. Simey points out that for Rathbone, 'the people' for whose welfare he was so overtly concerned were to be kept apart from himself and his like, never to be 'loved in life nor garlanded with white camellias in death'.[12]

Formed in 1863 the CRS was an amalgam of three established Liverpool charitable societies. Committee members were mainly 'business men' but included Edward Whiteley the Tory MP.[13] Rathbone's affinity with COS ideas on investigation and organization made him prime-mover in the 1874 decision to change the CRS's full title to the 'Liverpool Central Relief and Charity Organisation Society'.

The abortive attempts to introduce the Elberfeld system into Liverpool's crowded and squalid suburbs demonstrate how few among the Merseyside middle class were really prepared to get involved in CRS practicalities. The town clerk of Liverpool, Mr Joseph Raynor, while supporting an early CRS Elberfeld-style initiative, warned that 'any perceptible improvement in the conditions of the lowest classes might take a long time'.[14] His prediction proved painfully accurate as the project was quickly abandoned through lack of middle-class interest, let alone participation. A later attempt to introduce Elberfeld techniques has been dismissed as 'a heroic, almost quixotic, scheme of recruiting an army of friendly visitors'.[15] Rathbone calculated that the scheme needed some 2500 visitors but it had no chance of survival with only 300 half-hearted, quickly disillusioned volunteers. Like other Victorian cities Liverpool was 'abandoned in its congestion, filth and disease'.[16] Dr J. Stopford Taylor, the city medical officer, attributed their 1884 fever epidemic on 'overcrowding, destitution, intemperance and debility'.[17] Taylor claimed that parts of Liverpool had 1210 persons packed into an acre in the old courts. He reported visiting one family where:

> ...the intense foetor of the room in which the sick people lay necessitated waiting outside until the window was open. The occupants of the bed, which is about 3 feet by 6, were five in number, and all exceptionally filthy. The mother is a fish hawker and the fish were in a basket under the bed. Three persons, the father and 2 children, are sick in this house, which is miserably furnished, filthy and foul smelling from the dirty skins and clothing of the inmates. The mother states that for 17 weeks the income of the family, derived from the father, has been 7s per week.[18]

Taylor commented that 'the public are shocked to hear of a few hundred deaths from fever, smallpox or scarlatina; but thousands who die from lung diseases are never thought of and that nearly half of the children born die before they reach the age of one is forgotten.'[19]

Another prominent CRS member was the Revd. H.V. Mills, a Unitarian minister and founder of the Home Colonisation Society with its proposal for state-controlled, self-supporting, non-competitive, co-operative, agricultural and domestic-industrial estates. Charles Loch dismissed the Merseysider's scheme for its 'economic primitivism' and concluded that 'the whole thing is airy, unsubstantial, the refuge of the destitute of religion'.[20]

Demands of business, religion, education, district nursing and Parliament, where he represented the constituency as a Liberal, diluted the time and energy William Rathbone could apply to the CRS which became caught 'between theory and practice, moral precept and economic possibility'.[21] Simey suggests that early heralded CRS intentions of forging harmonious relationships between rich and poor were forgotten by Rathbone's more mundane successors and precedence given to mandatory investigation. For many in Liverpool the CRS seemed to have drifted from their founding ideals and appeared 'even harsher than the Poor Law'.[22] However, the starkness of CRS charitable response as perceived by

Merseysiders was soft-centred when compared with the London COS's standards and caused friction between them. Much to London's annoyance William Grisewood confirmed in 1890 that as their name implied the CRS would always be primarily concerned with relief which he claimed they extended to all 'classes and creeds, the only limitation being that the distress must be such as is removable by temporary aid and the recipients must be of deserving character – the words "temporary" and "deserving" here being interpreted in a very generous sense'.[23]

Manchester and Salford

The many nineteenth-century Manchester operatives engaged in warehousing, manufacture and construction were similar to those in Liverpool by being tied to unpredictable job patterns having casual, cyclical and seasonal characteristics.[24] The last quarter of the century was not significantly different from when Engels noted in 1844 that manufacturers needed an 'unemployed reserve army of workers' which was 'larger or smaller according to the state of the market'.[25] Perhaps Engels painted the scene in dark colours but later commentators have confirmed that the 'conditions of the slums of Manchester ... can only be considered appalling'.[26] Fred Scott's contemporary survey of the Manchester and Salford poor warned that anyone not accustomed to the deficient ventilation would be met with a:

> ...mephitic atmosphere the like of which is not to be found in the domicile of any other animal. Stables and shippons, and even pig-styes, have their peculiar smells, but they are not poisonous, or repulsive, or offensive as these.[27]

The formation of the Manchester and Salford District Provident Society (DPS) in 1833 was inspired by Dr James Kay (later Sir James Kay Shuttleworth) and Mr William Langton, both of whom 'felt the impulse ... to do something immediately as private citizens to help their weaker fellows'.[28] According to Kidd the DPS 'remained the most prestigious and influential philanthropic body in Manchester' throughout Victoria's reign.[29] Two fundamental principles remained their touchstone, first was the encouragement of thrift and second was the giving of advice and help. The possibility that working-class morals and habits could be transformed by an effective middle-class society remained attractive to some of the city's prominent commercial and business families for the remainder of the century. As a consequence the DPS between 1870 and 1890 was greatly influenced by the Philips and Heywood families who were

Unitarians, and others such as the Reisses and Langtons mainly of Liberal, low-church or non-conformist persuasions.[30] Although these families had continued the bourgeois association with the DPS into the later decades of Victoria's reign, the representatives were then no longer originators of commercial capital. Instead, they personified the English 'process whereby the second generation of any parvenu bourgeois family could be assimilated into the "upper class" by the vehicle of a public school education'.[31]

Unplanned charitable disbursements were frowned on by the DPS but the exceptional distress associated with the 1860s downturn in textiles had found the society 'raising and dispensing of money by way of relief, an activity against which it had always set its face'.[32] The committee recognized how they had transgressed their own principles by misplaced emotion and reintroduced their more rigorous stance. They then became aware that by refusing to distribute emergency funds they risked losing local influence and motivated by 'the energy and enthusiasm of Mr Herbert Philips' instituted 'various new activities'.[33] These included a sick relief fund, a convalescent home and the development of the Manchester and Salford Provident Dispensary Association.

DPS decisions during the 1870s were made by surprisingly few members. For example, an average of only five members attended the monthly meetings of the general committee during 1875.[34] Although the DPS shared the Charity Organisation Society's objectives of encouraging thrift and suppressing mendicity, there was the important difference that the DPS did not concentrate on attempting to rationalize the activities of other charities. Some of the coolness and friction with other philanthropic agencies and the public at large which characterized most provincial COSs was therefore avoided by the DPS.

The first DPS committee in 1833 had sixty members each responsible for a district in the towns much on the style attributed to Thomas Chalmers in Glasgow. Committee members also performed the role of district visitor. Eventually other commitments coupled with the residential middle-class drift to suburbia slackened enthusiasm for personally administering to what often seemed an unappreciative and surly poor. The lack of volunteers led to a centralized structure with salaried officers.[35]

Like the London COS and the Liverpool CRS, the Manchester and Salford DPS were fortunate in retaining the long-term professional services of an extremely capable individual to head their salaried administration. Their agent James Smith, appointed in 1855, remained the senior executive officer for over 35 years. The respect afforded to Smith by the DPS can be gauged from their presentation in 1877 of a testimonial in 'recognition of his long and valuable services'; it comprised 'a handsome Timepiece and a Bank Book containing £1112 1s.0d.'.[36] In the same year the total relief provided to the Manchester and Salford poor by the DPS Sick Relief Department was valued at £877 divided between 601 cases.

Birmingham

During the first half of Victoria's reign the city of Birmingham expanded rapidly as a manufacturing centre without much middle-class worry about the jerry-building which by 1870 had created slum dwellings for many of its 450000 inhabitants. A mid nineteenth-century visitor compared Birmingham to an abominable domestic scenario:

> Select a large kitchen with an incurably smoky chimney and when the wind is in the wrong quarter cover the floor with a multitude of bricks, with here and there a fire extinguisher intervening, here and there a pepper box. Shut the door and look through the keyhole when the smoke is predominant, and you will have a bird's eye view of Birmingham.[37]

Joseph Chamberlain prior to becoming mayor in 1873 described Birmingham as 'one of the ugliest towns in England'.[38] During three dramatic years Chamberlain's much-reported infrastructure and public health schemes put the city on the way to becoming a more acceptable environment. In its social elites the city had similarities with Manchester in having a leadership caucus of middle-class Liberals with commitments towards Protestant non-conformism and few signs of a socially conscious local aristocracy. According to Briggs, three socio-economic characteristics distinguished Birmingham from other Victorian industrial cities: (a) work was carried out in small workshops; (b) many of the workforce were skilled; and (c) there was an unusual amount of social mobility.[39]

The Edgbaston Mendicity Society, started in 1870, developed within five years into the Birmingham COS with Joseph Chamberlain as its first president. The founding committee comprising eight males and one female was chaired by the Revd. J.C. Blissard. Their primary aims were 'repressing mendicity and assisting the deserving poor'. The society warned unsuspecting philanthropists about being hoodwinked by the pernicious poor amongst whom 'the professionals are fertile in lies' because 'to the public they tell one tale, to our officer a wholly different one'.[40] Compared with the growing prominence of Birmingham as a city, the local COS remained a low-key operation in spite of the Birmingham

Poor Law guardians applying a rigorous attack on outdoor relief throughout the 1880s.

In their formative years the society provided Edgbaston ratepayers with tickets entitling them to free advice on whether an applicant was deserving. From 1875 an annual subscription of ten shillings was imposed which 'would entitle the householder to a supply of the Society's tickets'.[41] Birmingham COS's ticket system was broadly similar to the procedures attempted by other provincial societies in its supply of tickets over-printed with their address to personal subscribers, charities, clergy and Poor Law representatives. The intention was that instead of the ticket-holder providing immediate relief they would offer the supplicant a ticket for presentation at the COS office. Searching examinations were then made into personal circumstances of the supplicant before the investigation results and recommendations were sent to the intermediate agency which had distributed the ticket informing them whether or not the case was deserving. At Birmingham those among the middle class who sampled the ticket system were given every assurance that the final recommendations had been compiled only after careful consideration by a Friday afternoon 'Committee of twelve gentlemen' after the COS agent had presented his report on each case.[42] The fact that a substantial proportion of supplicants were judged to be 'undeserving' satisfied COS ideas about the need to root out and reject imposters.

Brighton

Brighton was only a small seaside town of 3500 inhabitants when in 1784 the Prince of Wales chose to take up residence in the belief that sea-bathing was good for his health. The world of fashion followed him and the town quickly became a place of social importance.[43] The population expanded rapidly through Victoria's reign reaching 90 011 in 1871 before adding a further 30 000 inhabitants during the next twenty years. Most of Brighton's growth centred on its attraction as a fashionable seaside resort with ancillary industries like boat-building, fishing, brewing and house-building, mainly servicing the burgeoning demands of the pleasure centre.[44] The railways created an industrial base with the locomotive-works constructing many celebrated steam engines.

Along a three mile coastal stretch of 'palatial houses, gay shops and fine hotels' the wealth and fashion of England was displayed. The contrasting picture was in the town's back lanes of dingy slums of 'narrow streets and courts' which were 'for the most part ill-ventilated, badly-drained if at all and grossly overcrowded'.[45] When during winter the

Emergence of the Provincial Societies

holiday trade collapsed and the wealthy residents returned to town for the London season, life among the poor became precarious with a 'great deal of appalling poverty'.[46]

The Brighton, Hove and Preston Charity Organisation Society (Brighton COS) was one of the earliest provincial COSs and had the long-established Brighthelmston Provident Institution as its antecedent. A promising crowd at the first Brighton COS annual meeting in 1872 seemed to augur well for strong local support. The mayor presided over an attendance including members of the town's elite, the chairman and vice-chairmen of the board of guardians, the vicar and members of the ancient professions. Prof. Fawcett MP tendered his apologies for absence. The mayor regretted the 'lamentable fact that the excessively idle might be numbered in tens of thousands' but was confident that in co-operation with the local guardians the emerging Brighton COS would direct charity 'into the proper channel so that it might do real good and not mischief'.[47]

The vicar of Brighton, the Revd. Dr J. Hannah, saw the COS as having three objectives, namely (a) to bring organized co-operation among the various sources of charitable relief, (b) to investigate every case of apparent distress and (c) to suppress mendicity.[48] General Cavenagh commended the COS to Brighton residents and forecast with ill-fated enthusiasm that within a year or two every local benevolent society would be in communication with the COS who would then not need to spend one penny on relief but merely after investigation refer applicants to the most appropriate local society.[49]

Brighton COS adopted a consistent verbal formula in their subsequent annual reports. They adopted a habitual routine of self-congratulation on their attainments over the previous twelve months followed by a confession as to how disappointing their progress had actually been, especially in their failure to convert the town's charities.[50] Signs of public apathy about the COS had been soon apparent. The *Brighton Daily News* reporting on the COS second annual meeting in the Royal Pavilion mentioned 'the audience – which was a very small one'.[51] Years later Brighton COS admitted that 'the work of the Society is still only in its infancy'.[52]

Southampton

Southampton situated along the south coast from Brighton also bred a Charity Organisation Society which attempted to apply the London ideology as imitatively as possible. Socio-economically the two coastal towns were quite different as was reflected in the composition of the respective COS committees. Whereas Brighton COS was greatly influenced by the leisured classes and higher Church of England echelons, the COS at Southampton was controlled by active professionals and by businessmen.

The growth of Southampton as a port was fired by commercial pressures centred on its deep-water facilities which became all the more important as the size of ships increased. The population of Southampton which was 7629 in 1801 had grown tenfold a century later. There were no large factories in Southampton of the type found in the industrial north of England. Employers in shipyards, docks and building all offered jobs on a casual basis. A survey in 1883 suggested that only one-third of the dock labourers 'may be called able-bodied' with many earning wages so low and variable that 'women and children nearly starve', men 'drink more than they can afford' and 'it is a mystery how they live at all'.[53] Some years later an article in the *Southampton Times* claimed 'poverty was much more widespread than had been thought' and 'its causes more complex than the COS diagnosis' which simply blamed it on many among the poor having 'an idle and vicious character'.[54] Mr Tom McCarthy, organizer of the Dock Labour Union, speaking about the plight of Southampton dock workers claimed that whereas 'people talked about the country being proud of their workers and of the British working-men being the finest specimen of their class ... let them come to look at the specimens of British subjects fighting for bread at the Dock gates for themselves, their wives and their families'.[55]

Two of the most enthusiastic supporters for the idea of rationalizing Southampton charities and co-ordinating them with Poor Law activities were the Drs Griffin and Langstaff, both experienced Poor Law medical officers. In 1875 they attacked what they saw as the out-relief profligacy of local guardians and relieving officers. The Southampton COS inaugural conference of that year, chaired by the mayor, was attended by over sixty representatives from local relief agencies. Dr Griffin claimed that Southampton pauperism was extraordinarily high and that advantages would accrue to ratepayers and to the poor from combining the Poor Law and charity. Objections were voiced both from those concerned about the COS 'interfering with the action of charity' and from Mr C.C. Smith, clerk to the guardians, who challenged Griffin's claims about excessive Southampton pauperism.[56] The *Southampton Times* warned the COS about 'indiscreetly' magnifying the amount of pauperism and that 'anything in the way of an inquisitorial treatment of the subjects of charity would be most reprehensible'.[57] But COS stalwarts were undeterred. Within a few weeks Griffin was claiming that 'at present the knowledge that a lazy, a dishonest and a squandered life is as well rewarded by our laws and by indiscriminate charity, as a steady, hard-working frugal one is a great check to individual effort and thrift'.[58] Within a couple of years Mr Russell Gurney MP acknowledged that Southampton COS was gaining few converts and was attempting to establish itself in the face of a 'great many misgivings, a good many misrepresentations and perhaps prejudices'.[59]

In their reports the Southampton COS always allowed themselves a few eulogies about how favourably their principles had influenced local society before admitting their bewilderment that the general public were still inhibiting COS progress by failing to grasp the importance of their mission. The Dean of Winchester expressed 'the hope that the Society would be much more largely supported' because 'if they had larger funds they would do a great deal more good'.[60] Ideas about introducing Elberfeld principles at Southampton were still-born through lack of support. Worse followed in the 1880s with regrets about their subscription list 'falling off'.[61] The society's work was still being done by a 'few old members and that few of the younger members made a practice of attending the weekly meetings'.[62] The Committee admitted that owing to lack of funds they were 'often pained by their inability to relieve cases which cried out for aid'.[63]

Leamington

The popularity of medicinal springs plus the financial interest of London and Midlands property speculators expanded Leamington rapidly from only 315 inhabitants in 1801 to 15 723 fifty years later when the rate of population growth normalized.[64] The associated house-building boom was augmented by the demand for hotels and shops created by the influx of spa visitors. Two distinct residential areas developed. North of the River Leam was fashionable middle class whereas south of the river was the dingier downmarket old town. When in the 1850s enthusiasm for medicinal spas declined the local economy was hit by the shortage of health-seeking visitors and by the evacuation from north-bank properties of high-spending residents. This caused not only a slump in building activity but also a sharp fall in the need for such as stablemen, grooms, jewellers and tailors servicing the better-off. There were few compensatory jobs in local industry with nothing other than a small brewery and a minor foundry.

But it was not only the Leamington working class who found themselves threatened. There were also real economic dangers looming for local professionals and businessmen who recognized the threat to their livelihood from further deterioration of the town's image and sought means of shielding loyal spa visitors from images of local poverty. COS principles seemed attractive in being admirably suited to ridding the town of scrounging imposters and eliminating wasteful indiscriminate charity while possibly instilling self-respect into the squalid lives of 'deserving' working-class residents.[65]

The Leamington Charity Organisation and Relief Society (COS) was formed in 1875 to support the 'cause of charity organisation in Warwickshire and particularly in Leamington'.[66] Active support came mainly from local businessmen and professionals although the appearance of the committee was buttressed by the names of respected members of the community. There were also 30 founder patrons including dignitaries such as the Lords Leigh and Yarmouth, together with local gentry like William Willes and Richard Badger.[67] In addition there were 28 founding 'patronesses'. The first chairman was the Revd. T.B. Whitehurst, Rector of Redford, and early meetings were attended by the mayor who claimed that the same 'system of the organisation of charity has been in existence among the Jews for many years'.[68]

Annual reports from Leamington COS included a monotonous succession of member's obituaries but important exceptions included the Hon. Secretary Mr G. Cunnew and the Hon. Treasurer Mr J. Page who both retained their early appointments through to the 1890s. Another founder committee member with long-term association was the Hon. and Revd. J.W. Leigh, brother of Lord Leigh who himself chaired a number of annual meetings.

By the 1880s the all-male committee of around fifteen had the names of clergymen making up about one-third of their number with almost as many retired officers from the armed services. Because the Leamington COS management committee was small in number it created personal pressure on members to provide their time regularly at weekly relief meetings as well as sharing a daily duty-rota for urgent cases. Initially Leamington COS had two paid employees, a resident officer in Mr J. Gilliland and a Miss Palmer who was employed 'to use every diligence in collecting funds'. The society's financial frailty meant that Miss Palmer was soon made redundant and the two functions were combined in Gilliland.[69] As the years passed so the 'quality of the Enquiry Officer's reports deteriorated as did the statements from the applicants' referees, which declined both in number and detail' so that the 'genuine social-work activities such as the investigation of the moral and physical condition of the working class through personal contact disappeared'.[70] There were clear signs that Leamington COS assistance was frequently intended to ameliorate immediate distress with little relevance to the principle of motivating self-sufficiency.

From the start Leamington COS found the shortage of voluntary visitors and funds restrictive. The society regretted 'that its usefulness is still very much limited by the want of increased Funds to enable them more liberally to supply the intermitting and temporary wants of the needy, sick and aged poor'.[71] In 1882 the *Leamington News* referred 'to the want of funds' of the local COS and described the committee as 'gentlemen of experience, position and integrity'.[72] But the following year's COS report still lamely expressed disappointment that 'some kind-hearted and charitable persons support it but feebly, while others are prejudiced against it' before adding that 'such persons are earnestly requested to consider again the question of charitable aid'.[73] In 1890 a *Leamington Chronicle* editorial 'acknowledged that the Society is still decidedly unpopular and probably not even the Vigilance Association excites a more general sentiment of mistrust'.[74]

Birkenhead

The River Mersey had dictated the growth of Birkenhead even before the first metal ships were on the slipways in the middle of the century, but in the decade from 1871 the town's population of 42 997 almost doubled and reached 99 857 by 1891.[75] Docks, flour mills, corn warehouses, tanning yards and Thompson Bros' Gelatine and Glue Works all played a part in the phenomenal growth of what became a county borough in 1877. But it was the shipbuilding and ship-repair yards mainly associated with the Laird family which dominated the Wirral town. Generations of the Laird family not only represented Birkenhead in Parliament and headed the town council but also participated directly in developing the social fabric of the area. Much as William Rathbone dominated the founding of the CRS across the Mersey so the Laird family spearheaded attempts to inculcate workers with self-help principles and alert the middle class about the evils of haphazard charity.

Work along the Mersey was greatly affected by adverse weather which brought the 'utter stagnation of outdoor employment'.[76] Casual labour with violent demand fluctuations characterized Victorian riverside life. A contemporary local newspaper explained that 'an east wind, which keeps the ships out, means starvation and a west wind which brings them in means working day and night and an amount of prosperity often leads people into improvident, thriftless and foolish ways'.[77] Unlike northern mill towns which demanded female labour, few women were employed in the docks or shipyards. In the conditions of economic unpredictability it was sensible for employers to encourage provident schemes so that working men could accept responsibility for ironing out income troughs.

The Birkenhead Provident and Benevolent Society (PBS), formed in 1863, had Conservative MP John Laird as its first president and William Jackson, a Liberal MP, as vice-president. The PBS's 30 strong all-male general committee had representatives from business, commerce and the professions. Initially there were no clergy and an early resolution asked 'the Clergy and Ministers of all denominations ... to call attention of their congregation to the existence of the Society, inviting them to contribute funds ... '[78]

Although according to their rules the provision of relief was intended to be 'occasional' the BPS benevolent department were soon under pressure because of the exceptional distress in 1863. As well as becoming involved in a civic emergency fund they also provided relief from their own funds in the form of bread, oatmeal, groceries and provisions at a cost of £89 19s.8d. spread over 628 cases of which the nationalities were: English 294, Irish 233, Welsh 46, 'Scotch' 54 and one 'Alien'. Of these 476 had 'sickness or suffering from accidents' and the remainder were in 'temporary distress through want of employment'.[79] The BPS also issued 'recommendation notes' to hospitals and were tempted to construct a soup kitchen.

The PBS became the Birkenhead Association for Organising Charitable Relief and Repressing Mendicity (COS) early in the 1870s. By 1876, still chaired by John Laird and dominated by businessmen and professionals, it now had the names of local clergymen making up a third of its 51 strong committee.[80] The active clerical participants were mainly senior Church of England clergymen typified by the Revd. Canon W. Saumerez Smith, a vice-chairman for over a decade before being made Bishop of Sydney.

When in 1872 the Birkenhead COS became one of the first provincial societies to be affiliated to the London COS they took as their text 'Blessed is he that *considereth* the poor'. Unlike the Liverpool CRS on the other side of the Mersey, Birkenhead COS did not see themselves as being a 'relief' society and had rules much closer to the Manchester and Salford DPS.[81]

During their first year Birkenhead PBS had persuaded 1863 investors to deposit a total of £472 6s.3d.[82] Voluntary visitors were essential for the success of their venture but they admitted that they covered 'little more than half the town, owing to insufficient numbers of these zealous labourers'.[83] Their successors, the Birkenhead COS, also complained about being restricted through a shortage of volunteers but by usually being able to muster a group in excess of thirty actually fared rather better than many among their provincial peers.

At Birkenhead COS visitors distributed tracts entitled 'Thrift' together with handbills published by the Ladies' Sanitary Society aimed at promoting habits of cleanliness among the working classes.[84] COS ladies were put on guard against succumbing to misplaced pity and were warned that when dealing with the poor 'an expectation of gifts impairs or destroys the efforts towards frugality and thrift'.[85] A delicate line in personal relationships with poor families had therefore to be attempted by COS ladies as they were also told to establish 'a genial intercourse ... with their numerous clients' and lead the poor by example to providential actions so as to eventually make them 'independent of the fluctuations of the labour market'. Visitors were reassured that they provided 'above the spirit of thrift, a very healthy and refining influence ... in the homes of the poor people resident in the most degraded parts of the town'.[86]

Mr C.J. Ribton Turner of London COS informed his Birkenhead audience in September 1876 that as pauperism increased so did the decadence of the nation. This made it essential for reciprocity of action between charity and the Poor Law. Ribton Turner pointed out that benevolent persons often did more harm than good and that although not widely recognized the organized principles of the COS were 'more in the interests of the poor than in those of the donors'.[87]

Oxford

Demographically, nineteenth-century Oxfordshire was unusual in not displaying the population surges of most counties. What industries there were around Oxford city such as textiles, brick-making, quarrying, paper-making, marmalade-making and printing, were small-scale when compared with many northern factories. In Oxford the manufacturing trades arose either from 'purely domestic arts' or because they were made necessary by the 'presence of a large and ever-growing university, which naturally brought trade to a county that would otherwise have been purely agricultural'.[88] By the beginning of the twentieth century the University Press, which employed 650, was the largest industrial concern.

With the university as the biggest employer of labour the working class in Oxford suffered the same effects of irregular employment as did seasonal and casual workers elsewhere. The university divided the employment year into terms and vacations – periods of activity and of comparative stagnation. Workers in the lower echelons of college service rarely earned sufficient in term-time to tide them over the vacations. This was especially so for the women employed as college domestics.

The Oxford Anti-Mendicity and Charity Organisation Association (COS) formed in 1872–3 looked successfully to the university both for funds and committee members. They became affiliated to London COS in 1873 and saw themselves as a way of allowing undergraduates to learn something of the condition of working people as well as providing a 'safety-valve' against any misplaced generosity of young innocent university members. Furthermore by use of the ticket system it was hoped to induce undergraduates to trust the COS for the 'judicious relief of the numerous travelling poor who, in a district as central as Oxford, inevitably meet them in every walk they take'.[89]

It was not unusual in the 1860s for the COS's predecessor, the Oxford Anti-Mendicity Society, to annually relieve about 5000 poor travellers. There were mixed feelings among Anti-Mendicity Society members in 1872 about whether they should allow themselves to be 'coalesced' with the fledgling charity organizers. A leading protagonist for the amalgamation was Colonel the Hon. W.E. Sackville West. He claimed his experience with the London COS showed Oxford to be ideally suited to COS operations because everyone was 'playing his own tune on his own instrument' and being such a 'monstrous evil' that it could not be exaggerated.[90] The chairman of the Oxford Incorporated Parishes guardians hoped that Oxford COS would soon be directly related to the local Poor Law by the 1869 principles of 'Mr Goschen who had explained how these agencies could be worked together without any detriment to each other'.[91] The Oxford *Undergraduates' Journal* believed the emergent society 'to be taking a step in the right direction' and cordially commended their readers to finance the recruitment of a 'well-qualified officer' who would be more effective in supervising enquiries than would attempts by members of the university who had 'neither the time, opportunity or knowledge ...'[92]

Changes were quickly made in the modus operandi of the composite society. Reductions in anti-mendicity activities allowed concentration on charity organization. COS reformers arguing for a clamp-down on the former Anti-Mendicity Society's night refuge referred to a user-questionnaire which was interpreted as showing that only 17 out of 290 refuge users had supplied satisfactorily truthful answers. This allegedly confirmed that the vast majority of cases were 'either notoriously drunken and worthless characters, or people who impersonated other and more deserving people, or at the best were idle and vagrant'.[93] It was clear to COS vice-chairman Alderman Randall that in 1873 Oxford they 'were developing a system of hypocrisy'.[94] Within a short time free admission to the refuge was discontinued.

Emergence of the Provincial Societies 81

Oxford COS were convinced that if their principles 'were more acted upon' they would 'mitigate the frightful condition of the population' which, according to a report from the Poor Parishes Fund, was so bad as to compel more than half the residents at times of illness or distress to seek the assistance of richer neighbours.[95] COS public meetings in Oxford to propagate their principles had limited success. Typical was their 1879 conference 'kindly presided' over by Lord Jersey which 'failed to call forth ... much interest ...'[96] In the summer of 1888 two meetings intended to put 'before the wealthy district of Oxford the work of the Society in the poorer districts' were both 'for a variety of reasons ... thinly attended'.[97] The Revd. L.R. Phelps, Oxford COS chairman and Fellow of Oriel College, admitted in 1890 that 'we have not succeeded in recruiting many members or much support from outside the University, still less have we been able to enlist any of the working class'.[98]

Reading

The rapid increase in the Reading population during Victoria's reign resulted from its ideal geographical location as a rail and road link with all cardinal points. The commercial possibilities provided by the fast modernized forms of transport were recognized by local entrepreneurs involved in a miscellany of activities like biscuit-making, horticulture, brick- and tile-making, iron-founding and printing. Companies like Huntley and Palmer grabbed the opportunities eagerly. Their biscuit-making workforce of 50 at mid-century increased a hundredfold by the 1890s.[99] The Sutton Seed Co. gained prominence when consulted by the government about appropriate quick-growing crops to alleviate the 1846 Irish famine and Sutton's seeds became famous throughout Britain.[100]

A common characteristic of many burgeoning Reading firms was that most employees needed few skills and earned low wages. Low pay for low skills was still being identified in the early twentieth century by Bowley and Burnett-Hurst as the principal cause of primary poverty in Reading.[101] In spite of this disadvantage Reading's industrial growth continued as a magnet for the under-employed Berkshire agricultural labourers whose mobility was not discouraged by the stringent out-relief policies at nearby Poor Law unions like Bradfield, Wallingford and Faringdon.

When the Reading Charity Organisation Society (COS) was formed in 1874 their first chairman, the Revd. J.H. Jenkinson, alleged that 'the apparent severity of the Poor Law was found to be an absolute necessity' as the prevention of 'pauperism was the strict object of true charity' and explained why COS principles were 'disliked only by the bad and the worthless'.[102] Reading COS saw themselves as a 'Sub-Committee' of London COS with themselves a 'Branch' of the 'Head Society'.[103] Their first annual report stressed that 'the Society's first business is investigation' and claimed vindication of their approach by their discovery that 'not more than one fourth' of applicants deserved COS relief.[104] This stark interpretation of life among the needy could not be maintained for long in the face of public comment. The COS then softened their stance and claimed to have recognized that 'tact, firmness and tenderness' were also ingredients needed in the 'battle of Pauperism'.[105] The committee maintained that 'instead of trying to reduce beneficence to a mere system' they were endeavouring 'to make all Charity, as far as possible, personal and direct, based on intimate knowledge between the giver and receiver' with the encouragement of 'every emotion of pity and kindness' while discouraging the carelessness that leads to 'idleness and vice'.[106]

Long-term paucity of COS subscriptions and donations was a clear sign that the Reading middle classes were not enthused. Benevolent bodies preferred risking being hoodwinked occasionally rather than forcing their poorer neighbours through the rigours of COS examination and analysis.[107] In 1881 the Reading COS admitted their funds were 'at a low ebb' and overheads were reduced by an arrangement with their new agent Mr Crapp whereby their office rent would be included in his salary of £26 per annum.[108] It was much the same story throughout the decade with a catalogue of COS excuses attempting to explain their parlous condition.[109] Their Hon. Sec. Mr R. Worsley expressed concern that there still appeared 'to exist some misunderstanding as to the practical work of the Society' and quoted Lord Derby's recent comments about 'the constant attacks made on the Society by dishonest or ignorant persons ...'[110]

Before discussing responses to approaches by provincial COSs in their attempts to rationalize local relief agencies it is instructive to flavour the general impression provided by Mr George Whitcombe of Gloucester COS in his paper *Charity Organisations in Provincial Towns*. He described some of the 'difficulties and wants' of 'attaining co-operation with the Poor Law Guardians, the Clergy, other Ministers of Religion, and local charities which were considered to be of the utmost importance'.[111] Whitcombe enumerated the common provincial COS problems of inadequate funding, the ever-present 'want of sufficient voluntary assistance for private inquiry or as almoners', and with no 'ladies or gentlemen able or willing to devote sufficient time' to charity organization. He portrayed the general failure of provincial COSs to capture sufficient middle-class support or to generate trust among the poor.

In the remainder of this chapter discussion centres on the few successes and the many frustrations of provincial societies attempting to build close working ties with other relief agencies. The survey conveys the indefatigable COS optimism in the face of adversity sponsored by a public who believed COS investigative procedures took precedence over pity.

THE PROVINCIAL COSs AND POOR LAW GUARDIANS

In June 1871 the LGB surveyed 70 Poor Law unions in southern England and showed that 63 boards of guardians had no contact whatsoever with persons administering charity and that in the remaining seven unions contact was unsystematic.[112] There was shared confidence between the LGB and the COS that this situation would soon change with the expected widespread acceptance of Goschenian concepts. The Revd. E.F. Glanville, who was also chairman of the Incorporated Parishes Poor Law union as well as a member of Oxford COS, was quite certain in the heady early days that the society 'could only be successful by an unreserved and complete inter-communication with the Poor-Law Officers'.[113] Such close rapport was to be rarely even approached.

Prompted by the LGB there was an initial acceptance amongst provincial guardians about the need to proceed with the out-relief crusade together with a readiness to consider co-operating with local charity organizers. For most guardians any such willingness could never materialize in practical terms simply because there was no attempt by local worthies to rationalize charity. However, in a limited number of urban areas guardians were keen enough to become prime-movers in forming a local COS. Brighton and Oxford were two such centres.

The fact that at Brighton the chairman and two vice-chairmen of the Poor Law board were founder members of the local COS initiated early relationships that would have gained approval from George Goschen. Co-operation between the two institutions was illustrated by their joint handling of successful legal proceedings against a Mr Boon and family seen as emigration imposters skilled at extracting money by false pretences.[114] At Oxford the active involvement in the early 1870s of the Revd. Glanville might have been expected to have led to powerful early formal working relationships between the Oxford COS and the Poor Law officials. In reality, although there was mutual sympathy on crusade principles, it took about ten years to develop much liaison between the two agencies involving some semblance of co-ordinated action but even this was never 'formulated'.[115] The system eventually adopted at Oxford in 1882 involved the Incorporated Parishes Board referring likely deserving cases to the COS for investigation, the idea being that charitable relief would then be provided to deserving cases in 'temporary distress'. The COS believed that co-operation would guarantee 'a more thorough investigation of cases before assistance is given, and so check imposition, whilst after such assistance has been given, will insure personal visiting by members of the Society'.[116] The actual number of cases transferred was small. In the first nine months of the scheme 31 cases considered by the guardians to have a reasonable chance of being deserving were despatched to the COS. Thirteen were returned to the workhouse as not being worthy of charitable help. Subsequently the proportion of cases rejected by the COS remained so high as to lead to the transfer arrangement foundering.

In 1887 the Oxford COS complained that their efforts to diminish outdoor relief by 'pensions and grants to aged persons, to widows and to the sick have not always been welcomed' and asked themselves whether perhaps they were attempting too much in wanting to simultaneously 'relieve the ratepayers and to save the deserving poor from degradation'.[117] Whereas the level of co-operation achieved at Oxford might appear low key, Mr J.J. Henley complained that in the whole of the district for which he was the LGB general inspector, Oxford was the only place where the COS had made 'an honest attempt to take off the hands of the Guardians all persons who ought not to be receiving Poor Law relief'.[118] An important factor underlying guardians' hesitancy was that most provincial COSs did not fulfil their seminal objective of persuading other charities about the value of their principles. Therefore pragmatic guardians had little to gain from appearing too close to a society ostracized by other charities, many of which had members who could be influential allies at election time.

At Reading nothing would have pleased the COS more than to have been able to develop a closer association with their strict local guardians. With this in mind the COS regularly described how they and the guardians intended to co-operate.[119] Unfortunately for Reading COS their inability to gain financial or emotional support from the public meant they lacked resources. In most years the number of cases referred between the official and organized voluntary sector were numbered in single figures.[120]

Although provincial COSs soon discovered they were unlikely to gain a structured day-to-day relationship with their local Poor Law representatives, it was COS practice as at Reading to attempt a public illusion of closer affinity. Cordial references in provincial COS reports about their local board of guardians were commonplace and the COS harvested whatever publicity they could from any hint that implied favourable guardian response. As an example Birmingham COS included in their 1880 report formal thanks to the Poor Law representatives for consenting to 'mark upon lists' furnished to them by the society 'the names of those who are in receipt of poor relief'.[121] But Birmingham guardians declined entering into a more structured working partnership.[122] Henry Griffiths Jnr later admitted that Birmingham COS did not co-operate with the Poor Law officers except by referring to them 'chronic cases of poverty'.[123] At the other large cities of Manchester and Liverpool there were nominal relationships which were at their strongest when it suited the guardians. In evidence to a House of Lords Committee, it was said of both centres that 'persons are referred to the COS or to other Societies which administer charity among the people, but it does not amount to very much'.[124]

It was at times of exceptional distress that guardians were most amenable. Manchester DPS were reluctant after the 1860s cotton famine to again participate in doling out benefits to the jobless poor without investigation. Nevertheless their resolve weakened in the threatening circumstances of the late 1870s when they were persuaded to assist in the distribution of emergency funds.

James Smith, the DPS agent, contacted the guardians of Manchester, Salford and Chorlton unions 'bearing in mind the dangers of another unusually severe winter, inviting them to provide the names of all respectable and educated persons who might apply for assistance and whom it would be a pity to pauperise'.[125] In the event only in a few cases 'did the character of the applicants come up to the standard of, or seem to require the interference of the Society', particularly as 'during the last few months the Society has had to exercise the greatest caution in dealing with applications for relief'. These frugal attitudes were followed in the same report by information about the DPS adding another storey to their offices to provide a 'large and commodious Board-room, more offices, and increased accommodation in general, making the whole suite of offices as complete and perfect ...'[126]

It was when trade was weak that the Liverpool CRS scheme to help local people find more secure employment in factory districts outside the city was most welcomed by guardians. The CRS interpreted their job-placement function as obligating to them those among the poor who accepted their assistance to migrate. After a job had been accepted elsewhere as a result of a CRS initiative they then had no compunction about contacting the distant employer to check on the Liverpool family's progress. Details of wages received and comments on their performance as workers were published by the CRS with personal family details flimsily disguised by the use of initials rather than the emigrant's full name.

In Birkenhead the COS welcomed 'the courtesy and attention with which their communications have been received by the Guardians ...' but as the number of outdoor paupers in the town steadily increased from 1877 it seems unlikely that the majority of the board were greatly enthused by COS ideologies (see Figure 3.7).[127] In those few localities where there were relatively 'friendly relations', as at Brighton, the COS ridiculed guardians in other parts of the country where there was 'very much more to be accomplished' by a 'more just' application of the Poor Law.[128] Albert Pell, speaking on the same theme when chairing an 1890 COS conference, extolled his own special contribution as a guardian in virtually eradicating outdoor relief at Brixworth but had no doubts that for the COS generally the 'people who trouble our wheels are the Poor Law Guardians'.[129]

Guardians generally moved from viewing the COS with a certain cautious sympathy to a situation where apathy or opposition became the vogue. At Southampton any possibility of friendly co-operation was immediately jeopardized when the emerging local COS lambasted the alleged boundless mischievous generosity of the town's guardians. When in 1876 the Southampton COS did ask guardians for 'a periodical reciprocation of information' the board frigidly referred the request to an internal committee.[130] The universal rule that committee referral is a recipe for matters to be sidelined was not contravened. The best Southampton COS eventually achieved was permission to extract information from Poor Law documents made available weekly at a fixed time. Even this limited concession was achieved only because a number of Southampton businessmen, prominent in the COS, doubled as local guardians.[131]

Mr Dent of Bristol COS confessed in the 1890s that even with the advantage of four COS committee members being guardians on the Barton Regis Poor Law board, they had been able to establish only limited co-operation, and with the other two Bristol unions the COS were 'practically inactive'.[132] The Revd. Campion Mackgill of Croydon COS did not see 'much chance of our Society working with the Board of Guardians'.[133] Leeds COS approached local guardians asking them not to curtail the Poor Law outdoor child allowance to parents for the period the COS had arranged for a particular child to enjoy a rare country holiday. Charles Loch was infuriated by the Leeds COS plan which he ridiculed as being an unhealthy mix of voluntary relief and Poor Law doles. The mix seemed to him 'utterly – well – heretical'.[134]

RELATIONSHIPS WITH OTHER CHARITIES

Whatever may have been the obstacles against fruitful working relationships between Poor Law guardians and the provincial COSs, the fields of endeavour ploughed in attempts to organize existing charities were even more arid. George Whitcombe confessed that Gloucester COS wished for 'closer co-operation with the various local charities' and asked COS conference delegates for suggestions as to how this might be attained.[135] Solutions did not abound as most of his audience shared his problem. The early COS belief that other charities would be enchanted by the possibility of having their disbursements co-ordinated through the scientific methodology of organized philanthropy proved wide of the mark. Instead of the anticipated welcoming approval from charitable institutions the COS were shunned or ignored. They had insensitively missed the point that their methodology would be widely interpreted as attempting to override 'the charitable work of the clergy, ministers and Societies, often strong rivals of each other'.[136] In spite of this fundamental setback COS enthusiasts retained an unquenchable fervour to attain organized charitable structures but their quest remained a pipe-dream.

The COS would not compromise their organizing principle and in 1890 still proclaimed the same theme of 21 years earlier. The haphazard performances of endowed charities and managers of hospitals remained 'mischievous' and for the private 'miserable philanthropist' there was nothing the COS could do 'but to pray for him'.[137] Earlier they had cautioned 'the benevolent very earnestly against yielding even a moment's credence' to those 'who ply the public with their pitiful tales' and urged people to understand that 'to help such people *is only to perpetuate pauperism and to reward improvidence and drunkenness*'.[138] Their warnings were scarcely heeded.

Like their COS peers elsewhere, it was at times of exceptional distress that the Birmingham society were placed in the ideological dilemma of participating in the distribution of emergency funds. On such occasions the COS pleasure at being given the opportunity of temporarily joining with other charities was tempered by the knowledge that with the urgency of events they would not be able to impose their normal investigative criteria. Birmingham COS were delighted when the city Relief Fund Committee emphasized the desirability of some permanent organization by which the various charitable agencies could obtain 'mutual information' and 'co-operate to more advantage' but administrators of other charities would have none of it.[139] Whereas most were willing to allow the COS to busy themselves assisting in the distribution of funds raised quickly from public subscription, their response to COS involvement was completely different when it related to established long-term funds of which they themselves were the trustees.[140]

Liverpool CRS made a useful effort to get closer to other charities by allowing their offices to be used during January and February each year to collect subscriptions and donations for various Liverpool charitable institutions. Furthermore, to CRS minds it positioned them at the centre of the city's philanthropic stage. COS interest in the CRS collection system was sufficient to prompt their inclusion in a London conference on 25 May 1883 with an address by William Grisewood, the CRS Secretary. Somewhat to the disappointment of his audience Grisewood explained the limited scope of their scheme and emphasized the need for significantly more progress in approaching other charities on a broader front and in encouraging many more middle-class contributions. To support this last point Grisewood claimed that at least 20 000 Liverpudlians occupied premises with an annual rateable value of not less than £20 per year which he considered to be a reasonable symbolic level of wealth to expect charitable participation. However, supporters of Liverpool's 38 leading charities totalled only 6700 and of these 1200 contributed more than half the total subscriptions.[141]

In the larger cities other middle-class groups attracted to the idea of rationalizing charitable disbursements occasionally attempted to establish themselves in competition with the existing organizing society. Liverpool CRS were constantly alert to the danger of rivals intruding into what they took to be their own relief province. They put the 'public on guard against many of the so-called Charities' appealing to the public through spurious advertisements and collectors.[142] In September 1886 the CRS were dismayed that six different agencies were attempting to organize charity in poverty-stricken Toxteth. When they approached the most prestigious of the six, the Toxteth Relief Society, about the dangers of overlapping the ball was played back into the CRS court with a request for any information that might help the new society.[143] The *Liverpool Review* warned about the public 'feeling of dissatisfaction that had arisen on the method of working of the CRS' which had prompted the formation of the Toxteth Relief Society with Committee members including T.B. Royden MP, Dr Hamilton and Alderman J. Hughes providing 'sufficient guarantee that it will do good work'.[144] People would 'rather starve or go to the workhouse than apply to the Central Relief for aid' according to the *Review* while commenting that they themselves were appalled by CRS jealousy against rivals which unlike themselves would do all their work 'voluntarily and efficiently'.

The same protectionist attitude about their own position was demonstrated by the Manchester and Salford DPS. They were so concerned about the rumour that a competitive organization may be launched with the purpose of focusing more specifically on charity organization that to defeat the possibility they 'adroitly' renamed themselves the District Provident and Charity Organisation Society of Manchester and Salford.[145] But long before that decision they had seen themselves as being representative of the COS in Manchester. For instance when the recently enthroned Bishop Moorhouse wrote to the *Manchester Guardian* suggesting the formation of a committee including 'ministers of all denominations' to bring 'instant, sympathetic and effectual' attention because action from the COS was 'too slow, too clumsy or too unsympathetic', the DPS were spurred to sending a deputation to the Bishop to explain their own function.[146]

Provincial COSs failed to achieve the organizing format envisaged in the ebullient London days of 1869. Nevertheless, partly to avert the danger of diminished attention among fringe members and partly for public relations purposes, COSs published any detail they could about the occasional local charity providing a gesture of co-operation. Brighton clutched at every available straw that might indicate more widespread acceptance of their principles. When the Brighton Jubilee and Accident Fund agreed in 1879 that applications for relief would be 'received and dealt with' by the COS it was interpreted by the *Charity Organisation Reporter* as an excellent omen that they were gaining the confidence of the Brighton public.[147] But even south-coast optimists recognized that such co-operation was precious little to show for their eight years devoted to the principles of charity organization. Towards the end of the 1880s Brighton COS accepted reluctantly that few charitable agencies would co-operate with them and blamed 'popular prejudice, misrepresentation or studied indifference' to a degree that would have 'destroyed' societies with less 'true and just' principles.[148] They lamely admitted in 1888 that 'only one Charity in the town makes use of the Society for investigation purposes – the Jubilee and Accident Fund'.[149]

Much the same story was repeated elsewhere by provincial COSs with their seemingly endless catalogue of complaints that charities appeared blind to the benefits of COS investigative methodology. But there was little hope of developing harmonious working relationships when societies acted on the kind of advice given them by Ribton Turner, the London COS organizing secretary, that other charities be told to abandon their 'individual idiosyncrasies' which so often assisted the head of the family 'to go to the public house ... paying him a premium to beat his wife, put his children in rags and neglect his own duties to his family altogether'.[150] Southampton COS followed the line and told local charities that their haphazardly distributed alms encouraged 'the lies, the deceit and the fraud which laxity fosters, and which children from their earliest age are taught to practise'.[151] Interspersed with the verbal acidity provincial COSs tried to defend themselves from adverse criticisms by asking the public to disregard the frequently made accusation that they were 'an association of amateur detectives, bent on proving that all needy people were imposters'.[152]

The Revd. Phelps considered the COS's 'natural enemy' to be 'the Endowed Charity' when admitting that in Oxford they had not gained 'the administration of other charities' and that 'neither the Trustees nor the administrators of other Charities have ever made official use of the Charity Organisation Society for the purpose of inquiry'.[153] Birmingham COS accepted their isolation from the mainstream of charities and criticized 'the waste of charitable funds ... by the great charitable corporations of a town like Birmingham'.[154] In 1890 Bristol COS regretted the miserable size of their operations and Leeds COS lamented that there was only one local charity with which they had any dealings.[155] In spite of their repeated setbacks provincial COSs remained blinkered in their certainty that others were involved in a 'mean and cruel form of self-indulgence' by refusing to structure charity 'scientifically'.[156]

THE COS AND THE CLERGY

It was quite usual for committees of provincial COSs to include the names of a formidable number of local clergymen. As Charles Loch himself warned about charities in general, enquiry 'not infrequently proves that the display of names on the cover of a Society's report is entirely deceptive'.[157] There are sound reasons for believing that provincial COSs should be included in Loch's generalization. Few clergy participated actively in 'scientifically' organizing charity and some of those listed as COS committee members contributed little or nothing in subscriptions or donations.[158] Active support for the COS tended to be from sects like the Unitarians or from senior echelons of the Established Church. The latter because of their local prominence were quite often persuaded to fulfil a senior position in the provincial COS hierarchy. But Lynedoch Gardiner had no illusions about clergy generally being unresponsive. He regretted that although there had been inadequate co-operation with the Poor Law guardians, the point at which the Charity Organisation Societies had most signally failed was in winning the support of the clergy.[159]

As COS principles and practices became more widely recognized clerical support was eroded further when not only younger 'enlightened' clergy but also many 'old fashioned' clergymen resented COS attempts to intrude into the churches' traditional province of ministering to the poor.[160] The COS complained that even ostensibly sympathetic clergy 'so far from becoming co-operators in organised charity turn the local Committees into relief agencies'.[161] Curates were allegedly all too 'frequently guilty' of recommending support to people of whom the society had little knowledge.[162]

Provincial COSs bemoaned the unacceptably low level of response to their overtures and explained that clerics had 'great difficulty' in working co-operatively towards the rationalized distribution of charity.[163] They suffered from 'mistaken kindness' in seeking to 'gain the friendship of the poor ... by making the approach to charity easy and informal' instead of taking the 'wiser course' used by 'Miss Octavia Hill and her lady rent-collectors who make the taking and not the giving of money the occasion of making friendly relations with their poorer neighbours'.[164] COS commentators endlessly exposed erroneous clerical attitudes such as their mistaken tendency to regard 'hunger as the worst of all evils' rather than moral or spiritual considerations.[165] None of these alleged weaknesses should have been too surprising because Sir Charles Trevelyan had long foreseen that before the COS could be effectual 'every clergyman and minister, and every congregation must be content to work in subordination to a general committee of direction' and correctly predicted that 'the religious difficulty' would be an 'impediment'.[166] London COS seized eagerly on the possibility of gaining support from clergy from a provincial COS proposal that just 'as there is a Hospital Sunday, so should there be a Charity Organisation Sunday'.[167] The idea did not capture the general imagination.

As with other relief agencies the clergy were more prepared to co-operate with those attempting to organize charity when prevailing adverse economic and climatic conditions made it temporarily useful to inject more formal distribution patterns into hastily collected funds. Not only did the Liverpool CRS fill a co-ordinating role during the 1879 distress they also responded by extending their usual facilities for supplying soup, bread and cheese, and cocoa. Short-term support was provided by around forty voluntary 'Scripture Readers, Town Missionaries, and Domestic Missionaries'.[168] When the emergency had subsided, each voluntary helper received 'an illuminated lithographed copy' of the CRS's resolution of thanks for their 'valuable services' and were asked to a 'tea and conference'.[169] But the CRS 'Conference' ploy, commonly used by other provincial COSs in the hope of conjuring recruits, was no more successful than it had been twelve months earlier when the CRS had invited the Liverpool clergy with minimal effect to hear the 'principles and mode of working of the Society ... very fully explained'.[170]

Southampton COS attempted a similar recruiting exercise with their conference on 5 February 1877 which was intended to encourage a formal two-way transfer of information between themselves and clergy. Any sensitive interpretation of the mood of those clergy who did attend should have alerted the COS organizers as to how unlikely they were to get much favourable response for their plan to regularly circulate all local clergy and ministers, lists of poor persons, together with details of how the COS had adjudicated their worthiness.[171] When after two months the Southampton COS found only three clergymen showing interest, the London COS hoped they would not be too discouraged because Southampton's unresponsive experience was 'far from singular'.[172] London recommended that even when there was little reaction from clergy, provincial COSs should continue to bring 'the nature and method of the work of the Society' to their notice at every conceivable opportunity. When as usual such approaches resulted in nothing more than 'a dead letter' with 'information to the clergy ... largely one-way', provincial societies tended to ignore London's advice and abandoned similar procedures as ineffectual expenditure out of already tight budgets.[173]

Senior clergy who did support the COS admitted that many religious societies and parochial clergy had been 'unwilling to use the Society as an instrument of inquiry in their own parishes' and that COSs had 'hitherto only broken the crust' of getting others to take part in 'the Christian and patriotic work which lies open to them'.[174] Even at Oxford where a relatively high proportion of clergy were active COS committee members most were college representatives who accepted that parish clergy and district visitors viewed the COS 'with a certain amount of dislike and mistrust'.[175]

Nor were some clergy satisfied with passively ignoring the COS. Take for example the cutting clerical response to a COS report alleging that clergy would not co-operate, rarely sent cases to the COS and 'were perfectly impossible to organise'. A clergyman replied by asking whether it would ever be possible for 'heaven born charity to pass through the rolling, pressing, squeezing, drying process of a vast piece of machinery and still preserve some of the aroma and flavour of its divine origin'.[176] Another clergyman, the Revd. A.P. Purey-Cust, believed the COS 'over-emphasised the dangers of indiscriminate charity' because there undoubtedly were cases 'when immediate relief was indispensable'.[177] The Revd. H. Postance was convinced that the Liverpool CRS often excelled Poor Law representatives in 'their unnecessary painful enquiries' and believed the possibility of ever leaving the CRS with 'a monopoly of poor relief was too drastic to contemplate'.[178]

PROVIDENT DISPENSARIES

Provident dispensaries were one facet of the Victorian urban scene which were more likely to have rapport with any local society attempting to investigate the worthiness of the poor, develop thrift and organize charity. Occasionally, as in the case of the Manchester and Salford DPS, provident aspects dominated the organization. The provident dispensary concept of encouraging working people to contribute weekly sums towards their possible future needs was in complete accord with cherished COS self-help principles. As such they provided 'a vigorous onslaught on the vicious principle of wholesale gratuitous relief to outpatients'.[179] In addition provident dispensaries frequently shared an awareness about the alleged need for diligent examination of individual and family economic circumstances to expose those who were able to contribute at least part of the cost of medical attention.

Brighton COS described the 'threefold machinery of hospitals, dispensaries and provident dispensaries ... well adapted to meet the wants of the three classes – the pauper, the poor and the artisan; but there remained the difficulty of discriminating between the three classes'.[180] Provincial COSs believed their function was to persuade all skilled workers and as many of the poor as possible to contribute to a provident dispensary. Oxford COS saw provident dispensaries as primarily for artisans and labourers, and their wives, widows and children not in receipt of Poor Law relief, as well as for small shopkeepers and domestic servants.[181]

Provident dispensary contributors were usually given the right to receive home medical attention at times of serious illness at no extra charge, the opportunity to select from a panel of doctors and the means of having a voice in the management of the dispensary through the election of representatives. These advantages, together with what the individual gained in rectitude, usually cost around 2d. weekly, although this varied from place to place.[182] At Birmingham they suggested that 'bodies of workpeople should be invited to subscribe not less than an average of a half-day's wages a head per year' whereas the Manchester and Salford

DPS reckoned that a medical centre became self-supporting once it had achieved 2000 members each paying one penny weekly.[183]

After 40 years of developing the saving habit through the society's Penny Savings Bank some members of the DPS led by William O'Hanlon, Herbert Philips and Oliver Heywood developed the Provident Dispensary Association (PDA) which became a branch of the main society in 1879.[184] According to O'Hanlon the PDA would foster for the poor 'habits of prudence and forethought' with 'reliance on their own industry' in providing for sickness in times of health.[185] By 1890 there was a network of nine provident dispensaries across Manchester and Salford, seven of which were self-supporting. The total number of 'artisans and others' included by that time was well over 20 000.[186]

Leamington COS, like those at Oxford and Brighton, fully supported their local provident dispensary.[187] In Ward's opinion the Leamington COS favoured 'liberal medical aid when compared to the often minuscule aid offered in other forms' if for no other reason than being anxious 'to prevent the outbreak of serious epidemics ...'[188] Even though provident dispensaries shared some of the principles of their COS neighbours they were sometimes sufficiently apprehensive about the ill-feelings directed towards the COS from other relief agencies to emphasize that they were institutionally independent. The Southampton provident dispensary thought it appropriate to announce that although they rented a room to the COS this was strictly a commercial arrangement.[189]

Lady members of Oxford COS provided the driving force in the formation and development of the Oxford Working Women's Benefit Society. Although small-scale it helped to steer those who did join into the advantages of providence. After three and a half years it was self-sustaining with an accumulated fund of £90 collected from 110 members, mainly laundresses, kitchen-women and charwomen each contributing 2d. or 3d. weekly.[190] Within another four years the fund had grown to £222 held in the post office or in Consuls. Success of the scheme was helped by the robustness of members in that total sick claims of only £28 12s. needed to be paid in that year. Sickness benefits were between 5s. and 7s. for eight weeks with half-rate for four further weeks.[191]

Since the COS were so inflexible on principles, it was often difficult for them to create a working bond with medical charities who were usually not keen to use their rigorous methodology for examining individuals. Nevertheless there were occasional successes among COS attempts to convince others that their investigative techniques could show scientifically that a significant proportion of those currently receiving free medical attention were actually capable of making some financial contribution.

After the Queen's Hospital in Birmingham had allowed the COS to examine the worthiness of 366 cases they were informed that 34 of the applicants had been exposed as providing false addresses, 6 were parish cases, 2 had refused any information and 64 were dismissed as being 'unsuitable from idleness, drunkenness or otherwise dissolute character'.[192] The COS claimed that their investigation had been 'in every respect satisfactory to the patients, to the hospital and to the subscribers'.[193]

The COS attempted to persuade others that high-earning applicants were abusing the system. Dr Dawson told a meeting in Brighton town hall about the job details of 2283 cases he had attended at the free dispensary. The cases included: 121 charwomen, 18 clerks, 60 cabmen and stablemen, 284 laundresses, 242 labourers and labourers' wives, 195 needlewomen, 33 nurses, 890 mechanics, 97 railway servants and their wives and children, and 343 domestic servants. Dawson emphasized the large numbers of mechanics who, he alleged, 'each received 5s, 6s, or 7 shillings a day'.[194] Sir Cordy Burrows speaking as a 'medical man of long-standing and experience' claimed there were few medical charities in the country which were not being grossly abused.[195] After 21 years of endeavour Brighton COS accepted that 'vested interests proved too strong for much reform in the Medical Charities of this town'.[196]

The situation at Brighton was not unusual. Even in Manchester where the growth of the provident dispensary movement encouraged by the DPS had been so influential, there were substantial medical charities which chose to remain outside the DPS co-operative framework.[197] Furthermore those participating with the DPS did not necessarily function rationally together even though the DPS attempted to provide 'a certain extent' of co-operation.[198] London COS criticized Liverpool CRS for failing to develop a scheme whereby the city's free hospitals were converted to provident dispensaries.[199] Birmingham COS complained that there was 'no investigation worthy of the name' into 'the circumstances of the patients' by any of the city's medical charities, nor did they co-operate 'in any marked degree' with either 'general charity' or 'with the Poor Law'.[200] In addition to most medical charities continuing to supply sick-relief, traditionally there was the Poor Law system which the LGB steadily developed into a formidable infirmary network.

RELATIONSHIPS WITH THE LONDON COS

When addressing representatives from provincial COSs in 1881 the London contingent were anxious not to make the 'slightest claim' to have 'domination over their faith'.[201] However, comments in the London COS's various publications about the activities of the independent provincial societies provide a very different impression. The London society seemed to think it a moral imperative that they should augment any item of news from the provinces with their own critical comments rather in keeping with a headmaster's report. As regards matters of principle and their interpretation there was similarity between the relationship of the London COS and their provincial acolytes with that of the LGB and local guardians. In both instances the central institutions persisted in propagating concepts with which those outside of London ostensibly concurred but which in practice they not infrequently found it pragmatic to frustrate.

In the early years most comments from the centre were constructive but as the honeymoon rapport faded so failure of the provincial movement to gain a wider acceptance of their ideology increased London's derisive tendencies. Vitriol was frequently poured on the whole-hearted endeavours of their country cousins battling to succeed in unresponsive conditions. What opportunity there might have been to mould a mutually responsive network of Charity Organisation Societies was squandered. Most provincial COSs shied away from becoming too intimately embroiled as affiliates of the London pedants and preferred to retain the less onerous 'correspondence' status.

It soon became regular practice for London's *Charity Organisation Reporter* to co-ordinate and publish the quarterly details of affiliated societies with the verbal stick taking precedence over the carrot in editorial comments. As in their dealings with bodies external to the COS network the central administrators with their bullying tactics displayed no intuitive skills of how they should perform effectively in a supposedly democratic grouping or on how they might influence people by constructive persuasion.

Provincial societies were viewed as inferior by the London COS from their eyrie of imagined omniscience in 15 Buckingham St, Adelphi WC. The suggestion from Mr Cleland Burns that Glasgow COS had proved a greater success than their London counterpart was treated with scorn. London COS found it 'a pity that the [Glasgow] Annual Report has not been drawn up so as to exhibit the points of superior excellence' and that if indeed such points did exist they must be excused from 'repeating again and again that too little trouble is taken in setting forth the work done'.[202] Smaller COSs such as at Darlington received vilification in terser terms with their 1884 report judged by London as telling 'us next to nothing ...'[203]

In a broadly targeted criticism of provincial COSs a *Charity Organisation Review* editorial in July 1885 could not 'fail to contrast the witness borne by the speakers at the annual meetings and the evidence of the work done'. The article contrasted the frequent commendations on the 'vast amount of work done' from provincial chairmen with the reality when one turns 'to the body of the report and see that a number of persons, small in proportion to the place, have been relieved by food tickets or a very small amount of money'.[204] In London's opinion either the annual meeting was an affair of 'much butter and little business' or it was the lesser of the two evils in that the report only offered evidence of 'a very small proportion of the good really done'. The *Review* regretted that provincial societies all too frequently confronted the public with minimal attainment in stark contrast with their self-directed 'extravagant praise'.[205]

Comparison between the 'rules' of the Liverpool CRS and the 'objects' of the London COS show that although both documents were framed to eliminate the frivolous and immoral distribution of charity there were distinct differences of emphasis. The London 'objects' were primarily to 'bring into closer harmonious co-operation with each other and with the Poor Law authorities the various charitable agencies and individuals in the district' and 'to investigate thoroughly the cases of all applicants'.[206] In contrast the Central Relief Society emphasized the 'improvement in the conditions of the Poor by raising funds and dispensing relief to the distressed and deserving poor'.[207] Thus the basic CRS modus operandi contrasted distinctly with the seminal intention of the Charity Organisation Society that they should refrain from becoming yet another fund-raising charity. London COS were initially delighted to claim association with the established CRS and to have so impressed the Liverpool society as to have them change their title to incorporate their own principles. For some years the COS turned a blind eye to CRS activities like fire-lighter factories, penny dinners, soup kitchens and cocoa rooms which so blatantly transgressed their own code. London must have been delighted to learn from the 1877 CRS report that although the soup kitchens were 'convenient as a temporary expedient' they were recognized as being to a 'large extent indiscriminate' with the danger of encouraging improvidence and a weakening of self-dependence.[208] However, the exceptional distress on Merseyside the following winter brought a reversal of the recent CRS decision to double the price of their sago soup to 1d. per quart in an attempt to make their kitchens 'more nearly self-supporting'.

From around that time the London COS sniped persistently at what they saw as certain thoughtless CRS inadequacies. London noted that of the few CRS loans dispersed 'not half were refunded' and sarcastically anticipated 'the further history of that interesting experiment, the workshops ...'[209] Owen believed that no one could charge the CRS 'with administering relief with overlavish hands' but he overlooked the London Charity Organisation Society.[210] According to them material relief provided by Liverpool CRS such as penny-dinners and soup kitchens were 'a very serious flaw' and they hoped they would eventually learn that 'our friends in Liverpool had burnt all their bread and soup tickets and put their bronze penny tokens into the melting-pot'.[211] When London criticised the haphazardness of CRS penny-dinners for schoolchildren it meant little to them that their Merseyside colleagues were of the opinion that without such meals 'many children otherwise would be starving' or that some parents could not even afford 1d. for the child's dinner preferring to give 'a slice of bread at home'.[212] The CRS were advised to turn 'their minds from the distribution of groceries to permanent help'.[213]

Manchester and Salford DPS accorded with London's ideas about the rejection of indiscriminate relief methods like soup-kitchens, cocoa-rooms and night-shelters. They were also likely to receive London's accolades when they expressed a determination to keep an alert eye for worthless charlatans even when again drawn into exceptional distress situations, as in the late 1870s. Nevertheless Kidd describes how tensions simmered in their never 'entirely amicable' relations with the London COS.[214] A main bone of contention for London was that the DPS made little effort to organize other relief agencies. It was irrelevant to London that similar attempts, which they were constantly demanding elsewhere, had proved so fruitless. Another DPS weakness, in London's opinion, was their determination to centralize their administration instead of diversifying into districts. The COS were certain that the DPS administrative system could never develop the same closeness with the poor that they themselves claimed to have achieved.

There was disappointment in London at the relatively stunted activities of the Birmingham COS which they blamed on the erroneous devotion of excessive time to relieving the poor. They were most displeased when Birmingham COS informed members that 'your Society is now primarily a benevolent institution and nine-tenths of the time of your Committee is taken up in devising the best means of relieving those who are temporarily disabled or in distress'.[215] The *Charity Organisation Reporter* commented that they saw little evidence from Birmingham of 'that practical benevolence which strikes at the heart of pauperism' in that they seemed to be merely concentrating on relief without any indication as to whether they had ascertained the results of the distribution.[216]

Brighton COS from time to time received considerable praise from the metropolis. The seaside society's decision to publish monthly leaflets providing details of COS objectives, work, membership and general

Emergence of the Provincial Societies

arrangements was commended. London considered the leaflets to be 'short, clearly printed and easily read'.[217] But there were few provincial societies which totally escaped carping London criticism and according to the *Reporter* the Brighton COS showed 'little approach to the larger work of the Society' and 'little, if any, attempt to watch the future of the applicant and ascertain the results of what had been done ...'[218] Brighton were also advised that they may well 'consider carefully whether the £16 9s.10d. spent on bread for vagrants could have been used in no more useful way'. Brighton's defence was that they only gave bread when it was too late in the day for applicants to receive any from the workhouse.[219] They could also have added that although each wayfarer was provided with a pound of bread to 'guard against abuse' it had to be consumed on COS premises.[220]

When Southampton COS first became affiliated to London their decision was applauded from the centre. It confirmed 'the advantage of federation with other Charity Organisation Societies' in that they 'pledge themselves, to a certain extent, to carry on the work of the Society on a uniform system'.[221] But the London paragons were soon complaining about the Southampton COS's low level of achievement. 'The work is still on a small scale compared with the size and importance of the place' and London regretted that the Southampton report 'should give meagre information as to the work of the Society and the charitable agencies of the town'.[222]

Mr W. Marjoribanks, the Leamington chairman, sought London's praise with his letter to the *Reporter* recommending that COSs 'throughout the kingdom' should become affiliated to London so that the movement became 'one large and powerful Society'.[223] Readers' comments were invited but later copies of the *Reporter* give no impression of them being deluged with favourable replies. Leamington COS courted criticism by using a miscellany of relief methods suspect in London's eyes and with the word 'relief' added 'boldly' to their title they could hardly escape the central wrath indefinitely.[224] So it was in 1887 when London scathingly commented that at Leamington 'there are tickets to be given to beggars, bread and soup tickets, and coal tickets in abundance, so that nearly everyone who asketh gets at least a loaf'.[225] Ward believes Leamington COS became more of a 'centralised agency of relief in the town' orientated towards social control rather than adhering to the London model.[226]

Birkenhead COS were criticized for showing a disproportionate generosity from their own funds. During 1879 the Wirral society enquired into 573 cases of which 177 were found ineligible or undeserving, while

67 cases were referred to the Poor Law. The number of rejects satisfied London by confirming an apparent thoroughness of investigation but the fact that only 34 cases had been referred to private charity 'and none apparently to institutions or charitable agencies' while 235 received grants from the Birkenhead committee's own funds implied that 'the true meaning of Charity Organisation is not fully understood'.[227] London's comments to Oxford COS on the same theme were similar. They were informed that 'there appears to be room for much more organising of charity and for less supplying of relief from their own funds'.[228]

Not all of those attempting to organize provincial charity were prepared to just accept the uninvited missives from London. Oxford COS's Revd. Spooner said it was a 'weakness of the London Society' to be 'a little too inclined to think that the needs of the country are the needs of London'.[229] He argued that whereas in the large urban conurbation of London it was necessary to lay stress on the need of thorough investigation in all cases there was not the same need in country districts. In Spooner's opinion the main difference lay in London being 'a hopeless community' whereas places like Oxford were 'manageable'. Spooner was correct in so far as London COS remained intransigent in the belief that it was the problems detected in the East End during the late 1860s and the solutions fashioned at that time which remained the focus of attention. They were not inclined to accept that provincial COSs might well have been confronted with difficulties foreign to their own experience.

As a recipient of the annual reports of organizing societies outside the capital, London COS must have been well aware that the provincial movement was stagnating. With their obduracy on principle and social status constraints on structure, there was little room in which COS idealogues could manoeuvre towards more public support. Any hint that a provincial society may have strayed from the narrow-principled path was jumped on. In London's eyes the provincial committees were always prone to error, especially when they yielded to misplaced thoughtless emotion if confronted with the human faces of distressed anguish and when they attempted some form of unapproved social activity lacking adequate investigative rigour.

The following chapter provides quantitative and qualitative details of how, faced with London's constraints and using a methodology viewed by others with widening suspicion, the provincial societies struggled with little success to achieve supportive acknowledgement from the middle classes in the forms of finance and active participation.

6 The Activities of Provincial Charity Organisation Societies, 1870–1890

This chapter centres first on the great importance placed by Charity Organisation Societies on the investigation and categorization of applicants and discusses which personal characteristics were believed to make the poor deserving of help. Discussion then exposes the misleading implications of COS ridicule about what they persistently claimed were the unfair inadequacies of Poor Law doles as a means by which the poor might attain respectability. It is shown that the annual and unit value of provincial COS relief was often worth less than that of the Poor Law. This was partly because of provincial COS failure to attract adequate monetary and material support which in most localities left them with less financial muscle than the traditional relief agencies. Within the limitations of their financial constraints the various organizing societies experimented with a catalogue of relief techniques. Some of these methods were contrary to COS principles on indiscriminate relief and moved embarrassingly close to replicating forms of outdoor Poor Law relief which the COS were so fond of deriding. Explanations are provided as to why, during the two decades, various societies modified their adherence to particular methods of poor relief.

The efficacy of the provincial COSs' miscellaneous relief efforts are then debated prior to considering the paradoxical situation faced by the societies at times of exceptional distress. Focus on the cautionary warnings circulated by the COS about alleged imposters illustrates the personal failings which excluded an applicant from COS assistance. The chapter concludes with a discussion on how provincial organizing societies grappled with their perennial problems of attracting volunteers and doggedly attempted to bolster sickly subscription lists.

COSs wrestled with the problem of how the actions of their paid agents and volunteers should be related in the process of investigation. They recognized that their agents were sometimes considered too rough by the 'better class of applicant' in not empathizing with their predicament. On the other hand the COS were concerned about their volunteers lacking diligence in checking references, previous addresses, relatives able to assist and failing generally in their investigatory objective on account of 'their sympathies being excited'.[1]

This COS intention of bringing the rich and the poor into harmony through close personal contact was rarely much more than illusory in the provinces. Most outsiders saw their technique as an obsession with probing and prying into poor peoples' personal affairs. Any early COS ideas for alleviating the suffering of the deserving poor became submerged in the 'scientific' methodology of charity rather than its substance. As a result where the COS had expected gratitude they found themselves confronted by apprehension, suspicion, anger and eventual antagonism.

Any hope provincial COSs may have entertained about conducting their affairs entirely with volunteers proved impracticable through lack of support. Unfortunately the economic constraints on provincial societies carried the danger of forcing them to appoint inappropriate inexperienced agents apt to get 'flustered and irritated', which did not alleviate the COS's 'reputation of dealing harshly with applicants'.[2] Figure 6.1 is an organization chart for a typical medium-size provincial COS with annual subscriptions and donations totalling some hundreds of pounds, as at Birkenhead.

CATEGORIZATION OF APPLICANTS AND COMPARATIVE RELIEF VALUES

The essential precursor to any possibility of a favourable COS intercession was that the applicant had been thoroughly investigated and categorized. No one in the COS doubted 'the usefulness, and indeed the necessity, of the careful investigation which always precedes any other action on the part of our Committees'.[3] COS assessments were based on methodological investigation carried out mainly by the professional 'inquiry agent' as discussed in the next section below. His advice on the treatment of the cases was rarely sought by COS Committees.[4] According to the COS nothing had fostered pauperism more than the widespread erroneous belief that Christian duty was fulfilled by giving relief indiscriminately. Dr Griffin of Southampton COS claimed that if organized principles were pursued there would be 'no hardship in practically abolishing out-door relief, for there is no contingency against which there is less difficulty for the poor to make provision than sickness, and what little difficulty there is, properly directed charity can overcome'.[5] The COS alerted volunteers about those people so spoiled by careless charity as to resent enquiries. They were urged to diligently acquaint themselves 'with all the circumstances of distress' because 'impostors living among the poor'

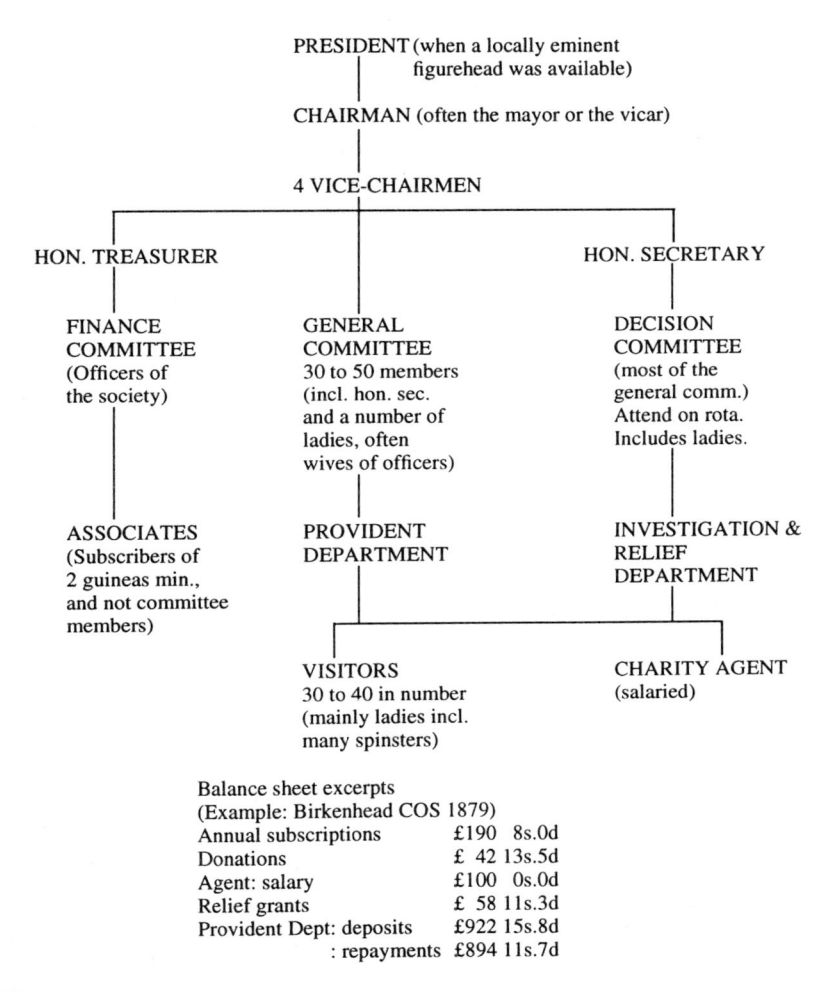

Activities of the Provincial Societies

```
                PRESIDENT (when a locally eminent
                         figurehead was available)

                CHAIRMAN (often the mayor or the vicar)

                4 VICE-CHAIRMEN
```

HON. TREASURER		HON. SECRETARY
FINANCE COMMITTEE (Officers of the society)	GENERAL COMMITTEE 30 to 50 members (incl. hon. sec. and a number of ladies, often wives of officers)	DECISION COMMITTEE (most of the general comm.) Attend on rota. Includes ladies.
ASSOCIATES (Subscribers of 2 guineas min., and not committee members)	PROVIDENT DEPARTMENT	INVESTIGATION & RELIEF DEPARTMENT
	VISITORS 30 to 40 in number (mainly ladies incl. many spinsters)	CHARITY AGENT (salaried)

Balance sheet excerpts
(Example: Birkenhead COS 1879)
Annual subscriptions	£190 8s.0d
Donations	£ 42 13s.5d
Agent: salary	£100 0s.0d
Relief grants	£ 58 11s.3d
Provident Dept: deposits	£922 15s.8d
: repayments	£894 11s.7d

Notes.
1. In some COSs all Officers served on the General Committee and in smaller Societies it was identical with the Decision Committee.
2. Day to day collecting for the Provident Department was mainly by Lady visitors, with the co-ordinating administration by the Agent. Not all provincial Societies had sufficient volunteers with which to establish a Provident Department but in such cases they encouraged the poor to use other thrift agencies.
3. The Agent usually conducted the investigative work, with volunteers used as appropriate in support.

Figure 6.1.   Organization chart for medium-size COS.

made a comfortable livelihood by 'deceiving simple-minded and carelessly benevolent people'.[6]

Provincial COSs perceived applicants as belonging to three main groups: the temporarily sick, those unable to get work, and habitual 'loafers and beggars'.[7] The sick, if assessed as 'deserving' and not in receipt of parish relief, were usually helped materially and lectured about the benefits of protecting themselves in future by joining a sick club. Those without a job were often ostracized in the early years of the COS movement but provincial problems associated with factory closures, trade troughs and adverse weather brought such surges in the numbers of innocent needy people as to negate the earlier assumption that work would always, somewhere, be available. 'Deserving' applicants were therefore seen as those who 'from illness, or failure of work, or other misfortune' were temporarily distressed but who allegedly with COS prompting could soon become self-sufficient.[8]

The rejected faction of COS investigations were mainly inveterate 'loafers or beggars', a description used in a cautionary way by the COS to warn unorganized charities that such people should be shunned.[9] However, these 'undeserving' types included not only criminals, vagrants and drunkards, but also significant numbers of those the COS judged 'hopeless to expect to become wage-earners again'.[10] This last condition meant there were 'innumerable instances' where the case was 'thoroughly deserving' but 'so desperately necessitous as to be incapable of adequate help' from private sources as to require despatch to the Poor Law.[11]

Provincial COSs accepted fluctuations in applicant numbers phlegmatically and with an underlying optimism. If numbers increased they were said to confirm an increased local awareness about the social good being provided by the COS. A downturn in numbers was seen as 'an index that the commercial depression which has existed during a series of recent years, and been more or less felt in the masses as well as the classes' was lessening.[12] It is also clear that the numbers of applicants to the COS were influenced by the tone of response they anticipated. The Oxford COS report for 1889–90 explained how applications had reduced from 445 the previous year to only 385. This was interpreted as the poor becoming aware that COS administration had knowingly become 'somewhat sterner'. For proof they pointed to their recent record of having helped only 64.4 per cent of applicants in 1889–90 compared with 67.9 per cent in 1888–9, 73.1 per cent in 1887–8 and 77.9 per cent in 1886–7.[13] Birmingham COS were convinced that investigation needed to be 'so thorough that those whose cases will not bear inspection do not care to go to the Society' which explained why 'only a very small percentage are reported as not a case for relief'.[14]

Table 6.1 shows for various locations the average annual number of the deserving poor relieved by provincial organizing societies in comparison with the numbers relieved outdoors by the nearest Poor Law institution. The gross value of the relief provided by the particular society relative to the annual value of the Poor Law out-relief given at each location is also displayed. The data indicates that the COSs in Birkenhead, Birmingham, Brighton, Leamington, Reading and Southampton were small, when compared with their nearby Poor Law institution, both as regards the number of applicants they helped and in the total value of relief they provided. On the other hand it should be noted that although they

Table 6.1 Numbers relieved annually and value comparisons between provincial COSs and Poor Law unions

Data Sources for periods between 1870–1890	Poor Law average annual out-relief numbers[a]	COS average annual numbers relieved[a]	Gross annual value of COS relief as % of Poor Law out-relief[b]
Birkenhead COS and PL union	3394	444	1.7%
Birmingham COS and PL union	8951	630	2.7%
Brighton COS and PL union	4293	322	1.5%
Leamington COS and Warwick PL	2290	613	3.4%
Liverpool CRS and PL union	8409	10 632	14.0%
Man. and Sal. DPS and PL unions[c]	8519	1 202	6.0%
Oxford COS and PL union	460	144	37.3%
Reading COS and PL union	1165	58	1.3%
Southampton COS and PL union	2656	144	3.5%

(a) The tabled annual average values apply only to those years during the period 1870–90 when data was available both from Poor Law and COS sources.
(b) COS monetary values used in calculating the relative percentages in the fourth column include the cost of the various forms of relief provided by the particular society, i.e. grants, loans, pensions, etc.
(c) The DPS normally only considered applications to their 'Visiting, Relief, and Investigation Branch' for direct support. Therefore only data from this branch are included above. Poor Law statistics refer only to the Manchester and Salford unions. Data from the other Manchester unions at Chorlton and Prestwich are *not* included.

Refer also to Appendix: General Notes on Poor Law and Organized Charity Data.

remained stunted compared with both the local Poor Law institution and traditional charities, some provincial COSs did manage to increase their local participation in the 1880s albeit from a low level.

Oxford COS, as a prime example, developed on a scale which was eventually comparable with the restricted outdoor relief from the nearby Incorporated Parishes union where activities were influenced by leading COS members who doubled as guardians. The constraints practised by this Oxford union contrasted with the more generous responses from the nearby Headington workhouse with which the Oxford COS had 'less close' relationships.[15] For example, the Headington guardians granted £2172 in outdoor relief during the 12 months ending Michaelmas 1890 which was more than three times the amount provided by the Incorporated Parishes union.[16] The tabled data shows that the two long-established societies, the Liverpool CRS and the Manchester and Salford DPS, both operated on a more meaningful scale than most provincial COSs. A factor which must be recognized when considering the Poor Law data is that guardians, encouraged by the LGB, despatched increasing numbers of the mentally ill to district asylums rather than housing them in their own infirmary.[17] Although these mentally disadvantaged people were classified by the LGB as outdoor paupers, they are here omitted from the tabulated data to provide more realistic comparison between the numbers relieved by organized charity and the outdoor paupers receiving doles in the immediacy of the local workhouse.

We turn now from comparing the overall average relief provided annually by the various Poor Law unions and their COS neighbours to an assessment of what the typical individual deserving applicant received during the year from each agency. Table 6.2 summarizes the annual values of relief provided to the average successful applicant at various locations in Poor Law outdoor relief and by the geographically nearby society attempting to organize charity. Assessment of what these gross annual values represented on a weekly scale is hindered because provincial COSs rarely published information about average periods over which the typical deserving applicant might expect to be assisted. However, Manchester and Salford DPS did indicate that their relief was stretched over a period of between four and five weeks for the average recipient.[18] Another clue, this time from the Liverpool CRS, suggested that the 'deserving' poor in Liverpool could expect relief for an average period of three weeks.[19] A further indicator, if somewhat outdated, comes from the records of the Liverpool Provident District Society, a CRS antecedent, which showed that 7476 'reliefs' in the year had been divided between 2978 families implying that on average, families were relieved two and a half times. The

Table 6.2 Annual values of Poor Law outdoor relief and the annual values of relief provided by a nearby COS to the average deserving applicant

Data sources	Poor Law outdoor relief: applicant/year[a]	COS relief applicant/year[b]
Birkenhead COS and Poor Law union	54s. 3d.	7s. 6d.
Birmingham COS and Poor Law union	34s. 0d.	10s. 9d.
Brighton COS and Poor Law union	48s. 7d.	9s. 0d.
Leamington COS and Warwick PL union	48s.10d.	5s.11d.
Liverpool CRS and Poor Law union	36s.11d.	4s. 1d.
Man. and Sal. DPS and PL unions[c]	39s. 5d.	22s. 4d.
Oxford COS and Poor Law union	47s.10d.	49s. 7d.
Reading COS and Poor Law union	36s. 9d.	9s.10d.
Southampton COS and Poor Law union	46s. 4d.	29s. 5d.

(a) The values tabulated for Poor Law and COS relief are the mean of the annual values provided to the average deserving applicant over the period. Therefore the COS values include grants, loans, pensions and costs of other relief forms.
(b) The values tabulated apply only to those years when data is available from both Poor Law and COS sources.
(c) Refer to note (c) in Table 6.1.

Refer also to Appendix: General Notes on Poor Law and Organized Charity Data.

same data shows that one-third of the families were relieved only once, and 60 per cent no more than twice.[20] The foregoing evidence augmented by data in the next section below on provincial COS grants and by a survey of various individual COS 'deserving' cases has been used in making the assumption that four weeks was the typical period over which relief was provided by provincial organizing societies.[21]

Comparison between the average unit value of Poor Law doles and the relief from organised charities is complicated by ambiguities as to whether relief was provided to an individual or to a family. In general Poor Law statistics focused on individuals with the father, mother and children in a family each being listed as paupers. In contrast COS relief was usually granted to the head of the family who alone was listed as an applicant. It can be argued that pensions, which became an increasingly important relief element in some provincial COSs, were mainly for the long-term support of elderly individuals. COS pensions will be discussed later but meanwhile, as grants remained the most frequently used form of COS relief, the data discussed so far has been assumed to be for the benefit of families.

Data supplied by the Manchester and Salford DPS is again useful in assessing the size of family benefiting from the relief given to the typical applicant. A survey of DPS annual reports over the period 1870 to 1890 suggests that the number of their applicants 'represented' about 4.5 times as many 'individuals'.[22] The result of applying this figure to other organizing societies is to emphasize that many more people actually shared the benefits of organized charity than the numbers of applicants published in provincial COS reports. Equally the same assumption implies that the unit value of the relief per person from provincial organizing societies would have been proportionately less than those shown in Table 6.2.

The COS ridiculed the allegedly mischievous 'haphazard trickle' of a few shillings normally given in Poor Law outdoor doles and delighted in implying more substantive COS support allegedly always 'wisely applied' to a recipient together with an appropriate dose of moral instruction.[23] For most provincial organizing societies this COS propaganda was unrealistic and misleading. Provincial COS relief was generally less in value than Poor Law doles. Exception to this generality may be claimed for Manchester and Salford DPS, Oxford COS and Southampton COS, but even in these centres the value of relief does not bear close scrutiny as being any guarantor of future self-sufficiency.

For example, if the average annual DPS relief in Table 6.2 is equated to weekly DPS relief of 5s.7d. for four weeks and is assumed to have been shared by an average family of between four and five people, then each individual would have benefited by 1s.3d. Making the same assumptions on size of family and period of relief for Oxford COS, their average annual relief of 49s.7d. gave a weekly benefit to the individual beneficiaries of 2s.9d. for four weeks, some of which was in the form of loans. When compared with the relief from the Manchester and Salford DPS and the Oxford COS the benefits provided by other provincial organizing societies were paltry. Using the same assumptions regarding the numbers of individual beneficiaries and the weeks over which benefits were provided the average weekly relief from Birkenhead COS would have been worth 5d. per person, from Birmingham COS a little over 7d. and from Brighton 6d.

It will be seen that COS relief generally compared badly with the Poor Law doles which the society delighted in criticizing for meanness. Although the scale of Poor Law out-relief doles varied across England it was quite usual to find a provision of between 2s.6d. and 3s. for adults, with an additional shilling or eighteen pence provided for each child.[24] It should be recognized that the average COS relief figures quoted hereto incorporate the miscellaneous forms of assistance discussed in the section following the next below but that grants remained the most commonly used type of COS benefit.

The inadequacy of provincial COS relief as a means of creating respectability becomes even more apparent when considered in the light of Booth's findings on poverty in London and Rowntree's in York. In Booth's opinion a weekly 'bare income' of between 18s. and 21s. was needed by a 'poor' moderate family 'living under a struggle ... to make both ends meet' while Rowntree calculated that a 'minimum weekly expenditure' of 21s.8d. was needed by parents with three children to maintain 'physical efficiency'.[25] Harlock's later evidence suggested that Poor Law doles, which as we have seen were generally of greater value than COS relief, were not only insufficient but 'impossible'.[26]

Even in Liverpool where the CRS claimed a certain dominance in charitable matters and were proud to emphasize that they were primarily a 'relief' society, their gross income in 1890 from subscriptions, donations, legacies and 'private case' donations totalled £4156 out of which had to be deducted substantial administrative expenditure. This was said to contrast with the amount 'upwards of £170 000' administered by other Liverpool charitable 'institutions' which 'by no means' included 'the whole of the benevolent agencies at work in the town'.[27] At Birmingham it was much the same. The gross COS receipts in 1888 were £819 whereas there was a 'current expenditure' of £43 260 14s.10d. by various Birmingham medical charities.[28] Bristol COS had looked forward eagerly in their early days to co-ordinating 'the enormous sum of £100 000 per annum' applied by the city's charities but by 1890 admitted that their own low level of involvement was 'inexcusable'.[29]

COS publicists stoically claimed that they should not be judged in terms of monetary disbursements but on their social worth in exposing the multitudes of imposters allegedly hoodwinking philanthropists at large. This line of excuse was undermined by the impecuniosity of provincial COSs which forced admissions about their inability to support many of those they investigated and judged to be deserving.[30]

The COS's reputation for harshness meant that in spite of their privations many among the poor were not prepared to suffer the rigorous COS prying. Johnson has described how the pawnbroker's shop, despite unattractive redemption charges, was often preferred by the poor to provide a short-term cash flow for household essentials.[31] An impression of the cool response to the would-be organizers of charity can be gauged by comparing the numbers applying for COS relief with those in the locality likely to be living in difficulty. From the evidence provided by both Booth and

Rowntree, around one-third of the urban population of later Victorian England struggled in poverty.[32] If this fraction were applied to the 1881 decennial census population of Birkenhead, 31 000 in the town were poverty-stricken. During that year the COS received 926 applications. Using the same assumptions for Brighton there would have been over 29 000 residents living in poverty during a year when the COS received 581 applications and at Reading 84 applications were received from the 13 000 or so likely to be in need. Looked at another way, at Oxford with its comparatively flourishing COS serving a population of nearly 22 000, there were 185 applicants assisted by the COS in 1890. Two further points must be considered when gauging provincial COS attractiveness. First is to remember that since many of the COS applicants enumerated above may have had family responsibilities, there would have been significantly more individuals receiving a share of whatever benefits were dispersed although, of course, the unit value would diminish accordingly. On the other hand, the above assessments of the likely numbers living in poverty do not include people in Booth's classification E.[33] This was the numerically large group just above the poverty line who attempted to save regularly. It can reasonably be argued that these people would be amongst those most inclined to approach the COS when times were difficult believing that their past thriftiness made them likely candidates for COS favours.

DIVIDING THE DESERVING POOR FROM THE UNDESERVING

Provincial COSs were annoyed by critics who likened their rigorous investigative procedures to those of Poor Law relieving officers. When Sussex people described Brighton COS 'as a board of ogres ... looking askance at every applicant for relief' the COS's Revd. Dr Hamilton and Col Baines both provided 'personal testimony to the kind and careful manner in which each case is enquired into'.[34] Public suspicion did not abate and the Revd. Hooper affirmed that throughout Brighton COS's history they had encountered 'obstacles thrown in the way of the Society, by systematic misrepresentation of the objects which it has in view, and this condition of things has by no means passed away ...'[35] Another provincial COS felt the need to let the public know that their enquiries were 'not made in any harsh or inquisitorial spirit, and cautioned others against believing a charge ... frequently made against the COS ... that deserving applicants are left to starve while investigations into their case are being made'.[36]

COS volunteers were constantly alerted to the danger of contact with the poor leading to them being misled by the seemingly 'deserving' characteristics of those who were actually shady. Sir Cordy Burrows was roundly applauded by Brighton COS when advising ladies 'whose tender hearts and sympathies were so easily touched by tales of woe, all too often indiscriminately relieved street beggars' that they were 'as bad as the beggars themselves – one being wicked; the other fools'.[37] The Manchester and Salford DPS were never slow to commend their investigators' vigilance because it was 'well known how extraordinary are the cunning and ingenuity manifested by impostors'.[38]

According to the COS the ordinary charitably-minded person was at fault by asking only superficial questions of the poor. As a result it was alleged their 'answers, together with their evident squalor and misery, were sufficient to loosen the purse strings; with not one person in ten taking even the elementary step of applying to the employer to learn what wages are going into a wretched-looking house, or to the relieving officer to know whether the inmates are in receipt of out-door relief'.[39] The COS accepted that 'to make these inquiries is indeed a difficult and rather invidious task' which 'a private person may well shrink from' but they argued, it was 'here that the COS comes in and offers to undertake this work for the benevolent'.[40]

Such explanations of COS purpose convinced few. A *Leamington Spa Courier* correspondent considered it 'a distressing thing to make the deserving poor feel their poverty'.[41] A letter in the *Birkenhead and Cheshire Advertiser* on 3 April 1882 claimed that the COS were 'much more interested in finding cases to be undeserving than in finding deserving cases and relieving them'. Complaints of this nature made against Mr R.J. Banks, the Birkenhead COS agent, were of sufficient force and repetitiveness for the society to be forced to give him three months' notice of dismissal. When told the charges against him related to 'unkindness and incivility of the poor' Banks claimed that such complaints were 'not confined to Birkenhead COS, but have from time to time appeared in the reports of most kindred associations ... including Philadelphia'.[42] Birkenhead COS were pleased with Banks's successor William Makin. He quickly made 'a favourable impression' on the committee 'by the kind and considerate mode of dealing with applicants'.[43] The committee later described how Makin had exposed impostors who had appeared 'deserving' to unskilled eyes but 'a visit at night often finds the clamorous applicant for relief comfortably engaged over his pipe and glass, sometimes in excess'.[44]

The COS preached that the family was the true nucleus of society and that morally relatives should shoulder as much as possible of any relief burden.[45] According to the COS no personal obligation was more important than that the poor accepted family responsibilities in caring for young and old, as well as in supplying mutual aid to other family members at times of sickness and emergency.[46]

Figure 6.2 portrays the recommended COS procedures on receipt of an application. Searching enquiries were intended not merely to centre on the applicant's own personal circumstances but to involve their whole family. Information was extracted about the parents themselves, earnings at their last employment, reasons for leaving the job, children's ages, whether children were at school or working, previous addresses, debts, rent, references, savings club membership, whether the home was clean and reasonably maintained, how many deserving applicants might be 'thoroughly helped' and which of their relatives should be persuaded to assist.[47]

COS enquiries when conducted to the prescribed format usually occupied about one week, during which time some limited help may be provided but destitute cases were directed immediately to the workhouse and no further interest taken.[48] The normal application for COS relief allegedly 'obliged' an agent 'to make three to five calls in different directions' then, until the applicant 'was again self-supporting or until referred to the guardians' they were visited twice weekly, once before the 'meeting of the Committee to ascertain progress and afterwards to convey assistance awarded'.[49]

The rigorous investigative procedures recommended by London must often have been difficult to apply provincially with widespread COS financial and staff constraints. COS propaganda about detailed examinations providing uniformly meticulous personal dossiers of applicants camouflaged more chaotic practices. For example, although the detailed format of Leamington COS record books provided a formidable framework from which minute details of an applicant could have been unearthed, it has been estimated that only about 10 per cent of cases were actually recorded so precisely.[50] At the 1881 COS conference it was admitted that nationally 'case-work too often' fell short of the required standard with reports 'slovenly and ill drawn' and failing to show the 'real merits or demerits of the case'.[51]

Although provincial COS form-filling did not always achieve the impeccable standard claimed, the theory remained inviolate that every applicant should be keenly investigated. Later in this chapter discussion centres on COS explanations as to why particular candidates were undeserving. More immediately concentration is on a sample of published cases intended by provincial COSs to illustrate how and why they had assessed applicants as being deserving of relief with the underlying implication that each selected case achieved a remarkable transition from

Activities of the Provincial Societies

```
                    APPLICANT IN DISTRESSED CONDITION
                                |
                       COS OFFICE: CHARITY AGENT
                                |
                           FIRST INTERVIEW
Limited short-term ─────────────┼───────────── REFUSED RELIEF
support in case of              │
apparent good                   ├───────────── REFERRED ELSEWHERE
        ┌───────────────── INVESTIGATION ─────────────────┐
        │              (in applicant's home, mainly       │
        │                        by agent)                │
```

PERSONAL DETAILS:

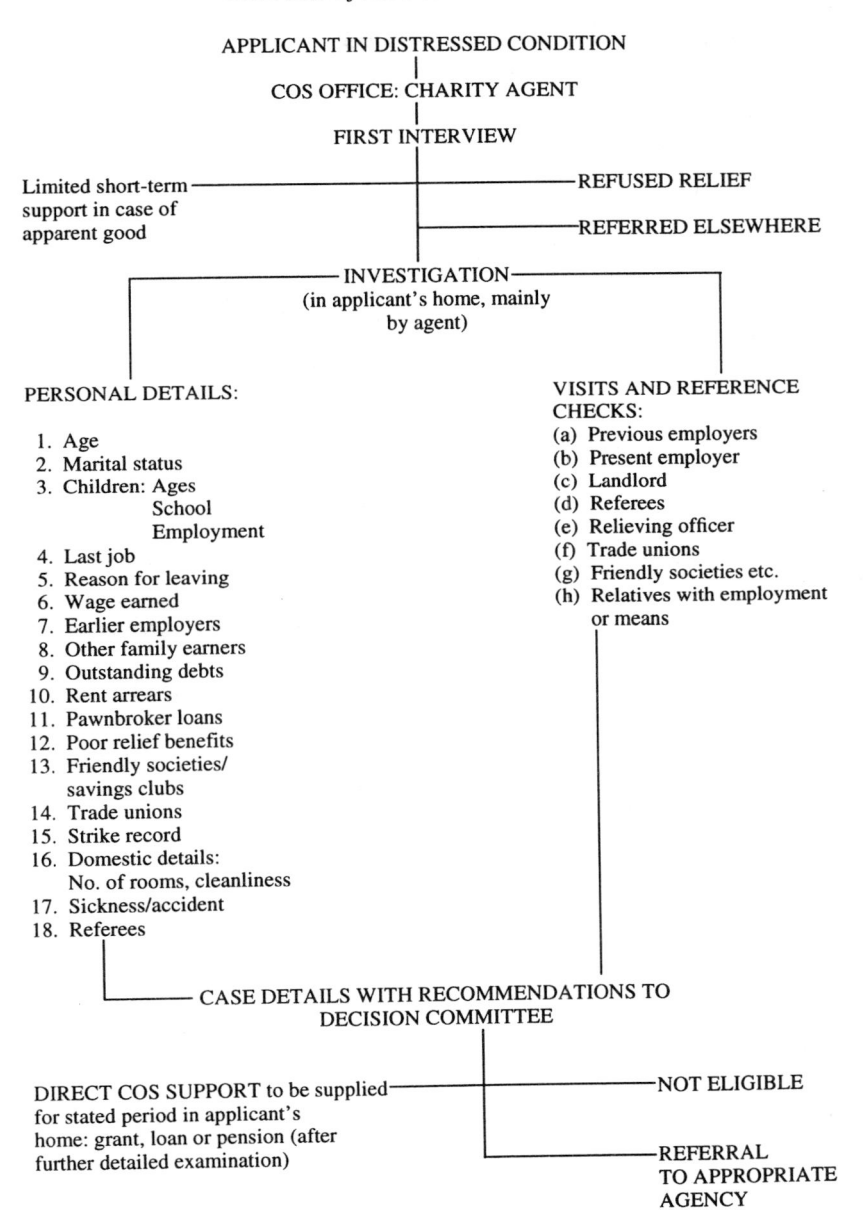

1. Age
2. Marital status
3. Children: Ages
            School
            Employment
4. Last job
5. Reason for leaving
6. Wage earned
7. Earlier employers
8. Other family earners
9. Outstanding debts
10. Rent arrears
11. Pawnbroker loans
12. Poor relief benefits
13. Friendly societies/
    savings clubs
14. Trade unions
15. Strike record
16. Domestic details:
    No. of rooms, cleanliness
17. Sickness/accident
18. Referees

VISITS AND REFERENCE CHECKS:
(a) Previous employers
(b) Present employer
(c) Landlord
(d) Referees
(e) Relieving officer
(f) Trade unions
(g) Friendly societies etc.
(h) Relatives with employment
    or means

CASE DETAILS WITH RECOMMENDATIONS TO DECISION COMMITTEE

DIRECT COS SUPPORT to be supplied ─────── NOT ELIGIBLE
for stated period in applicant's
home: grant, loan or pension (after   REFERRAL
further detailed examination)   TO APPROPRIATE
                                         AGENCY

Figure 6.2 Procedure recommended for provincial Charity Organization Societies following receipt of an application.

near-destitution to respectability. The following 'deserving' cases also provide a flavour of the quality and quantity of provincial COS relief discussed more fully later:

1. No. 3151. This was the case of a woman whose husband died suddenly, leaving her with a family of young children, one only a few days old. A grant in four weekly payments helped her until she was again able to undertake her usual occupation of a charwoman.[52]

2. No. 4056. This person, in consequence of long illness in her family, had been obliged to pledge her sewing machine; with some help from private sources (through the Society), she was enabled to redeem her machine and keep her work together.[53]

3. Case D. Widow, aged 67, with six children all grown up. Society granted temporary assistance; members of the Committee visited the case and induced the family to support their mother. Assistance now ceased.[54]

4. No. 12,608. In this case the family was composed of a husband, wife, and six young children. The man was in a sick club, but had received full benefit. He had tried to help himself as far as his means would allow, and ill health only prevented him from maintaining his family. The doctor gave hopes of recovery if suitable means were provided, such as change of air and nourishing diet. The Committee provided what was necessary, and gave the wife a weekly allowance during her husband's absence. He returned restored to health and went to work, the family being again placed upon a self-supporting basis.[55]

5. A poor woman whose husband has been ill for the last three weeks, and who has two children depending upon her, applied for assistance to tide her over for a short time. Character good. Granted 5 shillings a week for 2 weeks.[56]

6. A poor woman applied for 3s.6d. to purchase a kneecap for her husband, who has been a sufferer for a long time, and had been unable to work without one. Both bear good character. Granted 3s.6d. as requested.[57]

METHODS OF COS RELIEF TO THE DESERVING

After early COS optimism about other charities being delighted to pay for having their activities co-ordinated by scientific investigative methodology

Activities of the Provincial Societies

had proved to be misplaced, the movement was left with little alternative other than to attempt to raise their own funds. This was not easy and provincial COSs were regularly strapped for cash. Because other charitable bodies shunned them, provincial COSs were reduced, in contradiction with their founding aims, to becoming one amongst many other charities. The COS differentiated themselves from the other charities by a determination not to be budged from 'scientific' investigative principles. Table 6.3 summarizes for various provincial organizing societies the proportion of supplicants 'assisted', 'referred' and 'not assisted'. Although

Table 6.3 Percentages of total applicants who were assisted, not assisted and referred by various provincial societies

Data period	Society	Assisted[a] %	Referred[a] %	Not assisted %
1872–90	Birkenhead COS	58	16	26
1872–90[b]	do.	50	19	31
1873–89	Birmingham COS	72	12	16
1872–90	Brighton COS	45	13	42
1876–90	Leamington COS	61	23	16
1876–85[c]	do.	51	31	18
1875–90	Reading COS	42	22	36
1879–90	Oxford COS	49	20	31
1877–90	Southampton COS	37	28	35
1875–90	Liverpool CRS	69	14	17
1871–90[d]	Manchester and Salford DPS	82	–	18
1879–80[e]	London COS	34	22	44

(a) The percentages of applicants falling into the three categories 'assisted', 'referred', and 'not assisted' were calculated from the total number of applicants over the period stated in the first column.
(b) The second line of data for Birkenhead COS provides the percentages when the two exceptional distress years 1886 and 1887 are excluded.
(c) At Leamington, in the second half of the 1880s, few applicants were refused some relief although for many this was restricted to a grant for bread and soup. Alternative summary data is provided in the table for the period 1876–85 when this procedure was less in evidence.
(d) The Manchester and Salford DPS data refers only to applicants entered by the Relief Board of the DPS Visiting, Relief and Investigation Department.
(e) The London COS data are taken from their 11th and 12th Annual Reports, Appendices 1.

Refer also in this volume to Appendix: General Notes on Poor Law and Organized Charity Data.

the responses from provincial COSs were by no means identical the data suggests that, other than in the three largest connurbations, there was some broad consistency in maintaining ratios between the 'assisted', 'referred' and 'not assisted' of 0.5 : 0.2 : 0.3 respectively. The Liverpool CRS, the Manchester and Salford DPS and the Birmingham COS assisted a greater proportion of applicants. This was at variance with London COS which proportionally assisted fewer applicants than most provincials. Normally each provincial society maintained reasonable consistency in the percentage of cases they assessed as being worthy of assistance. This pattern tended to change at times of exceptional distress with the proportion of deserving cases increasing as the number of applicants also surged upwards. The next section includes discussion on the paradoxical circumstances in which COSs found themselves on these occasions.

COSs remained attached to the ideological concept that they should be consistently circumspect about the evils of relief profligacy. Pragmatism associated with their own scarcity of funds did nothing to challenge this attitude. Nevertheless, within these constraints, the provincial societies contrived to provide support in a miscellany of ways as indicated by Table 6.4. Inclusion of a tabulated relief mode does not necessarily imply that it was consistently supplied by the particular society but shows relief of that type as being provided on occasions during the two decades 1870–1890.

Some COS relief methods used in the provinces ran the danger of transgressing COS ideals. Facilities like non-commercial factories and soup kitchens were seen by London as veering dangerously towards being providers of indiscriminate relief. Provincial COSs drifting into forms of relief tainted with ideological dubiety often made the excuse that each recipient had been subjected to rigorous scrutiny but London COS remained convinced that the mere presence of facilities that transgressed organized ethics made it difficult to guarantee adequate investigation.[58] In their view, should soup kitchens and similar facilities be considered absolutely unavoidable they must be established on 'a commercial basis' and remained adamant that diversions like free dinners for children were 'unnecessary and inadvisable'.[59] C.S. Loch maintained that all charity must be meted out sparingly with certain things done only 'with very great precaution'.[60] According to London COS all assistance should be limited to that which was 'individual, personal, temporary and reformatory'.[61]

COS principles implied that relief should never take the shape of regular doles but should always form part of a definite 'plan' for the permanent benefit of the recipient.[62] Even when they wished otherwise some provincial COSs, because of their own lack of funds, had little

Table 6.4 Types of relief provided by provincial Charity Organisation Societies

	Birk	Bir	Bri	Lea	Liv	Man	Oxf	Read	Sou
Grants: cash	yes	yes	yes	yes	yes	yes	yes	yes	yes
kind	yes	yes	yes	yes	yes	yes	yes	yes	yes
Loans	yes	yes	yes	yes	yes	yes	yes	yes	yes
Hospital tickets	yes	yes	yes	yes	yes	yes	yes	yes	yes
Provident scheme	yes		yes			yes	yes		yes
Employment lists	yes	yes	yes	yes	yes		yes	yes	
Emigration help	yes	yes		yes	yes		yes	yes	yes
Coal fund				yes					
Pensions	yes		yes	yes	yes		yes		yes
Widows fund		yes	yes			yes	yes		
Railway tickets	yes	yes		yes	yes		yes		yes
Soup kitchens	yes			yes	yes	*	yes		
Cocoa rooms					yes				
Penny dinners					yes				
Convalescent home						yes			
Country/seaside lodgings	yes	yes							
Cast-off boots and clothing	yes	yes		yes	yes	yes			
Distressed seamen			yes				yes		
Tools and equipment					yes	yes		yes	yes
Blanket fund	yes	yes				yes			yes
Factories						yes			
Mendicity response	yes	yes	yes	yes	yes	yes	yes	yes	yes

Key to columns: Birk = Birkenhead COS; Bir = Birmingham COS; Bri = Brighton COS; Lea = Leamington COS; Liv = Liverpool CRS; Man = Manchester and Salford DPS; Oxf = Oxford COS; Read = Reading COS; Sou = Southampton COS.

* Manchester and Salford DPS investigated cases on behalf of Ardwick and Ancoats Soup Kitchen. On principle, the DPS were generally against soup kitchens, e.g. *Manchester & Salford DPS*, Monthly Committee Minutes, 3 November 1886 and 1 December 1886.

opportunity but to provide their relief sparingly. For example the value of Southampton COS grants during 1879 totalled £21 14s, loans had a gross value of £136, and twenty persons shared 45 lb of bread and 5.5 lb of cheese because they 'appeared to be starving and received immediate relief ...'[63] London COS applauded the Southampton committee for their 'vigorous efforts'.[64]

In spite of a COS aversion to grants because of their ideological similarity to Poor Law doles, they remained the most commonly used form of provincial COS relief. So much so that much of what has been discussed above about the average value of COS relief can be assumed as being broadly applicable to grants for most societies. Data on weekly grants are available from two sources associated with Birkenhead COS. Unpublished correspondence of Mr C.T. Gostenhofer, their Hon. Secretary, revealed a weekly allowance rate of '2/- for a single man not with his parents; 3/- for a man and wife or man and mother; 4/- for a man, wife and small family; 5/- if the children were more than 4 ... and something more in the case of sickness'.[65] Because the number of claimants increased at times of exceptional distress the tight limits on Birkenhead COS funds forced them to reduce their relief scale to 1/- for a single man, 2/- for a man and wife, 3/- where there were one or two children and 4/- if there were three children or upwards. Benefits were occasionally augmented for sickness, and in cold weather a lucky few were given a supply of coal.[66] Birkenhead COS annual accounts over an eighteen-year period suggest that even the foregoing modest grants exaggerate reality.[67] Their grants were usually in the form of shilling-orders on tradesmen for provisions because this saved the 'difficulty of audit' needed when their agent distributed money.[68]

Croydon COS disclosed that the value of their weekly grants was 1s.6d. with an additional 6d. for each child, usually 'not given in money' but in tickets on local grocers.[69] They normally helped temporary 'cases of sickness only' with further rare provision for 'chronic cases'.[70] At Birmingham they gave grants 'according to circumstances; food from the Society's stores, orders on provision dealers, butchers, or bakers, admission tickets to various institutions or homes, clothing and money'.[71] West Midlands COS contributors were told that 'the value of gifts of old clothes can hardly be over-estimated'.[72]

Oxford COS data makes it possible to calculate grants separately and there is strong indication that they provided the highest average unit grant amongst the societies examined. In the late 1870s Oxford COS decided to restrict the number of recipients and in the twelve months ending 30 September 1879 only 56 grants were provided with a gross value of £70 0s.9d.[73] As the number of cases assisted again began to grow in the 1880s the Revd. W.A. Spooner emphasized that the increased assistance had needed to be provided 'by the Committee itself' with few cases 'recommended to the Guardians for help, fewer for private persons, fewer to institutions'.[74] By 1886–7 grants from Oxford COS had rocketed to 146 during the year which cost the society £227 1s.10d.[75] The number of

Oxford grants again fell but increased substantially in unit value. In 1890 their typical grant to a deserving applicant over the year was nearly 42s.3d. which if assumed to be distributed over four weeks gave a weekly family benefit of around 10s.7d. When compared with most provincial COS relief the Oxford COS grants were munificent. Even then it is questionable whether even the Oxford benefit scale given for four weeks could be assumed as any guarantee that a recipient would achieve independence at a time when the local labourer's weekly wage was around fourteen shillings.[76]

Oxford COS congratulated themselves about what they saw as their 'more adequate assistance' in the late 1880s but became concerned because higher grants 'commonly meant a corresponding increase in the time and trouble devoted to a case' and believed they should 'consider seriously the probable limits of the increase'.[77] The success of their subsequent squeeze on grants was considered to be 'a most satisfactory feature'.[78]

Loans were considered by the COS movement as ideologically preferable to grants because they encouraged thrift and the building of individual responsibility. Loans also had the inherent advantage for penurious provincial societies that although they usually incurred a higher unit outlay than a grant, they had the great theoretical attraction of being a recoverable asset. Some loans were in the form of tools or equipment, especially of the household variety like 'wringing machines' with which women could earn wages. Other loans were monetary and intended to tide an applicant over temporary distress. When equipment was loaned it was indelibly marked as COS property to reduce danger of the society losing possession should there subsequently be distress levied on the borrower.[79] In addition the COS considered it highly desirable, if only for the borrower's moral good, that they should provide adequate security for repayment.[80]

Despite the ideological advantages claimed for loans the organizing societies in the large provincial cities like Liverpool, Manchester and Birmingham scarcely ventured into this form of relief.[81] This contrasted with London COS which as early as 1872 made 1039 loans in the year representing 18 per cent of deserving cases to tide 'over certain emergencies such as sickness'.[82] When Manchester and Salford DPS did occasionally offer a loan it tended to be for the likes of a widow with a family and took the form of 'wringing, mangling and sewing machines'.[83] Liverpool CRS were also hesitant about loans because 'not infrequently' they failed 'to recover the money' particularly when made to emigrants.[84] Elsewhere Leeds COS, Bristol COS and the Croydon Charitable Society either 'made no loans' or made 'very few'.[85]

Other provincial COSs were distinctly more enthusiastic about loans. Reading COS was one such society where their chairman, the Revd. J.H. Jenkinson, objected to clothing and footwear being granted to school children whose parents could not provide them.[86] Such a procedure was so 'productive of unmixed evil' that it entirely failed in its object and 'encourages everything which makes homes wretched and children ragged'.[87] Jenkinson's solution was to establish the Reading Destitute Children Aid Committee (DCAC) which provided footwear with insistence on weekly repayments and never providing 'a second pair till the first are paid for'. He claimed that the DCAC nullified a typical excuse for truancy of 'no shoes to go in' as when parents were legally summoned for not sending children to school the authorities would know that if they had been 'deserving they might have got help from us'.[88]

In the early 1880s the loans from Reading COS showed a marked numerical increase but their constrained finances meant that when lending peaked in the twelve months to 31 March 1883 their 108 loans were worth in total only £53 17s.0d.[89] When their enthusiasm for loans was dampened by widespread defaulting Reading COS responded with 'greater strictness in accepting persons as security for loans' as they had 'lost considerably by the failure of many of these to pay when called upon to do so'.[90] Debt recovery through the courts was a recommended option for COSs but there was little purpose in pursuing this course when legal victory for such small sums could be pyrrhic with the attendant danger of adverse publicity.

For some years the COSs at Southampton and Leamington both provided loans. Southampton COS developed lending hesitantly because the committee were afraid that any 'laxity in lending money or obtaining repayment would be most harmful'.[91] Nevertheless overriding these doubts was the idea that 'the regular weekly repayment of a loan is as good a test of character and steadiness as can be found'.[92] When times were bad even the tight controls of the Southampton COS loan scheme cracked. They conceded that 'where distress is general, and due to causes over which the distressed have no control ... some of the loans granted by the Society were in arrears'.[93] Leamington COS loans were 'limited to £2, without charging interest or any other fees, and those who are aware how greatly the poor are plundered and oppressed by professional money-lending harpies' would appreciate 'how much good was being effected by this branch of its activities alone'.[94] The unit value of loans from the Midlands spa town was high relative to their grants which typified the pattern at other COSs. At Oxford, Birkenhead and other COS centres where loans were used their popularity peaked around 1880. Initially

Oxford COS were quite keen believing that loans provided a 'real and substantial good'.[95] Within a few years they were 'anxious to discourage recourse to repeated loans' and considered it desirable that the poor should learn to save for themselves.[96] By 1890 the Oxford COS chairman was admitting that 'loans are not a very popular form of help with us ... we have had great difficulty in the past in the matter of arrears, and have been compelled to write off several loans as bad debts'.[97] Kingston-on-Thames COS were hugely enthusiastic about loans in the 1880s and reported having found 'another way' to be 'helpful to poor people' by 'granting loans under proper security'.[98] Their publicized eagerness resulted over a period of three years in them arranging a total of 22 loans having a gross value of £29 10s.

Although a few COSs claimed excellent repayment records, such as at Leith where it was said only £9 had been lost of the £1152 loaned over eleven years, loans faded in popularity with other provincial societies when disenchantment was fostered by defaulting debtors. This widespread inability to recover their capital when considered together with their insistence on securities raises doubts about their much vaunted investigative procedures with their claimed effectiveness in spotlighting applicants deserving of COS support as well as impostors who were not.

Lending-in-kind was popular with some provincial COSs and the practice of lending blankets through the winter months was often adopted from earlier provident societies.[99] Birkenhead, Birmingham and Southampton COSs, together with Manchester and Salford DPS, were among the organizing societies having similar schemes.[100] The Birmingham COS 'Blanket Loan Fund' started in 1877 typified others in being managed by a committee of COS females. Their activities were featured in COS annual reports which described how the society's officers investigated the worthiness of applicants and distributed the blankets to those approved by the 'Ladies'. Rules at Birmingham included:

1. Blankets 'given out' in October and 'rented at 6d a winter or 3d for a shorter period'.
2. Each recipient 'signed a paper on obtaining the blankets'.
3. Blankets collected in May of the following year to be 'steamed and purified' with working expenses defrayed from the Fund.
4. 100 pairs of blankets were purchased initially and 'marked so as to be recognised in the pawn shops'.[101]

Mrs Elizabeth Mathews, Hon. Secretary of the Birmingham 'Blanket Loan Fund', reported that 'the recipients were, in every case, delighted to have the blankets, and showed much gratitude for the trust reposed in them. Several had asked to be allowed to wash the blankets before returning them'.[102]

A coal fund was launched by Leamington COS partly as an attempt to gain liaison with other charitable agencies. The COS collected donations, organized tickets, obtained sixpences from applicants and arranged the coal deliveries. In the fund's early years co-operation with clergy and nonconformist ministers was nurtured by the COS allowing them to distribute the coal tickets but by 1887 the COS had decided to discontinue tickets being 'simply sent to the Clergy and Ministers' as in the society's view 'many persons receiving tickets... did not require them'. The COS found the need to 'exercise some slight restraint upon this abuse' and in justification published case-studies of alleged misuse, including that of a man 'who tore up the ticket and spent the sixpence at the public house'.[103] But a correspondent to the *Leamington Spa Courier* ridiculed how the typical applicant for a coal ticket had become the 'victim' of repeated enquiries, '... and this is charity'.[104]

The ideological weakness of grants and growing disenchantment with loans encouraged more provincial COSs to provide pensions for a select few considered to be especially deserving.[105] Each 'special case' was usually made the focus of a COS public donations appeal, a procedure which complied with the COS principle that each applicant relieved with a grant from a general fund signified neglect of their basic tenet that attention must always be on the individual.[106] Against this they had to bear in mind that COS stalwart General Lynedoch Gardiner believed pensions to be the 'most costly' and 'most demoralising' form of relief 'because they loosen the ties and abrogate the duties of kinship'.[107] For similar reasons Sir Charles Trevelyan reminded COS members that the condemnation of private doles was 'one of the earliest conclusions at which your Society arrived'.[108]

In spite of the in-house objections 'special case' pensions grew in number. They were said to be for a 'deserving person' whose circumstances made them unsuitable for treatment under the 'ordinary rules of the Society' and yet who justified charitable relief rather than being pauperized.[109] Manchester and Salford DPS sympathetically detected applications from 'that class which of late have been steadily increasing namely clerks, warehousemen, respectable and educated people brought to want through misfortune, and very often through no fault of their own ... for whom the Parish and the Workhouse Hospital have a most wholesome dread'.[110] There were also a number of 'respectable widows in distress through inability to let furnished rooms upon which they have depended for their existence' and persons of 'good social positions, but through some unforeseen circumstances have been suddenly compelled to seek the means of living'.[111] The DPS urged that some 'kind benefactor' would in each case see fit to establish a fund to alleviate such distress.[112]

The provision of a COS pension was not made lightly. Because of their long-term implications cases were subjected to especially rigorous investigation. If the agent's initial report was favourable a temporary weekly provision was made and a liaison COS visitor appointed to co-ordinate further intense probing into the person's circumstances. Relatives were questioned more rigorously and 'as much as possible induced to help' with the clergyman, district visitor and employers asked to 'corroborate essential details'. It was only if each constituent part of the investigation proved satisfactory to the COS committee that the case became 'special' and an appeal launched for supportive long-term donors.[113] After a pension had been provided the recipient was kept under constant surveillance. Oxford COS claimed that their regular visits were 'warmly welcomed' because although the visitor rarely gave direct help they were 'soon regarded as a friend and counsellor by the family assisted'.[114]

For their 'special cases' Oxford COS concentrated on: the aged, respectable widows with young children, confirmed invalids and orphans.[115] Public response in 1876 to appeals for their first two 'special cases' was 'disappointing' but over the years increased enthusiasm was engendered.[116] When their pensions were not completely publicly underwritten, Oxford COS attempted to extract additional contributions from their members, failing which they raided their general fund. In the later 1880s pensions monopolized Oxford COS finances so that by 1890 they accounted for £635 out of £1115 gross income.[117]

Southampton COS and Leamington COS were amongst those favouring pensions for those who 'in spite of age and ill-health, have succeeded in keeping themselves out of the workhouse'.[118] Southampton COS explained that in the past such cases had frequently been supported by a circle of friends but gifts had been irregular and fluctuating in value. The COS saw their role as that of collecting the variable gifts from well-wishers and marshalling them into a regular small pension. By 1887 the gross annual value of pensions paid by Southampton COS reached £89 12s.9d. shared between 'eleven old deserving persons'. Although Southampton COS shunned such comparison their average pension of around 3 shillings per week was virtually identical with what an elderly person might expect by way of a Poor Law dole. Sponsorship for Southampton COS pensions was always lukewarm and they confessed that were 'sufficient aid forthcoming they could readily, and would gladly, double and treble the recipients of this fund'.[119] Leamington COS pensions had few pretensions to adequacy. They gave one shilling weekly to 'meet the wants of persons who from a position of comparative affluence, have by misfortune, fallen into distress' and involved 'a class of persons who are often reluctant to make their necessities known'.[120]

Birmingham COS favoured long-term weekly allowances for 'specially-deserving' widows with families. In 1882 they established a widows' fund 'from which to make weekly allowances to women on whom had been thrown the burden of supporting a young family, through the death or disablement of their husbands'.[121] Deserving widows were provided with weekly allowances varying from 2s.6d. to 7 shillings depending on family size. The COS claimed that 'small as these sums may appear, they bridge over the great, wide gulf between actual want and bare sufficiency, and stimulate and encourage the otherwise disheartened women in their efforts to bring up their families in respectability'.[122] According to Birmingham COS 'with pauperism staring her in the face, the woman has to be cook, housemaid, nurse and breadwinner' and claimed that for 'assistance to be effectual must be continuous for months and, perhaps, for years'.[123] The following Birmingham COS case-study again illustrates how easy it was for outside observers to detect close similarities between COS pensions and Poor Law doles which they so frowned upon:

> M.A.A. Widow. Age 27. Three children, the eldest 7 years old. Came under Society's notice, January, 1881, when the woman and children had been ill from fever, and, in a very weak state. Has had 3s. per week for 35 weeks, and is still receiving that sum. Will be a long case, but will eventually become self-supporting.[124]

COS pensions tended to be class-divisive through often being reserved for fallen members of the middle class or at least the 'cream' of the working class.[125] When recipients were elderly, as was often the case, COS pensions were virtually for life. As such they had the same faults of value-inadequacy, permanence and deterrence to an independent lifestyle, which frequently were targets for scurrilous COS comments about Poor Law outdoor relief. In evidence to the 1895 Royal Commission on the Aged Poor the COS sought to demolish similar accusations by claiming that COS pensions, in contrast with Poor Law doles, were always taken to the house of 'the old people by some lady visitor' who would visit them 'in a friendly way, taking them in the summer time some flowers, and in the winter time little comforts ...'.[126]

But by 1890 there was growing provincial COS acceptance that they had moved perilously close to duplicating aspects of the Poor Law system they so despised. By then the number of pensions called for 'serious consideration' because 'unless they were given with great care they tend inevitably to discourage persons from making provision for old age, to lower wages ... and, in short, to reproduce the recognised evils of an indiscriminate administration of out-door relief'.[127] Oxford COS's excuse for their pensions was that there were 'a large number of persons who grew up in days when the opportunity and zeal for thrift' was 'far smaller' and that it was unfair to penalise such individuals.[12]

Not all provincial COSs became enamoured with pensions. In these localities, when societies did encounter 'special cases' they hedged long-term commitment by avoiding the word 'pension'. The Revd. J.A. Cross explained that Leeds COS did not provide pensions but that 'in some cases aged and feeble persons who need permanent assistance are placed upon what is called the Deserving List'.[129] At Bristol the COS preferred the term 'allowances' but whatever the label their involvement was small-scale.[130] Other provincial societies, while occasionally detecting 'very deserving cases' which were 'ineligible' in the 'normal way', were unable to commit themselves to pensions through not having 'money enough'.[131]

The common distinguishing characteristic of the various 'special case' pension funds was that the COS focused directly on a specific deserving individual in the hope of attracting donations from middle-class subscribers who may then develop a personal ongoing commitment with the unfortunate person. The same technique is currently used more than a century later by charities wanting to attract help for disadvantaged individuals in the UK and in the Third World.

A rather different form of relief practised by some provincial societies involved giving direct nourishment to the suffering masses.[132] COSs such as those at Leamington and Croydon followed the Liverpool CRS example by occasionally supplying sustenance such as soup, cocoa and meals at non-commercial prices much to the irritation of London COS. Leamington COS admitted that when throngs clustered around their soup kitchen in the cold winter of 1878–9, the applications became 'so numerous and pressing in their nature that our principle of previous investigation was obliged to be somewhat relaxed'.[133] Next year Leamington COS were satisfied that because of the 'less protracted winter' it had been 'unnecessary to distribute soup and bread in such large quantities' but they still supplied them to the most needy.[134] In mild winters when the kitchen was less used, the Leamington committee occasionally found it appropriate 'because of the unusual amount of sickness among the poor' to draw money from the soup fund to supply benefits.[135]

In the bad weather of 1870–1 Liverpool CRS provided 123 312 quarts of sago soup at one halfpenny per quart. Only 4476 quarts of the more nutritious but more expensive meat soup at 1d. per quart were sold.[136] A letter to the *Liverpool Lantern* described CRS soup as a 'sort of lumpy material of a bluish yellow tinge, and looked very much like bill-sticker's paste ... the sort of stuff that Uncle Sandy used to feed his pigs ...'[137] During the dock labourers' stoppage of 1879, CRS kitchen staff were required to exert 'great circumspection ... to avoid giving relief to those on strike'.[138]

Another relief method practised by Liverpool CRS was the establishment of their own fire-lighter factories which caused them aggravation from different directions.[139] On the one hand London COS ridiculed them because the factories regularly traded at a loss and because the low wage rates allegedly disturbed market equilibrium. At the same time the CRS were often cold-shouldered by out-of-work labourers partly because of the miserable wage rates and also because of unwillingness to 'undergo the severe and humiliating labour test which the Society applies indiscriminately and without regard to the fitness or capacity of the applicant'.[140] The *Liverpool Lantern* reported 'more than one case in which a starving family have been refused relief because the father or husband has been physically incapable of chopping wood'.[141]

Yet another form of assistance provided by provincial COSs was a facility to help the unemployed find work. There was general COS agreement with the maxim that 'the first objective of all aid should be to introduce those wanting employment to the labour market.[142] A number of provincial COSs created job registers which were a step towards the state-sponsored 1909 Labour Exchanges and present-day Job Centres. However, there was the interesting difference that whereas contemporary establishments concentrate on the display of job vacancies it was not unusual for COS registers to also feature, for the benefit of potential employers, the names of people ascertained by the local COS to be of 'good character' together with an outline of their work experience.[143] Leamington COS's Labour Register was freely available for those needing employment as nurses, labourers, gardeners, laundresses, charwomen and 'persons accustomed to jobbing work'.[144] Birkenhead COS concentrated more on providing skilled charwomen 'of which ladies have largely availed themselves'. They welcomed the co-operation of the Mersey Ferry Committee in placing 'employment notices' at the ferry entrance without charge.[145] Kingston-on-Thames COS hoped that their plans for creating a 'free labour registry ... might become a valuable help' for employers because the society would contribute their 'intimate knowledge' of an individual's character, capacity and circumstances.[146]

Mr M.W. Moggridge warned against the COS giving the impression of being employment agencies. He maintained that the task was 'impossible in most cases' because 'if a man cannot find work for himself, no one else can find it for him'[147]. Moggridge's comments had some validity in that when large factories closed even the most capable worker could often not find a local job. This encouraged some provincial COSs to provide migratory help. Leamington COS assisted workers to move away from the district because 'it was of very doubtful kindness to encourage him to remain in a state of chronic poverty competing with others and lowering the rate of wages'.[148] They believed that 'migration and emigration, which are so largely practised by the rich', represented the only permanent and effectual remedies.[149]

In 1883 the Oxford COS showed transient keenness about emigration but explained that the thoroughness of their investigations had exposed the need to dismiss 'a considerable number of applicants ... as unsuitable'.[150] Nevertheless the COS did satisfy themselves by carefully selecting 15 deserving applicants. The efficacy of their investigative procedures and their skills in assessing the would-be emigrants' integrity were called into doubt when 'again and again' they found the cash had been 'frittered away' or had been used 'for other purposes'. Oxford COS abandoned further participation after concluding that claimants for emigration assistance provided, 'no more fruitful source of dishonesty and mendicancy'.[151]

Southampton COS developed mechanisms for assisting migration but soon announced a 'considerable diminution' in their ability to help.[152] This did not stop them informing the Southampton middle classes in 1886 of their wish to find jobs not only for 'domestic servants, charwomen, washerwomen and such-like, but also for clerks, artisans, labourers, errand-boys and others seeking employment'.[153] When trade was low the Southampton COS helped a few workers to emigrate believing that 'such assistance almost invariably proved permanent and substantial'.[154]

Fundamentally much of provincial COS relief was orientated towards assisting the speedy recovery of an applicant's health so that they would soon become independent. To this end it was quite common to issue hospital tickets to deserving sick people. Some societies went further and developed their own convalescent schemes.[155] The outstanding example was the Manchester and Salford DPS's convalescent home established in Southport after a fund launched in 1876 attracted £3783 17s.0d.[156] When the home became operational, James Smith, the DPS agent, reported how he had visited Southport and addressed the first 14 patients. After asking for divine blessing he explained to the sick 'that this building had been bought by a number of good and rich people of Manchester for the benefit of such as yourselves and trusted they would appreciate the generous kindness'. Smith recalled how 'one poor fellow ... with tears in his eyes' affirmed the patients' thankfulness that 'such a beautiful place had been provided for the poor in the time of their convalescence from sickness, and the blessing it would be to them all to be restored to health, and return to their own homes, and be able to work to support their families'.[157] In Smith's opinion even these appreciative words did not adequately express the patients' looks of gratitude. By 1889 building extensions had allowed for the provision of 80 beds, with the home catering annually for over 750 patients staying three and a half weeks on average. The Southport facilities became a regular photographic feature of DPS publications. Male and female patients were accepted at Southport for a weekly charge of fourteen shillings 'paid either by themselves, by some sponsoring body or out of the Sick Relief Fund'.[158]. Table 6.5 shows the impressive increase in the number of admissions to the home and how they were categorized. The DPS explained that those termed cured 'went home in full health, and returned to work straightaway', those who were relieved were in 'nearly every case suffering from more or less chronic complaints, but at the end of their stay at the Home were so much better as to be able to resume their various occupations on their return home', while those categorized as improper cases included 'persons far advanced in consumption, heart disease etc., whose complaints had reached the stage that their medical advisers should not have recommended a visit to an institution established for convalescents'.[159]. Provident departments were developed by provincial organizing societies in the belief that 'the good done to the indigent classes by this system is incalculable'.[160] Personal contact with the lower classes was mainly by lady visitors. Each was assigned a

Table 6.5 Manchester and Salford DPS Convalescent Home, Southport: number of admissions and their categorization

Year	Number of patients admitted (A)	Cured %A	Relieved %A	Improper cases %A
1881	229	68.25	27.25	4.50
1885	472	73	26	1
1890	763	70	28	2

number of poor homes from which to collect small monetary deposits 'of any sum not including halfpence' to be eventually repaid for a specific purpose or even better transferred to the Post Office Savings Bank.[161] No interest was provided, nor was any administrative cost deducted. Ideally visitors called 'for money at the door' but when over the years the numbers of active volunteers tailed off so did this part of the COS service.

Around 30 000 collection visits were made during 1879 by the Birkenhead COS Provident Department.[162] Table 6.6 shows that the annual deposits of the Birkenhead COS Provident Department grew marginally from 1873 to 1890 even though the limited number of helpers was restrictive. Approximately thirty visitors engaged themselves during 1876 in collecting £1358 with distinct differences in the value of the deposits the various visitors attracted. Whereas a Miss Brown gathered savings of only £1 19s. 6d. during the year, Miss M.E. Minns collected £143 5s. 2d., while another entry in their report for a Miss Minns, possibly the same person, showed she gathered deposits of £104 6s. 10d.[163] At times of economic blight the appeal of visiting was further diminished when subscribers found even greater difficulty in scratching together a few pennies for a rainier day that it was painful to imagine. As the *Charity Organisation Review* reported, 'who shall persuade Lady Bountiful to emulate the zeal of the Prudential Agent, and go her rounds with an empty purse?'[164]

The Manchester and Salford DPS was the doyen of provincial provident societies and their principles, sacrosanct since 1833, were an unmistakable influence on COSs such as Birkenhead. The DPS did not consider it fundamental that they should organize the activities of other charities, more than offering their investigative skills to medical charities and others needing to test the wherewithal of patients. Nor did the DPS see themselves primarily as a relief agency as did the Liverpool CRS. The number of DPS volunteers willing to undertake direct contact with the poor through their Savings Department by home visiting gradually reduced. The hundreds of enthusiastic visitors envisaged by the society's

Table 6.6 Birkenhead COS Provident Department: details of deposits

	Year ending 31.12.1873	Year ending 31.12.1890
Deposits during the year	£1207 2s.	£1310
On hand at beginning of year	£ 167 10s.	£ 255 17s.
Returned to depositors in year	£1179 2s.	£1356 13s.

founders in 1833 had in practice become the more modest numbers shown in Table 6.7. In spite of the band of DPS visitors in 1890 having dwindled to being less than a quarter of what it had been twenty years earlier the society contrived to maintain broadly the same level of deposits by educating the poor into their own use of savings banks.

Another COS with a provident scheme was Oxford. In their early flush of enthusiasm they heralded their Penny Savings Bank as another way in which they would inculcate providence among the poor but the venture foundered through insufficient investors.[165] After having allowed the scheme to dribble along for a few years the Oxford society eventually decided that because the post office offered superior facilities for saving there was not sufficient public gain 'to compensate for the great labour in account-keeping which an independent Penny Bank entails'.[166]

In 1882 the Liverpool CRS attempted to stimulate local providence with the distribution of pamphlets about sick clubs, penny savings banks, post-office savings banks and the District Provident Society. They aimed to convince the poor that with appropriate foresight and tightness of purse-strings the lowest wage earners could protect themselves against needing to seek outside assistance even when they were out of a job, were sick or had a death in the family.

EXCEPTIONAL DISTRESS

In the eyes of the founders of the London COS, the Mansion House relief funds of the late 1860s caused such disastrous confusion in the distribution

Table 6.7 Manchester and Salford DPS: Savings Department details[167]

	1871	1890
Number of lady and gentlemen visitors	25	6
House visited weekly	995	431
Number of Saving Banks opened weekly	15	21
No. of depositors' accounts open on 1 Jan.	4 679	6 723
Number of accounts opened during the year	7 672	6 242
Number of accounts closed during the year	7 492	5 968
Amount deposited during the year	£3 147	£3 378
In separate sums totalling	54 475	40 955
Amount repaid during the year	£2 980	£3 424
In separate sums totalling	8 206	8 034

Activities of the Provincial Societies

of charity as to be a catalyst towards their establishment.[168] It was natural therefore that there was hesitancy in the provinces about becoming embroiled on such occasions, especially when COS principles were often concerned with proving that the distress was not exceptional and could therefore be ignored.[169] However, some provincial COSs were tempted to co-operate in the distribution of emergency funds by the possibility of them achieving, if only temporarily, a working relationship with relief agencies who normally rebuffed them.

Over the years the Birmingham Corporation invited the COS to participate in the administration of a number of mayoral distress funds. In 1881 the intense January frost caused an almost total cessation of outdoor employment in the city. According to the Birmingham COS report, crowds 'flocked to your Society for help' but the 'task of administering to the needy out of a population of half a million was truly very great'.[170] The COS admitted that for a day or two there were so many applicants 'and the cold so intense, that the rule that enquiry should precede relief had to be placed in abeyance, otherwise the injury done to the hungry and poorly clad by the exposure to the cold would have been very serious'. For Birmingham COS 'the sight of able-bodied, respectable-looking labourers reduced to begging ... caused sad reflections not easily forgotten' and convinced them 'that the methods of relief which would be effectual in a village were not only futile, but perhaps harmful, among such overwhelming crowds of utter strangers'.[171]

In explaining why their 1884 report had not been published, Birmingham COS claimed to have been 'under so severe a pressure of work in connection with the administration of the fund for the unemployed in the winter 1884–5, that finding it impossible to prepare the annual report at the usual time thought it better to defer it'.[172] Although the public relations attraction of sortieing into relief funds was important to Birmingham COS, their chairman Henry Griffith Jnr still cautioned in 1890 about their participation. He reflected that 'the excited sympathy at such times is too impatient, and the Society is in danger either of offending some of its constant supporters by endeavouring to enforce its habitual discrimination, or of violating its fundamental principle "no investigation, no help"'.[173]

The same attitude prevailed with Manchester and Salford DPS. After their experiences at the time of the 1860s cotton famine they were loath to become entangled in what members saw as a masquerade of organized charitable distribution. Despite this, when memories had blurred towards the close of 1878 when another trade depression arrived with a long severe winter, the DPS again agreed to assist with a special distress fund which exceeded £26 000. This temporary return to widescale relief was subsequently viewed as a 'mistaken divergence' and 'numerous further attempts to get the Society to continue its relief organisation were therefore resisted'.[174]

When there was intense local distress in 1885–6 Southampton COS attempted to satisfy need from their own resources. They were 'gratified to be able to report that a sum of £82 5s.7d. was subscribed by grants, i.e. free gifts – a much larger amount than the Society ever before received in one year for that purpose' but 'if the amount at the Committee's disposal had been far greater, there was no lack of deserving objects to relieve whose sufferings they would gladly have devoted it to'.[175] In 1879 when serious distress occurred in Birkenhead, the COS helped distribute the mayor's general relief fund. At the COS offices 807 persons were relieved with orders for the supply of food, coal and other 'necessaries'.[176] Five years later Birkenhead COS described how the 'unfortunate state of things continued and was even accentuated during most of the year' so that 'unemployed men gradually consumed their savings, pawned their watches and furniture, obtained credit from the shops they habitually dealt with, and were often helped by their more fortunate neighbours, some receiving allowances from their clubs'.[177] During the 15 months of distress in 1884–5, Birkenhead COS claimed to have organized the relief of 2403 families and individuals representing about '8000 souls' at a total cost of £1145 5s. in food and coal. They were confident that no other system of management could have made the money last so long.[178]

C.T. Gostenofer detected hesitancy among the Birkenhead poor about becoming involved with the COS even when conditions were especially bad. He was conscious that many among the labouring classes were 'well entitled to relief but omitted to apply for it, and some who were offered refused it, preferring to pawn everything they had'.[179] The *Charity Organisation Review* commenting on Gostenofer's opinion recognized the care taken at Birkenhead in 'minimising allowances and frequently reviewing the magnitude of the relief so as not to weaken the incentives to seeking employment' but warned against the evils of 'providing artificial employment in times of emergency' because any scheme that reduced the mobility of workers must be 'mischievous'.[180]

Exceptional distress on the dramatic scale experienced in the industrial and dockland centres was not suffered in Oxford but when foul winter weather coincided with the university vacation there was much hardship for the casually employed, lowly paid college workers. Oxford COS were delighted when other local charitable agencies asked their opinion 'as to the extent of the distress and the best way of dealing with it'.[181] The

Oxford society also found it possible when living conditions were especially vicious to supply 'hot soup' with bread for vagrants.[182]

During exceptional distress in North East England COS methodology was occasionally welcomed by other relief agencies. During the mid 1880s the shipping, shipbuilding, ship-repair and ironworks along the north-east coast were savagely depressed. West Hartlepool COS was established during the winter of 1885 when exceptional distress was being suffered across the region with Poor Law guardians 'totally unprepared' and 'ill-equipped to cope'.[183] For some months the newly formed society 'sparingly and carefully' distributed £100 a week but by February 1886 the COS funds dried up. Responsibility was then thrown back to the guardians, a situation repeated a few miles along the River Tees at Darlington. Elsewhere in the North East 'confusion and lack of co-ordination increased with the crisis' with Middlesbrough relief a 'scandal', charitable contribution at Gateshead 'pitifully small' and a member of Newcastle COS setting up 'a small but well-organised soup kitchen'.[184]

In general then, despite the ideological hesitancy, it was not unusual at times of exceptional distress for provincial COSs to temporarily abandon their cherished investigative principles when faced with the raw tragedy of the starving poor. The conflicting pressures associated with exceptional distress instigated the formation of a London COS committee in 1886 which reiterated that however desirable 'spontaneous charity' may appear to relieve destitution in emergencies 'evils resulted from the want of sufficient organisation'.[185] Before the provision of relief, co-operation with guardians was seen as 'indispensable' as were visits to the applicant's home and the obtaining of references from employers or 'trustworthy local sources'. It was COS suspicion about the motives of the poor that compounded adverse public criticism about their activities even at times of exceptional distress. For example the Lord Mayor of London was advised to decline the COS 'assistance(?) so generously offered' and was reminded of 'the mischief and cruelty which these organising busy-bodies have from time to time been guilty of ...'[186]

THE UNDESERVING: CAUTIONARY PROCEDURES

There was always a COS fear that their visitors may be outwitted by a devious residuum feigning poverty. Even the formidable Octavia Hill was anxious about what she saw as the wiles of the cunning poor. She reported to the 1888 House of Lords Select Committee that 'the people are exceedingly sharp and the more their homes look miserable the more they expect to get'.[187] Similar concerns were expressed at the formation of the Liverpool CRS back in 1863 when Sir William Brown emphasized that 'every great care ought to be taken to enquire and examine the character' of all relief applicants. An active man was always needed to visit and expose imposters applying for charitable support and Sir William was proud that he himself was 'hard-hearted enough' never to allow such people to hoodwink him.[188] He would have been pleased that the same alert attitude remained with his successors in 1890 with the CRS's Everton Committee reporting that although the working classes required 'very little monetary help' the committee 'fully justified' their own presence as 'an agency for sifting evidence and exposing undeserving cases'.[189]

Outside the big cities about 30 per cent of COS applicants were categorized as not being suitable for their assistance. Provincial COSs were proud that their investigative diligence identified the undeserving residua of society and prevented them receiving unwarranted and dangerously immoral benefits. Mr Sheriff Le Feuvre of Southampton COS was reassured that one-third of their applicants 'prove to be ineligible or undeserving' as this confirmed that their investigations had prevented money from being 'wasted on undeserving objects'.[190] The Southampton COS ground rules for investigators included:

> ... the rejection of undeserving drunkards and incorrigible idlers; those who were careless and improvident; those who for other sufficient reasons the Society felt it was out of their power to help so making them ineligible; and those who were in an absolute state of destitution fit only for the workhouse.[191]

Canon Wilberforce's experience had 'unfortunately' showed him that 'in a large percentage of cases' the applicant's statement could not be relied upon'.[192] Later Southampton COS reiterated that 'the evils of indiscriminate almsgiving are great and grave – so great and grave as wholly to surpass the belief of those who have had little or no opportunity of acquiring knowledge of its ill effects'.[193] These pronouncements were not infrequently accompanied by a plea for the public to recognize that COS principles were not 'as some imagine to gratify censurable inquisitiveness into the circumstances of poor folk'.[194]

A common COS technique was the circulation of 'cautionary cards' intended to guide peer societies and the public by the inclusion of names of organizations and individuals described as 'unworthy objects' of 'a parasitical class'.[195] The cards were also published as 'evidence' by which those who doubted the authenticity of charity organization might be

Activities of the Provincial Societies 135

convinced about the reality of a surfeit of malingerers determined to deceive the naive and unguarded. The Dr Barnardo law suit was a well publicized example of the damage caused to the society when one of the defamed objected with the force of law.[196]

COS investigations were claimed to be just as infallible in detecting ne'er-do-well applicants as they were in deciding who were deserving. A selection of rejected cases published by COSs show how their methods were applied:

1. Brighton COS alerted the London COS about James Smith, an impostor who had lost his right hand and right leg, apparently in military service. They considered that other affiliated Societies should be warned that Smith used his physical losses to win charitable hearts to supplement his 6d a day pension.[197]

2. A lamentable case of ingratitude and bad conduct illustrative of the difficulty of helping people whose vices prevent them helping themselves involved a man who had been financially assisted to buy a barrow which he had eventually sold for half its value and indulged in drink, judged by the COS to be his fatal propensity.[198]

3. A man stating that through slackness of trade, he had been out of work four months, applied for a loan of £2 to redeem from pawn clothing belonging to himself, his wife and three children, which he had parted with for food. He was found to be a widower, and the woman and the three children he mentioned did not belong to him. He was otherwise found to be undeserving.[199]

4. A man and his wife who obtained in one day 13 tickets for food and coal and got riotously drunk on the proceeds of their sale. This demonstrated the abuse made by imposters of unorganised charities and confirmed that relief should never be dispensed before enquiries were made in which the donor should place full reliance.[200]

5. Labourer 45, wife 38, son 13. Husband applied for help saying he was soon to get work but meanwhile had no food. Said he had been 6 months in the hospital. Discovered to have been in constant work until he went on the spree during which time he went to the Isle of Wight. Returning applied for admission to the workhouse. The Governor states that while there he was idle and full of cunning dodges. Agent found the family in comfortable room and saw food and fire. Decision – undeserving'.[201]

6. Cases 4034, 4035, and 4036. These were men who in the winter applied to one of our Subscribers for assistance and who according to

his usual practice sent them to the office for investigation, the result of which was that they were all found to have been in prison at various times and utterly undeserving.[202]

7. Case 4127. This man was a native of Reading, and had been in the Army. By means of very plausible manner and appearance, and the deplorable tales of distress he told, he imposed on the benevolent and earned a good living, however the police were put on his track with the result that he has left Reading. He was a thorough scoundrel.[203]

When Henrietta Barnett and her husband were becoming disillusioned with some aspects of the Charity Organisation Society in 1884 she asked incisively of her COS audience 'what does 463 cases thrown aside as undeserving and ineligible mean in last month's returns of work?'[204]

LACK OF COS VOLUNTEERS

The COS believed that the systematic visiting of the poor at their own homes was an indispensable basis of effective charity. Helen Bosanquet considered that visits should be for some definite errand by persons in a higher 'rank of life'.[205] Frustratingly for the COS they found the recruitment of visitors a persistent problem. In addition, because the COS failed in their bid to organize the activities of other relief agencies, they not infrequently discovered that their visits clashed with those of other charities. It irritated the COS that the poor were sometimes inundated with an army of representatives including relieving officers, school board visitors, clergy, dissenting ministers, almoners of the Society for the Relief of Distress, city missionaries, bible women, scripture readers, gospel missioners and Sunday school teachers, etc.[206] There was no worthwhile response from other relief agencies to the Revd. M.S.A. Walrond's proposal that miscellaneous visiting processes should be rationalized under COS auspices.[207]

COS attempts to prove their work 'better on every point' than that of other agencies led to their visitors being supplied with forms, record books and *Occasional Papers*. Allegedly all COS investigations were scientifically designed to expose the fraudulent rascal and ensure that the more deserving received constructive, purposeful support.[208] The paperwork unleashed from London central office undoubtedly helped to guide provincial COS workers on the rudiments of visiting but there was little formal induction training before the 1890s. Even at the end of the century Helen Bosanquet believed it remained true that 'many a devoted visiting-lady' felt bewildered because the 'whole system of social organisation which is moulding the lives of the people she has taken under her care' remained 'entirely unknown quantities'.[209]

Provincial organizing societies suffered increasingly from their shortage of visitors. Leamington COS inclined towards dispensing relief through their office to minimize dependence on volunteers.[210] Birkenhead COS warned in the 1880s that even the well-being of their lively Provident Department was being endangered by the shortage of volunteers.[211] They admitted in 1887 that 'appeals which have been repeatedly made for additional help have not been answered as could be wished ... and this most excellent branch of work languishes for want of workers'.[212] Recruiting drives were not helped when a newspaper usually supportive of the COS commented that the experience of coming face to face with destitution had 'blunted' the feelings of COS officers and 'their natures hardened' so as to make them 'unpopular with the poor'.[213] Brighton COS were reasonably well supported by influential local society factions prepared to serve on their committees but shared the dearth of visitors with other COSs. London COS discouraged Brighton's intention to economize on voluntary effort by sanctioning distressed persons to tout their COS-authenticated petitions themselves and recommended instead that Brighton increase their salaried staff.[214]

The repeated dramas at times of economic depression demonstrated by 1890 to more and more better-off people that the plight of workers had not been satisfactorily ameliorated in recent decades and in some respects was becoming dangerously worse. Socialism seemed to be taking root and the threats of New Unionism now made it feasible for great ports like Liverpool and London to be halted by casual workers. No longer was it an acceptable ingredient for social harmony that an inquisitorial COS should decide that so many of those unemployed, underemployed or underprivileged people were also 'undeserving' of assistance.

The shifting social attitudes did not leave the ordinary COS visitor untouched. The difficulty of retaining their services intensified as the individual consciences of COS visitors wrestled with conflicting social ideas. Ladies having little stomach for social theory found it bewildering and unattractive to reconcile the moral benefits promised eventually from the COS's confrontational methodology with the simpler less restrained Christian pity preached from most Sunday pulpits. Public opinion had veered towards accepting that less authoritarian solutions to social problems were needed to placate dissatisfied masses. A middle class with diminished self-confidence now accepted that the wider scope of urban disharmonies more often needed alleviation by state involvement even though this transgressed cherished laissez-faire ideals. By the late 1880s there were fewer ladies willing to accept that the cause of noxious working-class squalor was being correctly analysed by the COS in persisting to blame the very people suffering the discomfort, ill-health and indignity.

In an earlier recruitment drive Manchester and Salford DPS republished a letter from the *Manchester Guardian* which expressed the need for 'more visitors to visit the homes of the poor to induce habits of sobriety and thrift'.[215] Appeals of this nature were increasingly nullified by the reports of organizing societies being phrased in ways unlikely to attract well-intentioned ladies. As Simey observed, Liverpool CRS reports were couched in terminology more appropriate to the addressing of company shareholders with emphasis on the state of trade of their ventures together with tabular information on how many cases had been investigated, rejected, referred or relieved with 'never a word of pity for the anguish of a bitter winter, never a sigh for the fate of those sent empty away'.[216]

It was a fundamental flaw in COS structures that their volunteers were 'almost entirely ladies coming from at least moderately well-to-do homes' with little direct knowledge of the sort of life lived by most applicants.[217] The petit bourgeoisie scarcely featured in provincial COSs let alone the working class. As the COS admitted in the 1880s 'the class of retail dealers and working people were still hostile to them'.[218]

ORGANIZATIONAL FINANCES AND ADMINISTRATION COSTS

Even the *Charity Organisation Review*, usually so ebullient about the movement's beneficial influence on social affairs, admitted in 1890 that the COS had 'suffered from the cold and inclemency of a long Spring'.[219] By then the finances of provincial COSs had often become the focus of adverse public comment.[220]

It was an uphill struggle for provincial COSs wanting to present a gentler more appealing image when propagandists like Major C.C. FitzRoy writing from the comfort of the Army and Navy Club claimed that 'every penny' given directly to the poor set free 'a like sum to be viciously employed' because it was a direct 'encouragement to vice' in providing 'money to spend at the public-house'.[221] Oxford COS asked for public recognition that they were not 'hard-hearted' and that they were 'often misunderstood'.[222]

COS failure to gain wide acceptance for their ideology meant that fund-raising was extremely difficult and for many societies their weak finances were of repeated concern and restrictive to their activities. Table 6.8 shows the annual receipts and administrative costs for various provincial societies for the average year through the 1870s and 1880s. Most of these societies remained slight in financial muscle compared with many longer established traditional charities surrounding them. There was increased growth in some COSs over the years but this was not always apparent from their conventional subscription lists as any increased donations that did occur tended to be for specific purposes and in particular the 'special cases' discussed on pp. 123–5.

Provincial organizing societies were commendable in keeping their administrative costs tightly within the budget parameters set by their management committees but because their investigative procedures demanded salaried input their working expenditure remained stubbornly

Table 6.8 Provincial COSs: annual income and administrative expenditure[a]

Name of Society	Average annual receipts £	Average annual administrative expenditure £
Birkenhead COS	486	199
Birmingham COS	847	338
Brighton COS	806	332
Leamington COS	674	150
Liverpool CRS	4684	988
Manchester and Salford DPS[b]	2156	867
Oxford COS	595	141
Reading COS	136	52
Southampton COS	214	87

Note:
(a) The average annual receipts tabled here generally include subcriptions, donations, bequests, special funds, investment interest and, where used as part of the society's accounting procedures, items such as the balance brought forward from previous years.
(b) Manchester and Salford DPS data includes 'general receipts' and sick relief subcriptions and donations, but not contributions specifically for the convalescent home or the provident dispensary branch. Nor does it include costs incurred directly by these activities.

Refer also to Appendix: General Notes on Poor Law and Organized Charity Data.

high relative to the funds disbursed. It was no longer acceptable for COS stalwarts like Francis Peek to dismiss as 'foolish' public perceptions that 'the total amount of money relief given in one year was only equal to the Charity Officer's salary'.[223] The Revd. Dr Hamilton willingly accepted 'the criticism often made against the COS about its high administration expenditure' because he alleged that people consistently missed the point about the COS being 'an investigating Society'.[224] Mr J.M. Heathcote hoped the time had passed when 'the Charity Organisation was looked upon as a hard-hearted oligarchy, who assumed the offices of both poor-law guardian and policemen, but failed to perform the duties of either'.[225]

A series of biting public attacks were launched on the Liverpool CRS administrative expenses in 1878. The *Liverpool Lantern* expressed incredulity that the society had contrived to spend £1000 in distributing £1600 of relief and argued that the reality was even worse than the CRS's published figures because they had omitted certain subsidies.[226] The CRS attempted to defend themselves by claiming that their administrative expenditure covered not only the provision of relief but also other operations such as the investigating, organizing and distributing of charity, together with the management of their workshops and soup kitchens. Eight years later the *Liverpool Review* was prepared to accept that the CRS had 'done some good work' but believed 'the expense of such working has, in our opinion, been far greater than it need have been'.[227] The newspaper was also concerned about harsh CRS procedures, the following being one of the 'instances' they provided to demonstrate CRS 'unreasonable attitudes':

> A widow sempstress with family could get no work because of the 'slackness of trade' and applied to the CRS for relief. The kind-hearted wiseacre Inspector said, when visiting her house to check circumstances, that she could not expect support when she could 'easily sell her sewing-machine' the proceeds of which could be used to keep her family until she got work. 'It will be time enough to come to us when you have nothing to dispose of'. The poor woman was to sell the means by which she earned her scanty living, before she could get relief to help her along.[228]

These attacks in the local press did nothing to alleviate the CRS's reputation for having an uncompassionate approach or to improve the public response to CRS financial appeals.

Although the high provincial COS ratio of administrative costs to relief was generally a fair target there could be little justifiable criticism about them paying lavish salaries. The agent of a medium-size COS earned an annual salary of about £100 for which he was expected to possess 'considerable skill as an accountant' and maintain 'an elaborate set of books' as well as undertaking investigative and distributive work.[229] In contrast, a relieving officer in a union of modest size who was probably the nearest Poor Law equivalent would expect around £150 per annum and could expect an assistant on an annual salary of £50.[230]

Birkenhead COS had the assurance of being told by London that their business was 'being conducted' with 'increased vigour and efficiency' but Wirral observers were less impressed.[231] The Birkenhead COS found it difficult to refute 'the objection that was urged against them more than once in the newspapers ... that the amount distributed bears no proportion to the cost of the administration'.[232] Letters to the local press ridiculed the high Birkenhead COS overheads and hinted at their mishandling of donations.[233] Newspaper jibes in 1879 were well-timed and not easily answered because COS accounts needed to be published unaudited following administrative chaos subsequent to the death, illness or departure of senior officers. Years later there was renewed criticism with the *Birkenhead News* reporting that the COS were spending '£180 in making investigations prior to the distribution of £80 in charity'.[234]

Birmingham COS were proud of regularly avoiding an operating deficit, a record attained by 'the exercise of the most rigid economy' and by 'confining the help' to only the 'most distressing cases'.[235] They considered themselves 'almost unique in the history of charitable institutions' in never having shown a negative annual balance through their respect for the 'old fashioned assumption that debt is an evil'.[236] When making that claim in 1882 the Birmingham COS could look retrospectively with some satisfaction in that whereas the income of the society in 1873 had been £177 16s. 3d. with 561 cases investigated, their revenue had grown by 1881 to £1843, much of which was in the form of 'special case' donations together with exceptional distress appeals.[237] They were not to know that their financial progress had reached an apogee. By the end of the decade their income had dropped to £713 and fewer than 400 poor people were applying for assistance. The modest receipts of Birmingham COS contrasted with the various wealthy charities in and around the city.[238]

Oxford COS retained a rigorous grip on administration expenditure when their income increased through the 1880s.[239] Their efficiency as measured on an overhead cost : relief ratio basis was helped by them having the potential of input from undergraduates whose social consciences could be sufficiently awakened to recruit them as volunteers. It could also be argued that Oxford's favourable expenditure : relief ratio was partly explained in the 1880s by an increasing part of their outgoings being 'special case' pensions which once, established, were usually less demanding on salaried staff time.[240]

A cursory look at Brighton COS accounts gives the impression of healthy income throughout the 1880s but a high bank balance annually carried forward masked a less vigorous underlying pattern.[241] Early in the 1890s the Brighton COS chairman bewailed their decline in membership and suggested that if each member 'would endeavour to obtain one other subscriber, our funds would soon recover their former flourishing condition'.[242] T.H. Birtley expressed his regret to the Manchester and Salford DPS in 1879 that subscriptions were lower than they had been when he had joined the society thirty years earlier.[243]

Southampton COS constantly suffered from tepid support and in 1885 indicated their 'sincere hope that the people of Southampton would rally round the Society, and give it all the help it needed, and so thoroughly deserved'.[244] The meagre relief provided by the Southampton COS partly resulted from their own impecuniosity but still gave them license to pontificate that 'the primary object of dispensing charity should be to raise the recipient out of the mire – to enable him or her to be self-reliant – rather than to merely assist them to exist in it'.[245]

At a meeting chaired by the Very Revd. G.W. Kitchen the Southampton COS reported how there had been frequent assertions that 'such Societies were hard and inquisitorial' but claimed that these complaints invariably originated from a person 'who for very sufficient reasons was unwilling to have his circumstances investigated'.[246] But things did not improve and the Southampton COS remained 'surprised and grieved, after sixteen years' strenuous advocacy of principles which they all genuinely hoped would have been adopted by ... their fellow townsmen, ... to find their supporters numbered less than one hundred'.[247] A report on the condition of the Bristol poor indicated in 1884 that the local COS was 'not liberally supported' and it had been 'intimated that unless help is forthcoming it must cease to exist'.[248]

Leamington COS's frail subscription list led them to consider 'it advisable to remove to a less expensive house' for their offices.[249] Later they appealed that over 'the past year about twenty subscribers ... have died, or removed from the town ...' and in a vain attempt to bring themselves 'more prominently before the notice of the general public' the COS changed their annual meeting to October.[250]

The minuscule operations of Reading COS were surprisingly described by London COS as 'vigorous'.[251] When asked in their early days by the Revd. S.C. Gordon who would pay for the 'machinery of their Society' the

Reading COS had confidently answered they 'would leave the question to the public'.[252] Their confidence was to be misplaced. After years of lacklustre performance the most robustly committed COS supporters in Reading had to acknowledge that their society was not being generally accepted as a social panacea for rectifying the shortcomings of the poor. Reading COS could only plead that 'if the evils of indiscriminate out-door Relief were more generally recognised, the value of a responsible administration of Charity would be readily appreciated by the public'.[253] Their message was scarcely heeded and the society's annual subscriptions regularly dipped below £50.[254] There is little doubt that other provincial COSs shared Reading's frustration at not being able to persuade sufficient peers to their way of thinking.

7 Ideological Change in Late Victorian Britain: The Response of Provincial Charity Organisation Societies and the Local Government Board

With the evidence of previous chapters about the inability of provincial COSs to create change in the pattern of Victorian charitable disbursements this chapter discusses COS failures and provides explanations as to why their members clung so resolutely to their early ideals in spite of growing isolation from their social peers.

COS ADHERENCE TO PRINCIPLES

By the early 1880s COSs were acknowledging that they were not winning sufficient supporters among the middle classes and London COS appointed a committee 'to consider and recommend the best means of stating and systematically propagating the views of the Society on almsgiving'.[1] Under the heading 'Propagandism' the *Charity Organisation Reporter* concluded their main task to be convincing 'the charitable public that it is wrong to make charity the plaything of the rich and leisurely classes'.[2] Provincial COSs were encouraged to arrange press coverage for their meetings and to get the opinions of COS committee members published on each news item that might bear on pauperism, charity, mendicity or on the general condition of the lower classes. Other charitable bodies were to be 'strenuously canvassed' in the hope they would recognize belatedly that even the most durable social difficulties would soon disappear once COS doctrines were applied. COS members were encouraged to infiltrate committees of other charitable institutions because they were often 'more susceptible to influence from within than without'.[3] The COS also advised members to become guardians so as to speed the elimination of outdoor relief.

COS failure to convince sufficient of their peers about the benefits of organized charity led to them viewing themselves as akin to missionaries preaching to unresponsive heathens diverted from the exclusive scientific

COS truth. COS methodology alone allegedly provided the basis with which to convert others and lead to a 'Church of Charity'.[4] Should this imaginary body ever materialize it would do more than 'parliament, or preaching, or books, or pamphleteering' to enforce legislation and favourably influence churches, guardians, friendly societies, residents of a district and the 'common people'.[5] By disciplining the poor through 'a nobler, more devoted, more scientific religious charity' Charles Loch believed the COS would make 'the part instrumental to the good of the whole'.[6]

The COS remained implacable in their conviction that they alone were the omniscient possessors of the 'Science of Charity' and in the 1890s were still receiving encouragement from establishment factions including the Archbishop of Canterbury.[7] He preached that it was 'an evil thing to be charitable for the sake of giving careless and idle relief to one's feelings' at a time when the COS's 'philosophy of charity' had been formulated using Newtonian concepts. He urged the universal adoption of COS ideas so that the 'unhappy, suffering, miserable, neglected part of society' could be brought within the habits of civilized social behaviour.[8] Another appellation welcomed for the COS by Charles Loch was that they were attempting the 'work of the social physician'.[9] The blinkered Loch did not see that although the phrase was high-sounding it could be dangerous in enemy hands as it reinforced existing impressions of the COS's cold clinical attitude.

COSs assumed that the essential qualities needed for their visitors to instruct the poor were acquired naturally by way of their superior social status. As had Thomas Chalmers in the 1820s they believed that, for the poor, there was 'a substantial though unnoticed charm in the visit of a superior'.[10] They were also convinced that their visitors quickly gained social expertise after their inherent class-enriched qualities had been fortified by simple COS guidelines. Representatives of traditional charities without the benefit of COS science allegedly lacked the necessary qualities of detachment from unhelpful emotional involvement with the poor. Consequently charitable affairs should not be 'entrusted to novices, or to dilettanti, or to quacks' because any charity fulfilling the 'natural duty of others' was wrong and deceptive.[11] The COS saw themselves as the one society established to 'protect those willing to give their money for charitable purposes against imposture'.[12]

COS visitors were told not to contemplate the possibility that poor families could encounter misfortune which would not quickly be overcome with their society's help. When Helen Bosanquet was asked what should be done to support the unfortunate family on occasions when social conditions prevented them resisting the rigours of life, she dismissed the possibility as a 'vain and idle hypothesis' because always 'the social conditions *will* permit them ...'[13] Bosanquet explained that even in apparent distress, by use of 'the resources of mutual helpfulness' the poor should always have on hand the 'wise' middle-class administrator of charity with his wider outlook so that 'often the mere knowledge of his presence would be enough to give the courage for another effort'.[14] Sir Charles Trevelyan affirmed that 'the evils which affected the East End were not caused by want of work so much as by the abuse of charity, and by the abuse of the out-relief system'.[15]

CHANGING CIRCUMSTANCES AND ATTITUDES

The COS held doggedly to their founding principles throughout the 1870s and 1880s, a period of exceptional social, economic and political change. Some historians suggest 1870 as the fulcrum of most change while others detect greatest movement in the 1880s.[16] Compared with the leadened responses that were to follow, the early 1870s were the COS's 'golden years' before changing socio-economic circumstances prompted public realization of what the strict application of their principles meant in human terms.[17] After acceding to LGB pressure for five or six years most Poor Law guardians for their own local economic, social, political and compassionate reasons from around 1877 chose to largely ignore the continued LGB exhortations to ever more rigorous out-relief strictures. This guardian recalcitrance further diminished the chances of provincial COSs forging similar close relationships at local level as wrought between the senior hierarchies in Whitehall and Buckingham Street, WC. The failures of provincial COSs to create working frameworks with their local Poor Law were not broadcast widely in the forlorn hope that eventually more guardians would join them. In any case it helped COS esteem to encourage a public myth of close institutional association. Such deception could not continue indefinitely and the COS admitted in 1889 that 'with few exceptions the Poor Law authorities have remained impervious to the influence of the Society'.[18]

After the Barnardo setback of 1877 the COS found it more difficult to maintain their pretention of philanthropic omnipotence. The LGB circular on 15 March 1886 from Joseph Chamberlain added to the disillusion with the clear rejection of COS fundamentals by a member of government who earlier had supported the COS in the West Midlands. Out-relief for temporarily unemployed 'artisans and others' could now be related to public works programmes which would be non-stigmatic, non-skilful and non-competitive.[19] The apparent permanence of the 1869 liaison between the COS and the central Poor Law authorities was firmly laid aside by Chamberlain's simple device of making no mention of charity and offering no acknowledgement of a possible role it might have in placating the burgeoning unemployment problem. The COS later ridiculed Chamberlain and 'other clever gentlemen' for 'flying their pretty kites, with statistical tales'.[20] Public relief works were 'very undesirable' because 'works started for the relief of the unemployed' discouraged the real spirit of work and according to Charles Loch thereby diminished self-reliance so as to 'usually intensify the evil rather than remedy it'.[21] Other legislative amendments launched by central government in the late Victorian era brought improvements in public health, sanitation, education, employment of women and children, prisons, police and widened parliamentary franchise. The COS were themselves a motivating force in some of these reforms while remaining resolutely against any innovation which savoured of unselective relief. This included opposition to the provision of better housing for people the COS judged to be unworthy. In Bernard Bosanquet's opinion 'in order that putting a family out of a bad house into a good one' should give rise to 'an element of the best life' it was essential that within the individual 'there was a better life struggling to utter itself'.[22]

In 1886 the COS asked the public to choose between their own 'sober patience of charity, building up character, fashioning brave strong men and women, and the impatience of alms-flinging, which tempts to idleness, beggary, hypocrisy, and lying'.[23] At the root of this COS attitude was the certainty that the poor were inherently lazy. They recalled Thomas Chalmers's warning decades earlier that 'benevolence meets with much to damp and discourage her; and more especially in a certain hardness and unthankfulness among its objects, which it is the direct tendency of the reigning system to engender'.[24] It seemed sinful for so many among the middle class to ignore their responsibility for inculcating in the lower orders the Smilesian principles of personal responsibility, especially as the COS had diagnosed the problems of the poor as stemming directly from their own moral ignorance. According to the COS, it was this mental void among the lower classes which encouraged them to look for any means of existence which did not require them to actually participate in the sweat of genuine waged work.

COS exhortations failed to prevent the middle-class majority gradually abandoning strait-laced individualism and acknowledging the need for sufficient state participation to allow fuller development of citizenship.[25]

Governments became less comfortable about the validity of COS claims that the condition of the urban poor was being effectively alleviated and needed nothing more than wider application of COS concepts. Although there were only limited statistical data available on living conditions in the 1880s the state prudently recognized that working-class dissatisfaction, if aroused, was an ingredient for social unrest. Millions of workers continued to be employed on a casual basis with all its financial uncertainty and there was fear of urban instability as convincing pamphlets described the squalor of filthy unhealthy environments in cities like London, Liverpool and Manchester.[26] Governments were perceptive enough to recognize that although some contemporary commentators may be exaggerative the social tension of threatening aggregates could worsen explosively should a disgruntled residuum be reinforced by angry unemployed workers.[27] Even a member of the London Charity Organisation Society Council, Mr Allen Graham, warned his colleagues against hastening the revolution by 'their unwise and ingenuous actions' at a time when COS members 'were all living in a padded state of society'.[28]

The disquieting quantitative evidence eventually produced by the likes of Charles Booth and Seebohm Rowntree, together with other less publicized provincial social investigations, left little room for uncertainty about the real size of the problem.[29] Even then Charles Loch attacked the statistical accuracy of social surveys and doggedly reaffirmed that 'Charity Organisation' alone provided the crucial key to further social improvement and that already 'there has been great progress in the condition of the people; the people are better, and better able, to provide for themselves'.[30] This attitude which typified the COS as a whole was 'afflicted with a complacent and quite incurable optimism' distorting the 'perception of facts'.[31] Loch did admit that the 'concentration and organisation' of charity was still lacking but there was scant response to his appeal in *The Times* for church and charity leaders to meet 'without regard to any sectarian differences'.[32] In academia the hereto impregnable classical political economic theories were being dismantled and discarded by emerging idealists. Earlier criticisms of COS philosophy by John Ruskin and others had kept within the classical ethos whereby 'wealth' was a fundamental concept governed by inviolable 'natural laws' outside the power of man and beyond his conscience.[33] Occasionally classicists had discussed 'the poor' but rarely ventured to the question of 'poverty', seen as nothing more than a distinguishing characteristic of a group of inadequate people. According to classical economists, laws of society conformed to a framework of natural phenomena and were not greatly concerned that their explanation of societal mechanisms included little cognisance of the reality of life for the nineteenth-century poor.

Idealist campaigns made such inroads into classic economic doctrines as to cause a paradigm shift in the dominant philosophy taught in British universities in the late Victorian era. Thomas Hill Green at Oxford, together with Henry Sidgwick and Alfred Marshall at Cambridge, were among those who evolved logical reasons why the state should intervene in order to maintain the socio-economic status quo. Green aimed to erect a 'moral platform so broad that all men of goodwill could stand on it ... so as to transform liberalism from the social philosophy of a single set of interests ... into one which could claim to take account of all important interests seen from the point of view of the general good of the community.'[34] While retaining many Manchester School concepts Green softened the class bias by advocating the need for active participation of persons from other social sectors who would be prepared to acknowledge their obligation to contribute to the social good.[35] The traditional assumption whereby it was natural for there always to be lower classes was refuted.[36]

Many of Green's disciples discarded what they saw as archaic ideas about the social structure of modern society. It was to be no longer preordained for the majority of people to inherit at birth the expectation at best of a lifetime of ceaseless badly paid work so as to provide a refined and cultured life for the few. The COS dismissed such concepts as totally irrational and argued that since the lowest paid workers made goods suitable only for the poor, they were not involved in making luxury articles for the rich.[37] It was this lack of realism which left the COS intellectually stuck in the 1860s and fuelled the general impression of their 'remoteness and imperviousness'.[38]

Although Green was inspirational in explaining the need for change, he was not explicit on the crucial question of how far individualism should succumb to interventionist actions. This ambiguity allowed room for competing interpretations of his ideas as to what was actually needed to bring improvement in the condition of the poor. The COS disagreed fundamentally with interventionist concepts pursued by those who were becoming the dominant group of idealists. At the same time, they made it plain through Bernard Bosanquet and Charles Loch that they were highly sympathetic to Green's general ideas, and claimed that COS values accurately interpreted his idealism. The COS reminded cynics that Loch had been Green's admiring student at Balliol and that this was a major influence in Loch devoting his life towards helping the poor through the propagation of COS principles. Loch remained committed through the

COS to transform individuals morally but had no wish to recast the economic framework of society with creeping socialism.[39] Bernard Bosanquet had also been an outstanding student of T.H. Green and before reinforcing the London COS staff in the early 1880s had been a Fellow of University College and a generous contributor to Oxford COS funds. When he became London COS's 'resident philosopher' dealing with the more intellectual matters, Bosanquet enabled Loch to concentrate on propagating COS ideas on any contemporary event bearing on the condition of the poor, charity, the Poor Law and exposure of imposture.

Of course, the mainstream idealists were themselves far from being collectivists in the socialist sense of advocating extensive government intervention. Expressing themselves politically through the New Liberals they retained a fundamental belief in the freedom of enterprise, the strength of self-reliance and an alert suspicion of proposals for increasing state power in matters that did not have an overwhelming case in their favour.[40] They developed a middle-class logic for redressing certain glaring social grievances of workers so that traditional economic frameworks would remain dominant with the function of the state restricted to the regulation of external actions only and of dissolving hindrances to the general well-being. State action should be confined strictly to matters needed for conditions by which all men would be sufficiently liberated to accept and enjoy whatever positive rights and freedoms the market economy could allow. All individuals were perceived as social beings and as such were free, rational and moral persons each ethically committed to participate in the larger 'common good' which itself supplied a criterion of the individual's rights.[41]

Idealists came to believe that for many poor people, inhibited by negative constraints, aspects of the cherished freedoms had been illusory with life little more than ceaseless drudgery. No longer would it suffice to merely offer the relatively meaningless structural independence of individual actors free from outside influence and assistance.[42] According to Toynbee the freedom of the poor was 'under ordinary circumstances only a liberty to starve'.[43] The public concern about how the physical inadequacies of the residuum threatened national well-being helped mould New Liberal policies. Middle-class fears of incipient social disequilibrium encouraged acceptance of the need to improve living standards generally so as to placate the respectable working class and avert the danger of them combining with their poorer neighbours into a disruptive force. In Lynd's words, 'whatever the theory of individualism, health was not an individual matter' and although it had been possible to overlook the occasional sickly undernourished family, it was not so easy 'to overlook square miles of them'.[44]

Idealists now insisted that the development of individual character among the poor would proceed with more speed and certainty after the improvement of physical environments. It was the debate as to whether environment or morality was predominant in building individual character that was at the hub of differences between the COS and mainstream idealists. None doubted that both morals and reasonable living standards were required for the social good of the poor. Disagreement centred on COS insistence that only those among the poor who they judged to have the character to help themselves deserved an improved environment and that encouragement to philanderers by way of undeserved help was sinful. The COS were not inclined to accept that character faults indicated by their investigations may not be entrenched and may even disappear 'under less harsh industrial pressure' or that the mere removal of social stress may set 'some natures free to be better'.[45]

The crux of the debate was deciding at what point were the sacred tenets of individualism transgressed. The COS were themselves active in developing environmental improvement for those they classified as being deserving and campaigned staunchly for specialist help for disadvantaged groups such as the physically and mentally disabled. In their wish to improve conditions for deserving cases the COS also went so far as to accept that the demolition of slum properties could, with reservations, be entrusted to local councils. Further than this the COS could rarely be moved. For example, they opposed interventionism in house-building and criticized the 'cheapened rentals by the municipality'.[46] Private builders working under COS direction were seen as being the most efficient means of renovating or rebuilding slum dwellings for rental by deserving low-income families. Housing reform was an aspect of COS work which demonstrated Octavia Hill's exceptional management skills and improved the society's battered public image. Hill's efforts followed Hawksley's earlier recommendation whereby there should be 'improved dwellings for the working classes, at a rental practicable to the resources of the humble workman'.[47]

The loudly publicized good works of the London COS could not prevent the movement becoming increasingly isolated because of their determination that people must first show the character to help themselves before being given the chance to benefit from outside support. Bosanquet, in presenting the COS perspective, shunned more state intervention. He did accept that the state included 'the entire hierarchy of institutions by which life is determined ... and, in this sense, is, above all things not a number of persons, but a working conception of life',[48] and also that the state was 'in its right when it forcibly hinders a hindrance to the best life or common good'. Bosanquet recognised that because of these partial admissions, others may then ask why not go further and hinder unemployment by universal employment, overcrowding by universal house-building, and immorality by punishing immoral and rewarding moral actions?[49] His answer was that 'the promotion of morality by force' was an 'absolute self-contradiction' as what was always needed in 'the particular' was 'common sense and special experience'.[50]

Bosanquet argued that he and the COS had correctly interpreted T.H. Green's teaching and pointed out that Green himself had accepted that private property was essential in the development of character because it could provide 'a permanent apparatus for carrying out a plan of life' and was a means of 'giving effect to benevolent wishes'.[51] Others among Green's disciples maintained that if private property was of value to the 'fulfilment of personality' so common property was equally of value for 'the expression and development of social life'.[52] Hobhouse believed it was essential that whereas 'property for use' could be retained by the individual, 'property for power' must be in the hands of 'the democratic state'.[53] The Revd Hastings Rashdall accepted that Bosanquet had 'admirably' developed a case for the 'good effects of the present system upon character' but seemed 'almost blind' to the 'intense selfishness' it fostered.[54]

Bosanquet found no compunction in Green's teaching about a need to go significantly further along the collectivist road than had J.S. Mill. Bosanquet told how Green had maintained that the 'effectual action of the state, i.e. the community as acting through law, for the promotion of habits of true citizenship seem necessarily to be confined to the removal of obstacles'.[55] He chose to ignore Green's further explanation that these obstacles involved much that 'states had neglected thereto' including the provision of 'compulsory education, ... the massing of population without regard to conditions of health, unrestrained traffic in deleterious commodities' and the use of labour in 'particular industries' which raised the 'danger of an impoverished proletariate in following generations'.[56]

The COS were tireless in emphasizing that individual and national character would be destroyed by state dependence. They were adamant that everyone had not only the moral duty but also the opportunity to care for themselves and their family. The COS had no doubts that the prudent working man would always be able to save for the inevitable rainy day and so would recognize that thrift was 'the germ of the capacity to look at life as a whole and organise it'.[57] Bosanquet maintained that providence provided the way for each individual to enrich and secure from disaster the future of his family and others, not only for the immediate future but for years ahead. Life strengthened by thrift allegedly took on a higher meaning and adopted 'a more generous and not a more grudging acceptance of obligations'.[58] Through COS eyes, those among the poor who could not accept this contract of social obligation deserved nothing from charity, nor should they be provided with the relative freedom of outdoor relief but should be left to the legal constraints of the workhouse.

But mainstream idealists emphasized Green's view that the 'realisation of freedom in the state can only mean the attainment of freedom by individuals' through influences which the state supplies and that it was 'a mockery to speak of the State as a realisation of freedom' to 'an untaught and underfed denizen of a London yard ...'[59] Green contended that whereas in the past 'the idea of the individual's right to a free life has been strongly laid hold of in Christendom in what may be called an abstract or negative way, little notice has been taken of what it involves.'[60] Bosanquet considered that Green's statements, with their implication that the poor were unreasonably being expected to overcome exceptionally difficult socio-economic obstacles showed a 'pessimistic criticism of economic motive, political motive, and of every-day social motive' while insufficiently taking cognisance of the paradox affecting society 'from beginning to end'.[61] As an example of the inherent 'contradictions' besetting society, Bosanquet instanced the 'chaos of the medical charities of London' and claimed that without the 'material of organisation' their endeavours demonstrated that 'the maladjustment of adjustments brings out ever new contradictions which demand readjustment'.[62]

Bosanquet refused to accept that the COS differed 'profoundly' from Green on social issues and 'ventured' to 'assign a greatly diminished importance to his criticisms'. Bosanquet attempted to justify any apparent discord by calling on new social experiences which allegedly had only surfaced since Green's demise. These were said to explain how differences had followed naturally from the 'growth of a more intimate experience, owing in some measure to his [Green's] initiative, which seems to show the essentials of life to be far more identical throughout the so called classes of society than is admitted by such a passage as that ... about the dweller in the London yard'. According to Bosanquet, more recent experience had confirmed that character was distinctly more significant than environment in moulding the individual proving 'on the whole, a man is what he does'.[63] Bosanquet claimed that 'probably, in fundamental matters, there is as large a proportion of persons untaught and bred up between temptations among the rich as among the poor'.[64]

For tentative indication that they and not the rest of the world were accurately interpreting Green's socio-economic intentions, the COS could have pointed to the financial support their cause received after Green's death from his relatives and colleagues. Green's widow, for example, was among the largest donors to the Oxford COS, R.L. Nettleship (the editor of T.H. Green's *Works*) was a subscriber and Mrs Nettleship a committee member. Balliol College remained one of the most generous contributors to COS funds.[65]

Another aspect of the debate on the relative importance of character and environment in developing social well-being was to be later ignited when Helen Bosanquet attacked the soundness of Seebohm Rowntree's investigative techniques at York.[66] In his reply, Rowntree willingly accepted that as stated in his survey much of the immediate cause of secondary poverty was 'drink, betting, and gambling; ignorant or careless housekeeping; and other improvident expenditure' but claimed nothing was gained from ignoring the evidence that for 'a large section of the community' income was 'insufficient for the purpose of physical efficiency' so that their lives were as a consequence '*necessarily* stunted'.[67] Rowntree was prepared to agree with Mrs Bosanquet that individual character was important but thought it 'idle' to expect those 'suffering physical feebleness in a depressing environment' to have 'virtues and powers far in excess of those characterising any other sections of the community'. Bosanquet dismissed such comments and retained the inexorable COS belief that the primary aim of charities should be to stimulate the energy and improve the character of the sufferers rather than to make any change in 'adverse social conditions'.[68]

In spite of their differences there remained much agreement between idealist factions. None doubted the need to nurture individualistic attitudes in all sections of society. There was also unanimity that improvement in the condition of the poor would best be achieved through the active participation of an enlightened middle class prepared to sacrifice personal pleasures and not be satisfied by the transmission of an easily given gift.[69] Although focus on differences in motivation and attitude between the COS and Settlement idealists has made attractive historiographical copy, these did not represent a great gulf on socio-economic principles when considered over the whole political spectrum.[70] It is not surprising then that men such as Edward Caird, J.A. Hobson and Graham Wallas participated with Charles Loch and Bernard Bosanquet in the activities of the London Ethical Society, founded in 1886, by a small group of university men committed to gaining social improvement for the poor.[71]

Those COS members who transferred their main allegiance to the University Settlement movement did so in the belief that by actually living in a working-class neighbourhood they were closer to the ideal of developing, among the poor, an acceptance of the responsibilities as well as the rights of citizenship. The concept involved the active participation of all agencies by 'which they meant private, voluntary associations, as well as party politics'.[72] Arnold Toynbee was amongst those attracted to the Settlement idea and, like Samuel Barnett, transferred his main energies from day-to-day involvement with the COS. Before his premature death in 1883, Toynbee had advocated the need for closer physical association with the poor, for improved social conditions through supportive legislation, for wider educational opportunities and for enhanced worker mobility. He wanted to free workers from 'all vestiges of feudalism and custom' so that they could 'become like a middle-class in a working-class dress' and assisted by improved citizenship rights become 'in the true sense of the word ... gentlemen'.[73]

Settlement concepts provided a softer public image than did COS interpretations of T.H. Green's ideas on developing citizenship more widely. His proposals often appealed most to those who, because of religious upbringing, had sensitive consciences which he touched by turning any ebbing faith into personal guilt about the unfairness of their worldly privileges. Loch's life-long attraction to the COS had followed this general path but most idealists became turned off by the COS's parent and dependent child approach and were drawn to the more empathetic Settlement involvement with the poor.

The Settlement ideal was seen to involve 'above all else ... a spirit of neighbourliness, ... a very strong sense of civic duty, ... and a sense of responsibility for the standard of life'.[74] Even then it would be naive to expect that merely through living among the poor the Settlement idealists found themselves invariably championing the worker's cause any more than to believe they miraculously shed all signs of Victorian middle-class paternalistic moralism. Nevertheless, Settlements were seen by a number of university graduates as a natural next stage to the charity organization movement which, by the 1880s, seemed unnecessarily harsh and lacking sufficient personal association with the lower classes.

What inspired Samuel Barnett about the Settlement idea was that it enhanced opportunities for rich and poor to meet and talk in a less formalized way with the chance of some elements of fellowship entering discussions. The growing personal disenchantment of Samuel Barnett with COS activities surfaced in 1883. Barnett as a Whitechapel guardian, a parish priest and an avid COS worker had championed the Society's principles throughout the 1870s. He was a renowned activist in the crusade against outdoor relief which he saw as a system ignorantly cherished by the poor and remained the inveterate enemy of guardians who even bordered on being profligate. Somewhat contrarily, it was the stark effectiveness of the out-relief crusade at Whitechapel, compounded by COS principles whereby charity was 'given only to those who, by their forethought, or their self-sacrifice awaken feelings of gratitude and respect' that eventually prompted Barnett to transfer his main energies into the Settlement movement.[75] Barnett came to realize that despite his rigorous campaign against outdoor pauperism and improvidence, the lives of the poor had remained stubbornly miserable. He concluded that 'the outcome of scientific charity is the working man too thrifty to pet his children and too respectable to be happy ... the life of the thrifty is a sad life, limited both by the pressure of continuous toil, and by the fear lest this pressure should cease and starvation ensue'.[76]

Barnett's celebrated lecture in the autumn of 1883 at Oxford's St John's College called on his long COS experience but added the crucial proposal that a community be created in which the poor would have 'all that give value to wealth, in which beauty, knowledge and righteousness are nationalised'.[77] With the opening of Toynbee Hall, Barnett was quick to realize that the influence and benefits of University Settlements would have limited scope without state involvement in improving the environment which he now accepted as being an essential ingredient in the development of individual dignity. Barnett's 'practicable socialism' advocated a policy of better housing, national education to university level, organized medical relief, workhouses as schools of industry and state pensions for respectable working people with graduated taxation recommended to finance the improvements.[78] Many of these proposals, with their implication of state involvement, were anathemas to the COS because they were seen to erode individual character. The COS thought Barnett's coupling of the words 'practicable' and 'socialism' was like 'yoking an ox and a zebra to the same plough' but they were quite willing to accept his view that for the 'artisan and labouring classes life is, at best, grey and dull, and too often intolerably bitter'.[79] A *Charity Organisation Reporter* editorial published Barnett's belief that as 'no thrift, sobriety, or combination on the part of the men themselves can be expected to remove the mischief, some other force must be brought into play' and considered his views neither 'startling' or 'revolutionary' and socialist only in 'the sense that Lord Shaftesbury is a socialist'.[80]

Although Barnett abandoned his daily involvement in COS operations he remained strongly supportive of the desirability in principle of organizing charity. Barnett shared their horror at what he saw as the blight of promiscuous charity associated with the 1886 Mansion House Fund believing that 'every penny has eternal issues on the character of the recipients, yet pounds are given and scattered without prayer or thought whether these issues end in heaven or hell'.[81] The *Charity Organisation Review* claimed that 'Mr Barnett's devotion and experience' had 'won him the right to speak with authority' on the sinfulness of haphazard charity and because 'his independent judgement' was not 'exposed to any cheap imputation of jealousy'. Barnett's comments on the allegedly profligate Mansion House Fund had expressed 'perfectly' all the COS wished to say.[82]

But with passing years, the schism between Barnett and the COS widened. Initially his drift from total COS alignment was because he contended that the changing urban circumstances of the 1880s had found the Society hidebound in systems which confounded their true purpose. In Barnett's opinion the COS were increasingly falling short of the spirit and substance of those that once prevailed.[83] In an invited address to the Society in 1895, Barnett, who was still a London vice-president, claimed to retain endearment to the COS while regretting how their hierarchical structure had insistently put 'words and forms in the place of principles' so that charity was as 'disorganised, and poverty as prevalent, as in the year of the founding of our Society'.[84] On this occasion COS responses were decidedly more bruising than in the verbal sparring of previous years. Mr. R. Barrington criticized Barnett for changing his mind on fundamentals like state pensions. He pointed out that the COS 'had never committed itself absolutely to oppose the giving of out-door relief, but Canon Barnett had done so, and yet he was now proposing to extend it under another name'.[85]

Charles Loch's response to Barnett was vitriolic. In a lengthy harangue, clearly prepared prior to Barnett's address, Loch attacked Barnett's need of always wanting to 'be in harmony with the current philanthropic opinion of the moment or perhaps just a few seconds ahead of it' which had led to his disloyalty to 'old friends' and principles.[86] Loch scorned what he described as Barnett's interventionist ideas on school meals, refuges, shelters, emigration, hospitals and pensions, although most of these subjects had scarcely been mentioned in Barnett's address. Even then some resolute COS supporters, such as Octavia Hill, remained lifelong friends of the Barnetts.[87]

There remained a great deal of COS goodwill towards University Settlements generally. They were united by the shared awareness of class and of conscious superiority. More than a decade after the opening of

Toynbee Hall when the COS had wished the venture 'every success', the *Charity Organisation Review* continued to publish sympathetic articles about Settlement aims.[88] The COS recognized their shared objectives in the desire to get acquainted with the poor, to relieve the 'terrible monotony of their lives, ... to elevate, ... to give them ideas', which in their degraded social condition they might be willing to take advantage of and suggested that it may be approaching the time when it would be fruitful to study the beneficial effects of 'this modern lay monasticism'.[89]

Although the New Liberals had an important influence on sociopolitical changes in late Victorian Britain, there were other important forces eroding the tattered classical economic doctrines still being defended by the COS. Periodicals like the *Contemporary Review*, the *Fortnightly Review* and *Nineteenth Century* published warnings about the need for immediate social reforms if an alleged impending revolutionary threat was to be averted.[90] In reality, none of the main oppositional factions represented a meaningful challenge to the fundamental political structure of the established British state. On relatively benign socialist platforms, there were proposals for a more equitable distribution of the nation's wealth launched by various groups including the Social Democratic Federation (SDF), the Fabian Society and the Independent Labour Party. The first Fabian Tract called on those who lived 'dainty and pleasant lives' to abandon their 'superfluities' and help the workers who had the power of change in their hands while at the same time emphasizing that this was not intended as incitement to bloody revolution.[91] Heated debates between the Webbs and senior COS hierarchy continued for decades but with nothing more than an occasional hint at fundamental institutional overthrow ever entering their exchanges.[92] Admittedly, H.M. Hyndman had brought the SDF to the fore by propounding economic revolution but he lacked mass support. By 1890 socialist activity was dominated by people committed to progress by democratic evolution. Many were even prepared to consider right-wing ideas, generally shunned by the COS, like the social imperialism borrowed from Bismarck's Germany 'designed to draw the classes together in defence of the nation and empire'.[93]

Socialist tracts on social welfare and the Poor Law in late Victorian Britain usually concentrated on limited objectives. They rarely did more than advocate the need to reorganize Poor Law relief on a local authority basis and for there to be destigmatization of its operations. Nevertheless the COS were conscious that even in its less virulent forms socialism was a threat to their own principles and considered it politic to air in their publications selected mild interpretations of the socialist creed, which they could then criticize and control. For example, in a *Charity Organisation Review* article on the 'spread of socialism among the clergy' the Revd. W.W. Edwards argued with regard to economic structure that the 'whole system is wrong' while warning 'most earnestly against revolutionary attempts'.[94]

THE COS AND THE LGB: OBJECTIVES AND ACHIEVEMENTS

COS and LGB traditionalists scarcely wavered from the individualistic principles which had brought them together in 1869 in spite of trends towards an interventionist state having gained wider public acceptance by 1890. COS leaders refuted modernist criticisms about their rigid attitudes on outdoor relief and indiscriminate charity by claiming that as experienced professionals, in both the official and the organized voluntary relief sectors, they had remained consistent in their opinions for two decades. They alleged that the moral health of the nation was being jeopardized by the drift towards socio-economic state mechanisms likely to undermine the building of individual character.

Whether or not the COS were justified in retaining their unshackled Smilesian principles on the basis of what they had actually achieved in the social arena will now be debated. As a framework for discussion various seminal early assumptions and predictions made by the LGB and the COS are reviewed. They involve claims about how their social formulae would improve the condition of the lower orders and are discussed in the light of evidence over twenty years from data largely produced by the LGB and the COS themselves.

The formation of the Charity Organisation Society in 1869 a few months prior to the Goschen Minute, their commitment to co-ordinate actions of other charities, their determination to co-operate intimately with local Poor Law authorities and the early appointment of Goschen as a COS vice-president left little doubt that the new society was the privately sponsored institutional vehicle upon which the government pinned their hopes of constraining outdoor relief under a moral cloak. They would claim that those refused outdoor relief by guardians always had the freedom of applying to their nearest COS as an alternative to entering the workhouse. According to the joint plan there would be a great reduction in the number of people balanced 'on the verge of pauperism' by the provision of selective, restrictive charity designed to inculcate self-support.

The Local Government Board launched its crusade in 1871 and urged all provincial unions to pursue its principles regardless of the reality that little of the anticipated supportive network of COSs was in place let alone effective.[95] Organization of charity was to be attempted in about one hundred provincial locations in England and Wales during the next two decades with a focus on urban centres.[96] As the COS themselves admitted in the 1890s 'this number is very small in comparison with the many important towns and districts which are unrepresented'.[97] The consequence was that the majority of the six hundred or so provincial Poor Law unions, including many where the crusade was applied most stringently, had no COS nearby to even provide a possibility of influencing the destiny of those refused Poor Law out-relief.

Furthermore, in those localities where provincial COSs were attempted they generally failed to persuade charitable agencies to modify their traditional disbursement patterns. We also now know that when provincial COSs attempted to raise their own funds they rarely mustered sufficient revenue to pursue their ideas as they would have wished. COS excuses about their inability to attract sufficient subscriptions often included a reminder that the disbursement of charity was not their primary purpose but this has been exposed as partial. Repeated financial appeals from provincial COSs included public admissions that they were 'often pained by their inability to relieve cases which cry aloud for aid'.[98] In 1890 COSs still regretted their continued failure to reform what they saw as the indiscriminate wastefulness of the many charitable bodies possessing much greater economic power than they themselves.[99]

The COS and LGB shared the contention that the Poor Law crusade was motivated by the highest morals in being directed against the evil of feather-bedding hordes of lazy, able-bodied men for which outdoor relief extinguished 'every incentive to self-reliance and prudent forethought'.[100] As discussed earlier, these emotive innuendoes were grossly misleading as the adults most hit by the crusade were overwhelmingly 'not able-bodied' or were widows with dependent children. This must have been well known to the Poor Law authorities since they published much of the data discussed in this volume.

The idea that every available means be levied to make each relief applicant the responsibility of a family member or neighbour was a cornerstone of COS and LGB thinking. They alleged that there had been an erosion of traditional family values which had cut dangerously across the Smilesian concepts of providence, independence and respectability so as to now threaten individual and national moral standards, as well as being unfair to ratepayers.[101] In spite of these establishment concerns about moral deterioration among the working classes, it had remained quite common for relatives and neighbours of poor people to band together with a 'whip round' to avert a friend becoming a workhouse inmate even though they themselves were often in a parlous state.[102]

The COS and LGB accepted that the additional economic and emotional pressures on caring relatives may occasionally create some level of hardship but they were reassured that those who suffered uncomplainingly in supporting less fortunate family members would benefit morally from the experience. In view of the importance they attributed to family life it is unfortunate that no meaningful COS or LGB research was conducted during the 1870s or 1880s about how poor families fared after being cajoled by moral authority into sharing their meagre possessions with aged, sick or otherwise disadvantaged loved ones. Later evidence indicates that few poor families could support additional kin without further serious erosion of their own tenuous physical existence.

It is to be expected that although the COS were generally unpopular, some among the thousands of out-relief applicants rejected during the crusade turned in desperation for help from provincial COSs. As we have seen these societies were usually badly funded but what assistance they did provide to the deserving poor was milked for propaganda value. In Simey's words, failures were 'hushed up and their successes advertised from the roof tops'.[103] But even if we were to assume the correctness of COS claims about individual successes it has been clearly shown that in practical terms the social impact of provincial COSs was small when contrasted with their ceaseless verbiage.

The COS argued that any shortcoming on their part in applying organizing principles stemmed from the ideological myopia of other charities but it has been amply demonstrated that the COS themselves were insensitive to the likely responses of their social peers and miscalculated three factors basic to their own well-being. First was their misjudgement in assuming that other charities would applaud Thomas Hawksley's proposals for them to finance an emergent COS.[104] Second was the COS's tactless, haughty and repeated condemnation of conventional charity as being inefficient, unscientific, naive, disorganized, misdirected and sinful. Third was their inability to empathize with charitable bodies regarding their conceptual difficulties on being confronted with charity organization methodology. COS leaders lacked the humility or persuasive skills with which they may have reconciled their 'scientific' structures with simpler traditional interpretations of Christian compassionate charity. Their difficulty in convincing others towards an organized framework of charity was not eased when it became generally known that around one-third of provincial COS applicants were regularly branded as 'undeserving' of any form of charity and were sent packing.

The inability of the COS to debate social affairs from other than an arrogant conviction of superiority also contributed to them being unable to fulfil another seminal assumption that as voluntary sector organizers they would quickly earn the significant co-operation of guardians. The LGB in Whitehall shared the COS opinion about it being 'essential to the proper treatment of the poor that there should be thorough and cordial co-operation between Poor Law Guardians and Charity Committees' but local guardians rarely shared this view.[105] They soon became aware that the overtures of emergent COSs for acceptance of their methodology were being rebuffed by most charities. Consequently even guardians with COS leanings recognized pragmatically that their position in the community was not likely to be enhanced by forging too close a bond with an outcast group.

Another shortcoming of provincial COSs was their widespread failure to improve quantitatively on Poor Law doles although according to COS propaganda they were shamefully low and provided no opportunity for an individual to gain independence. It is therefore strange that years afterwards Helen Bosanquet could still write 'unfortunately the conception of adequate out-relief was even more remote from the Guardians' minds at that time [1872], than it is today...'[106] In much the same way, Charles Loch continued not to be embarrassed in the 1890s by his line that 'the community cannot afford to provide such relief on any sufficient scale' and that as a consequence the Poor Law benefits 'given to meet the ordinary contingencies of life, such as outdoor relief must be, is by the nature of things inadequate'.[107] The hollowness of such a statement is demonstrated by the realization that the unit value of provincial COS relief was often distinctly less than a Poor Law dole. Extraordinary powers of persuasion would have been needed by their lady visitors for them to so succeed in uplifting recipients morally that self-sufficiency followed the miserable COS material assistance. The reality was that the poor who did benefit from the COS learned how to display the expected gratitude and to suffer their privations in silence.

Some commentators have argued that it is misleading to consider the COS as being the archetypal expression of nineteenth century individualism. According to Vincent there were 'almost imperceptible changes between 1870 and 1909' in COS attitudes and that they were not 'simply antistatist'.[108] It is of course correct that even the most pedantic philosophies are eventually modified by their milieu and it is to be expected that some conceptual transition occurred in COS attitudes over a period of decades. Nevertheless in relative terms the COS adherence to self-help ideologies and belief in the overriding dominance of individual character remained its strong distinguishing feature. It may also be argued that the COS decision in 1886 to abandon the classification 'undeserving' for the more nebulous 'not likely to benefit' was a sign of fundamental change. The likelihood of this being correct was not enhanced by the tone of the COS announcement modifying their categories when they explained that in future they would 'refrain from passing moral judgement' on applicants no matter how 'undeserving a drunkard, or a man who deserts his wife, may appear'.[109] Further indication that little had changed was provided at the 1890 COS conference when Leamington COS proposed that the terms 'deserving' and 'undeserving', supposedly made obsolete years earlier, should be replaced by 'curable' and 'incurable'.[110] With the proportion of COS applicants not assisted by the provincial societies remaining essentially unchanged after the terminology change of 1886 the publicized modification can be seen as little more than euphemistic tinkering with retained emphasis that regardless of environment the character of supplicants was the paramount factor determining their current worthiness.[111] Octavia Hill accepted that it remained the 'fashion' to call the COS 'cold, formal, and inquisitive, and slow, and fifty bad things'.[112] It was the 'deep-rooted censoriousness' of the society about all viewpoints that differed from its own which remained the COS's determining defect.[113]

A drift in provincial COS procedures was their tendency around 1880 to supply a greater proportion of relief in interest-free loans. These had the ideological intention of instilling a sense of responsibility among the poor by steering them away from moneylenders and pawnbrokers. Loans were also theoretically advantageous to COS finances as non-deteriorating assets. According to the COS, loans gave the poor dignity through them not having to accept a non-returnable gift and provided the recipient with useful experience of a business transaction. The last point was emphasized by advice that provincial COSs should not shirk from issuing a County Court summons against defaulters.[114] In spite of their theoretical attraction the use of loans declined after some years, largely because so many remained outstanding. Whether failure to repay is blamed on poverty or craftiness it raises doubts about COS investigative efficacy. If it is assumed that recipients were trustworthy then the rigorous COS examinations into individual circumstances prior to the granting of a loan must have failed to detect the financial incapacity to repay. Alternatively if the default occurred from an unworthy rogue determined to cheat the lender, then the COS's allegedly foolproof investigative procedures had again been unsuccessful in not exposing the applicant's shadowy intent.

Although there were diagnostic failures, COS methodology can be perceived as a precursor for the twentieth-century analyses of state welfare applicants. As discussed in the previous chapter, it was not uncommon for COS organizational potential to temporarily became more publicly acceptable at times of local exceptional distress. The COS maximised the favourable publicity they manufactured on such occasions to impress decision-making elites about how their structured procedures had succeeded where unselective charity had foundered. Consequently when twentieth-century state schemes brought the need to confine welfare benefits within financial limits prescribed by the Treasury, the COS techniques attracted bureaucratic attention even though their use for collectivised welfare provision was an anathema to the COS. Perversely for the society, once in government hands COS investigative methodology formed a useful framework for the state to determine personal characteristics of applicants such as assessing whether or not they should be provided with benefits, determining the extent of individual and family needs and ensuring that relief was given in a precise amount from the most pertinent state source.

DISCUSSION

Although the COS failed to acquire the co-operation or public trust necessary to become the organizers of other charities the apparent integrity of their leaders, however misdirected, gained respect if only for the professionalism of their procedures. In spite of their differences with those of freer attitudes, the commanding presence in establishment circles of London COS apologists guaranteed they would continue to be invited to contribute on many important social forums.[115] Even in the early twentieth century it was difficult to find an official committee or commission bearing on the 'condition of the poor' which was without a COS contingent.

It was the implacability of COS leaders in retaining their air of self-fashioned omnipotence on social issues and individual morals which impeded their willingness to listen, let alone bend significantly towards other viewpoints. Had the COS been prepared to accept, in a modernizing world where man-made problems were exacerbating the difficulties of the urban poor, that the 'efficacy of charity for the redress of grievances' was inadequate without additional state correctives, the organizing potential of the COS may have enabled them to take a leading role in fashioning the later surge of twentieth-century social legislation.[116]

What was particularly disquieting to the COS was the realization that state interventions they had initially seen as irritating but blessedly short-

Ideological Change in Late Victorian Britain

term palliatives such as 'contrived' public works had become permanent appendages to society. By 1890 few among the middle classes were convinced that the demoralizing COS connotation of sinful idleness as applied to the unemployed was still valid. Most were prepared to recognize the depressing effects of environmental squalor and supported the 'degeneration' concept.[117] It was accepted that those without work must be cushioned by officialdom from any potentially dangerous drift into collective dissension rather than depending on the chance intercession of voluntary agencies. Frustrating as it was to die-hard COS members they had to acknowledge that in spite of their efforts over twenty years, strict individualistic solutions to the plight of the poor no longer received the automatic official seal of approval with which Goschen had blessed them in 1869.

A number of explanations will now be considered as to why provincial COS members remained obdurate about moral regeneration taking precedence over environmental factors which the middle-class majority had come to accept as being external to an individual's own range of response.[118] Five hypotheses, each aimed at explaining COS inflexibility, will be discussed:

1. that COS members were hard-hearted charlatans who blamed the poor for their own misfortune with little intention of helping them;

2. that COS members implacably propounded eccentric principles in their determination to retain the dominant role of morals in the making of individual character;

3. that COS members were opportunists intent on improving their personal aggrandisement;

4. that during the 1870s and 1880s the membership of COS provincial Committees remained essentially unchanged; and

5. that unlike what has been claimed for most of the Victorian middle class, COS members were miserly and used the society as an excuse to restrict their personal charitable contributions.

The first hypothesis assumes that COS principles were a cruel camouflage whereby the middle-class faction could justify their own privileged position by using a 'transparent ideology masquerading as expertise' to restrict the flow of charitable funds which traditionally had helped the poor in their daily struggles.[119] Criticism of alleged COS hardheartedness was not confined to their many foes in the public domain but also came eventually from the disillusioned in their own ranks. At a COS council meeting in 1891, Mr Allen Graham told the secretary Charles Loch that he had such a 'biased mind' as to be 'insensible to the sufferings of the poor' and because the COS had 'not even attempted to rescue the despairing classes' felt sure the 'inevitable conclusion' of others would be that 'the Society had very largely failed'.[120] The difficulty with this assumption of fundamental COS callousness is that to describe the actions of men like Denison, Solly and Hawksley who contributed so much to the COS formative values in terms that did not acknowledge their genuine personal intentions towards improving the condition of the poor would be terribly unfair. Equally since the single-minded devotion of these three gentlemen is not to be expected in abundance it would be unrealistic to expect many of those who later joined the COS provincial ranks to attain the same degree of personal application as their distinguished predecessors. At the same time it is reasonable to believe that with such celebrated role-models many COS recruits were genuinely prepared to contribute some personal effort towards mitigating the problems of the poor.

Another point is that whereas the huge gap between the earnings and wealth of the middle classes and the poverty of the Victorian majority made it easy for the better-off in momentary gestures to throw largesse to the needy, it was quite another thing to commit oneself as was expected of COS lady visitors to devote time, week after week, in visiting poor families. Undoubtedly there were distasteful syndromes arising from such actions including the Lady Bountiful image with its inbuilt condescension and its possible provision of a conscience-relieving hobby for ladies denied access to formalized employment.[121] But it must also be acknowledged that COS 'ladies', by having to engage in squalor, dirt, smell and danger of disease when on their sorties into the slums, showed an intention to help the poor at a certain personal discomfort to themselves. Helen Bosanquet's guiding principle for COS volunteers was for them to only 'give our money where we can also give our time and our trouble'.[122] Beatrice Webb after becoming disillusioned with the COS still believed 'these devoted men and women, unlike the mass of property owners, were yearning to spend their lives in the service of the poor'.[123] Even if these opinions are disregarded and it is concluded that COS devotees benefited from an intrinsic satisfaction in their activities among the poor it does not make them unworthy or guilty of charlatanism.

The second hypothesis explains COS ideological inflexibility by centring on the apparent eccentricity of their working values. This proposition was certainly not correct in 1869. At that time the COS were formalizing a firmly held government view that there would be advantage in organizing charity in favour of the deserving poor, an idea not viewed with aversion by much of the middle class. COS stalwarts such as Octavia Hill confirmed their early compatibility with contemporary social opinion by active participation in the influential 'Social Science Association' with its interests in 'the welfare of the poorer classes'.[124] The eccentricity of COS principles occurred with the passing of time and their refusal to remain in concert with the changing pattern of contemporary opinion. It is quite likely that some of those COS members who persevered with the same blinkered code of ethics in the more tolerant social environment of 1890 did so because their upbringing, their education and their persistent association with similarly minded individuals buttressed them against change. COS members would also be helped to feel comfortable while deflecting later accusations that they were harsh and out of step by their continued support from establishment factions among the aristocracy, the ecclesiastical elite and senior LGB officials. The confidence the COS retained among higher echelons of the Church of England seemed to supply them with justification for their belief that the society's principled steadfastness did not clash with Christian ethics. COS resolve was also strengthened by prolonged aristocratic support, including members of the Royal Family whose names continued to feature midst the COS upper echelons. Some senior LGB officials continued to back the COS in the 1890s because their philosophy was a useful model with which they still hoped to convert recalcitrant guardians about the wisdom of tighter constraints on out-relief.

Another factor cementing provincial implacability was the presence in the COS movement of outstanding individuals like Charles Loch, the Bosanquets and Octavia Hill who nationally maintained the society's high public profile. These propagandists placated the occasional provincial COS doubter with reassurance that the society's steadfastness not only had the blessing of prominent establishment figures but was also supported by the opinions of respected intellectuals who others had allegedly misconstrued. COS provincials were encouraged to eschew external economic factors as being the primary reason for the condition of the Victorian poor. This was made easier by recognition that few among the middle classes in the 1890s doubted that the success of the nation continued to depend on the concerted efforts of moral individuals. However, what the majority had also come to accept was that new economic factors related to modern urban communities made it increasingly essential, both for reasons of humanity and for national stability, to apply more consistent and dependable means of improving the condition of the poor than the inherent uncertainty of voluntarism. The position adopted by the COS in responding to these shifts of opinion was to agree with, and indeed activate, projects that may improve the lifestyle of those individuals who had satisfied the society after examination that they had the character and the willingness to help themselves towards independence. Equally, the COS felt justified in not bending towards collectivist trends which they saw as transgressing traditional morality by encouraging those among the poor they had categorized as being undeserving and likely to sinfully exploit thoughtless middle-class innocents.

The implacable stand against change adopted by the COS with its consequent drift into eccentricity is not unusual in societal circumstances of this nature. Shils argues in general that where articles of faith have been developed by such a group, holding what to them are a set of coherent and comprehensive beliefs, they develop the certainty that 'they alone' have the 'truth about the right ordering of life' and that their values are so central as to 'radiate into every sphere of life, that it replace religion'.[125] Beatrice Webb suggested that COS stubbornness to resist the mounting evidence about the welfare of the individual being closely related to economic environment implied that the mechanics of 'scientific' methodology were more easily taught than were intrinsic values like compassion or concepts like 'the consciousness of collective sin'.[126] Another possible ingredient explaining COS inflexibility is Harrison's more broadly based contention that 'nineteenth-century philanthropists seldom had the time or inclination to reconsider their fundamental assumptions'.[127] Where the line is drawn between social eccentricity, bigotry and a sincerely held faith is difficult to define. In the case of the COS, there is little reason to doubt that most of their members genuinely clung to their belief that socio-economic considerations were of secondary importance and that individual morals were primarily moulded by character.

The third hypothesis concerning COS rigidity was that their members were understandably motivated by self-aggrandizement at a time when Smilesian values influenced society. As a consequence it may be argued that provincial members were attracted by the society's elitist image and the possibility that they may gain personally from the association. Such an accusation has dubious validity. Any potential COS recruit conscious of the organization's high public profile must equally have been aware that the society had soon become the object of peer-group brickbats. There is also little indication that the general public perceived COS members as being self-seeking opportunists although there were many adverse comments about COS investigations, hard-heartedness, unrealism, weak economic management and excessive administrative expenditure. On the contrary, even when launching a blistering attack on COS insensitivities, Henrietta Barnett accepted that COS members could be characterized by their willingness for hard work, care for the poor, honesty about money, methodical application, business-like approach, thoroughness in detail, accuracy, eventemper, patience, painstakingness, even though their humility was tinged with conceit.[128] While there would be some black sheep in COS ranks, as in all institutions, it is unreasonable to believe that many who joined the provincial COSs were motivated primarily by the possibility of enhancing their own social position.

The fourth hypothesis hinges on the suggestion that during the 1870s and 1880s there was little change in the executive personnel of provincial COSs and hence no modification in policy. Such a possibility gains credence from the Southampton COS where a substantial majority of the sixteen senior COS executives in 1879 still occupied similar authority a decade later. Other provincial societies such as the Liverpool CRS and the Brighton COS where over the same decade about one half of the committee retained an executive role also provide some support for the hypothesis. This is especially valid when the mature age of many committee members made mortality or incapacity likely ingredients for attitudinal change. But among most of the provincial societies examined there is little correlation of committee names at the extremities of the same ten years. This destroys the general hypothesis that the permanence of provincial COS executive members explained their intransigence.

The fifth hypothesis implies that the COS was used by members as an excuse for meanness. It is based on historiographical impressions of the Victorian era such as 'no country on earth can lay claim to a greater philanthropic tradition than Great Britain' and that many millions of pounds were raised annually by 'a great network of charities'.[129] In contrast with the impressions of generosity provided by such statements the donations and subscriptions to provincial COSs were fragile and small scale. It was quite common for COS committee members to subscribe no more than one or two guineas annually to their society's funds. Some contributed only a few shillings and others nothing.[130]

One explanation for the low level of COS contributions could be that because COS members believed in the sinfulness of profligate charity, they consciously restricted their COS contribution to avoid the society committing the same error. But this excuse is unconvincing when provincial COSs regularly bewailed that shortage of funds inhibited their actions. There is also the evidence that provincial COSs such as those at Kingston-on-Thames and at Dorking ceased operations after financial failure.

Another argument in support of this hypothesis could be that COS members were not miserly with their charitable donations and that COS contributions represented but a small part of their total benefactions. But such a proposition would be irrational and in total conflict with the seminal purpose of the COS which was to prevent the distribution of charity until each applicant had been subjected to COS investigative rigours. Because these COS ideas on haphazard charity were general knowledge an interested observer could reasonably conclude from the COS's published subscription lists that a COS member's donation was a substantial part, if not all, of their total charitable contributions. In reality the general low value of COS subscriptions seemed to cause no public embarrassment to members. Nor were the subscriptions made the target of adverse comment from among their social peers who often offered virulent criticism about local COS activities generally and who themselves apparently offered so much more to charity.

This raises the question as to whether the assumed magnanimity of the Victorian middle class in respect of their direct support for the poor may not have been exaggerated.[131] Some historiographical misconstruction could have resulted from the common practice of interchangeably using the words 'charity' and 'philanthropy'. If a dictionary definition is accepted that philanthropy was 'charity on a large scale' and that reference to the charitable generosity of the Victorians includes the vast amount of capital used to build the public edifices that mushroomed in nineteenth-century Britain, this would have had little bearing on the provision of direct financial relief to the poor in the sense of providing an alternative to Poor Law outdoor doles.[132]

Another factor may be because a substantial part of Victorian charitable resources were medical charities which like much of philanthropy were often funded by endowments from the deceased. While these provided much needed support to the sickly poor they did not constitute an alternative to the majority of Poor Law dole applicants deemed to be in good health and which were numerically dominated by the elderly and disabled together with widows and their dependent children.

Thus, if it is accepted that the finance for constructing philanthropic public works together with the funds of medical charities accounted monetarily for a substantial part of Victorian 'charity', then the question is raised about the precise meaning of historiographical statements such as that charity provided ten times as much relief as did the poor-rates.[133] It also provides a possible reason why COS members seem not to have been perceived by their middle-class peers as being miserly on account of their modest subscriptions.

None of the five hypotheses explains in itself why members of provincial Charity Organisation Societies remained so rooted in their founding principles. The explanation is most likely to be an amalgam of the factors

Ideological Change in Late Victorian Britain 171

discussed with the influence of each varying in weight according to individual characteristics and to the localities in which they operated. It is likely that provincial COS members generally acted on what they believed were justifiable motives by maintaining concepts of personal morality in which they themselves had been schooled and which had stood them in good stead throughout their successful careers. What COS stalwarts could not accept was that by the 1890s their restrictive systematic individualistic social formulae should be dismissed as obsolete by a broadening public opinion convinced that social regeneration for the 'common good' required more than the injection of charity, organized or not.

SUMMARY AND CONCLUSIONS

Heretofore, there has been relatively little historiographical information on the activities of provincial Charity Organisation Societies in Britain. Opinions on the success of these societies have therefore mainly been guided by the claims disseminated by London COS. They implied that a vibrant network of flourishing organizing societies stretched across Britain during the later decades of Victoria's reign and talked confidently about the 'national character' of their movement which had become of 'imperial importance'. Helen Bosanquet asked convincingly that her readers should assess the society's reputation, not on the performance of London COS alone, but on it being part of a 'much larger movement extending throughout the country and beyond it'.[134] The misleading nature of these comments has now been exposed. It has been shown that although by 1890 many outposts of charity organization were being attempted, those in the English provinces were beset by failure, contradiction and anachronism.

We have seen how the inauguration and development of the London COS was based on a widespread acceptance of classical political economic ideology and by concepts shared with the President of the Poor Law Board concerning the diminution of individual character by easy outdoor relief. Although this volume has focused mainly on the crusade as practised in 'anti-outdoor relief' Poor Law unions and on those adjacent to a provincial Charity Organisation Society, it has been shown quite clearly that nationally the categories of outdoor paupers who suffered most from the crusade were not the able-bodied groups upon whom the Poor Law authorities concentrated public attention. In reality by far the greatest fall in out-relief numbers were among disadvantaged categories of pauper including the aged, the infirm, the disabled and widows with their dependent children.

Examination of provincial Charity Organisation Societies has left little doubt that they were generally rebuffed alike by guardians, charitable bodies, clergy and by the poor themselves. COS Secretary Charles Loch went a long way to accepting their failure when complaining in 1893 that unless more progress was made towards organizing charity it would remain 'what it has too often been, a poor stunted thing – a well-meaning tree in a smoke-laden atmosphere of dirt and dolefulness, whose fresh roots wither before hardening into serviceable wood, and whose branches fall off in premature decay'.[135] The widespread ostracism of the COS by other relief agencies provided scant chance for the consummation of G.J. Goschen's planned marriage of the official and organized voluntary sector. Study of the relationships between provincial organizing Societies and their London counterpart has shown how the latter soon adopted a superior stance and became increasingly impatient about the failure of provincial attempts to propagate their principles.

The categorization of applicants was a seminal requirement preceding all COS responses. Case-studies have illustrated the individual characteristics which made an applicant deserving or undeserving to the COS. Inability to convert charities to their ideology left the COS with little choice but to attempt self-funding and so become yet another addition to the hotchpotch of charitable bodies that were so frequently the target of COS virulence. When provincial COSs failed to attract the richness of funds often enjoyed by traditional charities they excused their deficiencies by claiming they were above mammonist values and demanding to be judged by the efficacy of their 'scientific' investigative methodology. This COS excuse was at best partial with its validity undermined by the need for impecunious provincial COSs to repeatedly make largely fruitless public appeals for funds with which to help applicants they had investigated and found thoroughly deserving.

At the first national 'General Conference' of those attempting to organize charity, held at Oxford in 1890, the London COS were unable to provide sensible answers to what was seen as the unsatisfactory 'diversities of detail' used by their provincial counterparts.[136] Their leaders confessed that after twenty years the movement was in its 'springtime still' with a continuing problem of getting members to realize the 'magnitude of their work' and a need to do 'more, very much more, to influence public opinion'.[137] By the very nature of national conferences it is likely that those who attended the Oxford get-together would be amongst the most loyal, active and influential members of provincial COSs. Yet the cold advice offered them by the conference organizers smacked of failure. Delegates were told to return from whence they came and that 'somehow, directly and indirectly, they must make the managers and almoners of charities, be they voluntary, endowed, or parochial, the Poor Law Guardian, the private donor and the philanthropist ... share their convictions'.[138]

Clouding of the COS early vision that it was to be their destiny to organize other charities soon forced them into a web of contradiction. From their formation the COS repeatedly criticised the low value of Poor Law outdoor doles and their inadequacy as a means of developing independence. Historians have therefore tended to conclude that by implication the COS provided 'effectual assistance on a fairly generous scale' which might make 'all the difference between dependence and independence'.[139] It has been shown that in the English provinces this powerful impression, received from the COS, that the monetary value of their benefits was far more substantial than Poor Law out-relief was a sham. The COS made little attempt to determine the efficacy of their scientifically measured relief portions. When Mr S. Fuller asked the COS council whether members knew of any 'inquiries into the results of cases that have been dealt with' he was told that 'no regular system' existed and that attempts had 'failed from want of a sufficient number of visitors'.[140] Major Fitzroy and Mr A.H. Hill went further and 'questioned the expediency of looking too closely into results on the ground that such action was calculated to impair the independence of applicants'.[141]

COS methodology was built on paradox. They claimed that its primary purpose was to nurture self-sufficiency but their methods demanded abject deference from applicants. Any hint of an unthankful response to the COS's uninvited advice was taken as ingratitude from an underling. The COS were economical with the truth when they projected idyllic scenarios in which a caring friendship was regularly fostered between the COS visitor and a grateful recipient. These images were based on the COS claim that their representatives, after rudimentary training in scientific investigation, would naturally conjure an ambience of cheery kindliness while delving unreservedly into the most personal circumstances of the poor. In reality, because the anticipated armies of middle-class volunteers failed to materialize, COS provincial visitors were often hard-pressed with little time for compassionate counselling. Even small provincial COSs found it necessary to employ a professional agent who, in a way remarkably similar to the Poor Law relieving officer, assessed applicants' credentials and disbursed whatever relief was decided upon by a remote impersonal committee.

Provincial COSs faced further contradiction at times of exceptional distress when indiscriminate charity was rife. Despite COS awareness that volume pressures would preclude their usual detailed investigations, they often succumbed to the temptation of having the chance of functioning, albeit temporarily, alongside relief agencies who normally shunned them. This was partly because the COS were flattered by an invitation to participate, partly because they believed that even in diluted form their methodology might prevent succour getting to the undeserving, and partly because they saw involvement as a possible means of building permanent bridges with other relief agencies. The COS propagandized what success they enjoyed on these occasions by informing government about the unique value of their techniques when rational decisions were needed in unusual socio-economic circumstances. Paradoxically, in the twentieth century the welfare state turned to the methods used by the arch anti-interventionist COS for clues about structuring investigative techniques which might allow civil servants to distribute precisely prescribed Treasury benefits only to deserving applicants.

Another contradiction shared by provincial COSs was an increased tendency to supply pensions which possessed the hallmarks of what they so despised most about Poor Law doles in being permanent, inadequate and a contrary influence to the creation of a thrifty lifestyle. COS pensions are shown to have often also had the distinguishing characteristic of being reserved for 'special cases' among the middle classes or for the 'cream' of workers.

The passing years marinated the contradictory elements of COS procedures into anachronism. By 1890, undisguised individualistic solutions imposed on the poor by a superior strata of society were no longer tenable. Social forces as disparate as the New Liberals and the New Unionists, influenced by burgeoning urbanization and the widened franchise, demanded increased state commitment to environmental improvements and to the fostering of institutions committed to universal civic, political, social and economic citizenship. The unbending COS were left socially marooned, obdurately indifferent to the changing tides of public opinion, still preaching obsolete philosophies which in practice had faint resemblance on fundamental issues to their early intentions.

We have seen how Charity Organisation Societies persistently attacked what they saw as the sinfulness of other charitable bodies in disregarding how their haphazard benefactions encouraged latent sin amongst the poor. Now that more is known about the misleading nature of COS propaganda and how inadequately the society matched their own prescription for adequately assisting deserving cases, it must be asked whether the COS themselves were morally equipped to cast the first stone on the question of sinful charity.

Appendix: General Notes on Poor Law and Organized Charity Data

1. Poor Law data has in the main been extracted from Parliamentary Accounts and Papers, or from the PLB and LGB Annual Reports and Appendices. For references to individual years: Peter Cockton, *Subject Catalogue of the House of Commons Parliamentary Papers, 1801–1900, Part III* (Cambridge, 1988), pp.580–1 and pp.591–8.
2. Poor Law outdoor relief financial data are for the twelve-month period ending Lady Day, 25 March, unless otherwise stated.
3. The tabulated number of outdoor paupers shown in the various tables has generally been calculated from the sum of the one-day count on 1 January that year, plus the number counted on 1 July of the previous year. This assessment is justified by evidence compiled by the LGB in 1881 and 1892, and by the 1905–8 Royal Commission on the Poor Law. Each of these sources indicate that the total number of paupers relieved in a particular twelve-month period can be conservatively assumed to equal twice the average of the succeeding one-day counts (BPP 1908, XCII, p.359). The data from 1 July of the previous year has been used so that the tabulated number of paupers in any twelve months is more closely equivalent to the financial data.
4. Poor Law costs and numbers are exclusive of lunatics, idiots and the insane in mental institutions. However, these paupers were classified by the LGB as outdoor paupers and their cost had to be borne by their settlement union. In 1871 the number in these mentally disadvantaged categories was nationally around 4.5 per cent of the outdoor pauper total. Over the next two decades there was a marked percentage increase to 9.8 per cent. This growth partly resulted from the crusade against outdoor relief for the mentally sound, and partly because of the increasing tendency to care more professionally for the mentally ill in asylums designed to suit multi-union needs. In cities and towns committed to anti-outdoor relief policies, the proportion of mentally inadequate paupers cared for in this way increased dramatically. For example, at Birmingham the total from the one-day counts for 1.7.89 and 1.1.90 was 1725, compared with the total of 2823 mentally sound outdoor paupers.
5. Data for the provincial COSs, the Liverpool CRS and the Manchester and Salford DPS were compiled from their annual reports, minute books or other documents relating to the particular society. Supplementary information and comments were derived from COS documents and publications including the *Charity Organisation Reporter* (*COR*), and the *Charity Organisation Review* (*COReview*).
6. (a) In the data from organizing societies, the category tabled as 'not relieved' includes those who were 'ineligible', 'undeserving', 'found not to be requiring relief', 'guilty of providing false information especially an incorrect address', and in the second half of the 1880s those 'not likely to benefit'.

(b) Those who were 'referred' include applicants sent with a favourable message to other charitable agencies, committees, private persons, guardians and to other COSs.
(c) The 'relieved' category includes those receiving grants, loans, pensions and other forms of assistance debited directly to the local COS accounts.

Notes

CHAPTER 1

1. Samuel Smiles, *Self-Help* (1859); Harriet Martineau, *Illustrations of Political Economy* (9 vols, 1832–4).
2. M. Simey, *Charitable Effort in Liverpool* (Liverpool, 1951).
3. Thomas Hawksley, *The Charities of London and some of the Errors in their Administration* (1869), p.13.
4. Charles Booth, *Life and Labour of the People of London, 17 volumes* (1902); Seebohm Rowntree, *Poverty: A Study of Town Life*; and J. Rae, *Contemporary Socialism* (New York, 1884), pp.57–8.
5. T.R. Malthus, *An Essay on Population, Vol. II* (1914 edn), pp.143 and 177.
6. C.L. Mowat, *The Charity Organisation Society, 1869–1913*, (1961), pp.10–19; also K. de Schweinitz, *England's Road to Social Security* (1975 edn), pp.135–8.
7. *17th Annual Report, COS Council* (1886), p.1.
8. BPP 1870, *22nd Annual Report, Poor Law Board, Appendix 4* (c123), XXXV.I, p.9.
9. *Charity Organisation Reporter*, 24 February 1881, p.50.
10. BPP 1870, *ibid.*, p.11
11. Charles Murray, *The Emerging British Underclass* (1990), p.22 and pp.1–35.
12. Russell D. Roberts, 'A positive Model of Private Charity and Public Transfers', *Journal of Political Economy, Vol. 92, No. 1*, February–June (1984), p.147.
13. C. Murray, *In Pursuit of Happiness and Good Government* (New York, 1988), p.112.
14. J. Moore, 'Welfare and Dependency', speech to Conservative Constituency Parties Ass., September 1987, cited in R. Jowell, S. Witherspoon and L. Brook (eds), *British Social Attitudes, 7th Report* (Aldershot, 1990), p.10.
15. C. Murray (1988), *op. cit.*, pp.260 and 289.
16. Michael B. Katz, *In the Shadow of the Poorhouse* (New York, 1986), p.280.
17. They include: C.B.P. Bosanquet, *The History and Mode of Operation of the Charity Organisation Society* (1874); T. Hawksley, *Objections to 'The History' of the Society* (1874); H. Bosanquet, *Social Work in London 1869–1912: A History of the COS* (1914); C.L. Mowat, *The Charity Organisation Society, 1869–1913: Its Ideas and Work* (1961); D. Owen *English Philanthropy, 1660–1960* (1965), pp.211–46; K. de Schweinitz, *England's Road to Social Security* (South Brunswick, 1975), pp.140–53; M. Rooff, *A Hundred Years of Family Welfare* (1972), pp.22–63; A.F. Young and E.T. Ashton, *British Social Work in the Nineteenth Century* (1956), pp.92–114; K. Woodroofe, *From Charity to Social Work* (1968), pp.25–55; Judith Fido, 'The COS and Social Casework in London, 1869–1900', A.P. Donajgrodzki (ed.) *Social Control in Nineteenth Century Britain* (1977), pp.207–30.
18. H. Bosanquet, *op. cit.*, p.392.

19. *COR*, 26 May 1881, p.124.
20. Jose Harris, 'Political thought and the Welfare State: ... ', *Past and Present*, 135 (May 1992), p.121.
21. David Owen, op. cit., p.215.
22. Attributed to G.V. Rimlinger in foreword to Chapter 6: Andrew Vincent and Raymond Plant, *Philosophy, Politics, and Citizenship* (Oxford 1974), p.94.
23. C.L. Mowat, *op. cit.*, p.91 *et seq.*
24. A.F. Young and E.T. Ashton, *op. cit.*, p.101.
25. Jose Harris, *Unemployment and Politics* (Oxford 1972), p.105.
26. A.W. Vincent, 'The Poor Law Reports of 1909 and the social theory of the Charity Organisation Society', *Victorian Studies*, 27 (1983–4), p.347.
27. Christopher Harvie, *The Lights of Liberalism* (1976), pp.195–6; and A.F. Young and E.T. Ashton, *op. cit.*, p.101.
28. K. Woodroofe, *op. cit.*, p.39.
29. *First AR, LGB, Appendix 20*, BPP 1872. (c516), XXVIII. pp.63–8.
30. W. Hanna, *Memoirs of the Life and Writings of Thomas Chalmers, D.D.*, 4 Vols (Edinburgh 1849–52); A. Doyle,'The Poor Law System of Elberfeld', *Poor Laws in Foreign Countries, Reports by H.M Sec.of State for Foreign Affairs*, BPP 1875 (c1255), LXV.I; Doyle's paper also published in: BPP 1872 (c516), XXVIII, Appendix 35, pp.244–65.
31. 'Why is it wrong to Supplement Outdoor Relief?', *COS Occasional Paper No. 31* (1893), p.1.
32. For example, Francis Peek, *The Uncharitableness of Inadequate Relief*, COS pamphlet dated 20 May 1879, p.1; and Sophia Lonsdale, *The Evils of a Lax System of Outdoor Relief*, COS pamphlet dated 30 April 1895, p.4.
33. Francis Peek, *ibid.*, p.10
34. A.J. Taylor *Laissez-faire and State Intervention in Nineteenth-century Britain* (Basingstoke, 1988 reprint), pp.50–1.
35. W.L. Burn, *The Age of Equipoise* (1964), pp.224–6 and pp.289–91.
36. Michael Freeden, *The New Liberalism*, (Oxford, 1878); Helen M. Lynd, *England in the Eighteen Eighties* (1968), pp.237–98; Henrietta Barnett, *Canon Barnett: His Life, His Work, His Friends* (1919); and Gillian Darley, *Octavia Hill* (1990), p.128.

CHAPTER 2

1. *The Poor Law Report of 1834*, re-published with introduction by S.G. and E.O.A. Checkland (1974), p.334.
2. W. Chance, *The Better Administration of the Poor Law*, Charity Organisation Series (1895), p.1.
3. The Poor Law Report of 1834, *op. cit.*, p.429.
4. K. de Schweinitz, *England's Road to Social Security* (South Brunswick, 1975 edn), p.131.
5. A. Digby, *The Poor Law in Nineteenth-century England and Wales* (1982), p.27.
6. The Poor Law Report of 1834, *op. cit.*, pp.475–6.
7. S. and B. Webb, *English Poor Law History, Part II* (1929), p.419.

Notes

8. A. Digby (1982), *op. cit.*, p.27.
9. D. Ashforth, 'Settlement and removal in Urban Areas: Bradford 1834–1871', in M.E. Rose (ed.), *The Poor and the City: The English Poor Law and Its Urban Context 1834–1914* (Leicester, 1985), pp.61-2.
10. BPP 1909, *Report of the Royal Commission on the Poor Laws and the Relief of Distress*, p.83 (c4499), XXXVII.
11. K.D.M. Snell, *Annals of the Labouring Poor* (1987), p.72.
12. *Second Annual Report, Poor Law Commissioners*, BPP 1836 (c595), XXIX, p.43.
13. *6th AR, Poor Law Commissioners*, BPP 1840 (c245), XVII, pp.16–18.
14. Report of the Royal Commission ... (1909), *op. cit.*, p.141.
15. Letters of the Poor Law Commissioners Relative to the Transaction of Business of the Commission (1847), cited in K. de Schweinitz, *op. cit.*, p.131.
16. Report of the Royal Commission ... (1909), *op. cit.*, p.142.
17. M.E. Rose, 'The Allowance System under the New Poor Law', *Economic History Review, 2nd Series, Vol.XIX* (1966), p.610.
18. *22nd AR, PLB*, BPP 1870 (c123), XXV.I, pp.xix/xx
19. J.A. Thomas, *The House of Commons 1832–1901* (Cardiff, 1939), p.9.
20. T. Mackay, *op. cit.*, p.355.
21. M. Caplan, *op. cit.*, p.290.
22. *Hansard 1865*, CLXXVIII, cc.277–358.
23. K. Williams, *op. cit.*, Table 4.5, pp.158–9.
24. *Ibid.*, Table 4.6, pp.169–70
25. Report of the Royal Commission ... (1909), *op. cit.*, p.191.
26. PLB Annual Reports (1858/9 to 1869/Sol.70) refer to *Subject Catalogue of the House of Commons Parliamentary Papers, 1801–1900, Vol.III* (Cambridge, 1988), pp.580–1.
27. *22nd AR, PLB*, BPP 1870 (c123), XXXV.1, p.9.
28. Gareth Stedman Jones, *Outcast London* (Peregrine edn. 1984), pp.101–5.
29. M. MacKinnon, 'English Poor Law Policy and the Crusade Against Outrelief', *Journal of Economic History, XLVII* (1987), pp.603–4.
30. K. Williams, *op. cit.*, p.144.
31. A. Digby (1982), *op. cit.*, p.25.
32. M. Bruce, *The Coming of the Welfare State* (1973), p.49.
33. M.E. Rose, 'The disappearing pauper: Victorian attitudes to the relief of the poor', in Eric M. Sigsworth (ed.), *In search of Victorian Values* (Manchester UP, 1988), p.67.
34. Michael B. Katz, *In the Shadow of the Poorhouse* (New York, 1986), p.41.
35. *22nd AR, PLB*, BPP 1870 (c123), XXXV, p.xviii.
36. *2nd AR, LGB*, BPP 1873 (c748), XXIX, p.249; and *Accounts and Papers*, BPP 1872 (c387), LI, pp.4–5. Also see *22nd AR PLB*, BPP 1870, *op. cit*, pp.xix/xx, for explanation of the causes of destitution.
37. *23rd AR, PLB*, BPP 1871 (c396), XXVII.I, pp.37–8
38. M. Fothergill Robinson, *The Poor Law Enigma* (1911), pp.75–8.
39. *First AR, LGB*, Appendix 20, BPP 1872 (c516), XXVIII, p.63.
40. *Ibid.*, p.67.
41. *Ibid.*, p.66.
42. *Ibid.*, p.xv.
43. *Ibid.*, p.64

44. D.W. Thomson, 'Provision for the Elderly, 1830–1908', (PhD thesis, University of Cambridge, 1980), p.208.
45. *Ibid.*, p.68.
46. *Ibid.*, pp.67–8.
47. *Ibid.*, p.68. For the opposite viewpoint see: *Plain words on Out-Relief* (pub. Knight and Co., 1893), pp.1–29.
48. Rev J.C. Cox, 'Outdoor Relief ...', *Poor Law Conferences, 1889–90 (1890)*, p.193.
49. K. de Schweinitz, *op. cit.*, p.156.
50. J.R. Pretyman, *Dispauperization* (1876), p.159.
51. A. Digby (1982), *op. cit.*, p.21; and M.E. Rose, 'The New Poor Law in an Industrial Area', in R.M. Hartwell, *The Industrial Revolution* (Oxford, 1970), pp.127–35.
52. H. Phelps Brown, *The Origins of Trade Union Power* (Oxford 1986 edn), p.285.
53. BPP 1873, *2nd AR, LGB* (c748), XXIX, p.xvii.
54. William Fowler, *The Poor Law and its Administration in Aston Union* (Birmingham, 1873), pp.14–15.
55. *3rd AR, LGB*, Appendix 20, BPP 1874 (c1071), XXV, p.62 and pp.72–3.
56. S. and B. Webb, *op. cit.*, p.150.
57. W. Chance, *op. cit.*, p.14.
58. The LGB described Longley's report as 'very exhaustive and satisfactory': *3rd AR, LGB, op. cit.*, p.xx.
59. *3rd AR, LGB, op. cit.*, pp.204–5.
60. *Ibid.*, p.145.
61. K. Williams, *op. cit.*, pp.98–9.
62. *Bradfield Poor Law Union, Administration, Pauperism and Expenditure Report* (1892), Preface.
63. *Accounts and Papers*, BPP 1878 (c352), LXV.49, pp.1–9.
64. *Ibid.*, p.7. For the diametrically opposite perspective refer to the evidence of Sidney Ward, Secretary of the Brixworth Out-Relief Association, to the *Royal Commission on the Aged Poor*, BPP 1895 (c7684.2), XV, pp.841–57.
65. *Ibid.,* p.7.
66. *Ibid.*, p.xiii.
67. G. Bourne, *The Bettesworth Book* (1920 edn.), p.viii.

CHAPTER 3

1. S. and B. Webb, *English Local Government 8, English Poor Law History 2:1* (1929), p.460.
2. Revd. J.C. Cox, 'Outdoor Relief, with special reference to Brixworth, Atcham, and Whitechapel', *Poor Law Conferences, 1899–1900* (1900), p.195.
3. W. Chance, *The Better Administration of the Poor Law* (1895), pp.80–1.
4. *Ibid.*
5. *20th AR, LGB*, BPP 1890–1 (c6460), XXXIII, pp.478–81.
6. *20th AR, LGB*, BPP 1890–1 (c 6460), XXXIII.I.

Notes 181

7. This could suggest that some of those professing sickness were receiving allowances to augment wages at the outset of the crusade. Even then, these circumstances could have applied to only about 2 per cent of the total number of outdoor paupers. See A. Digby, *The Poor Law in Nineteenth-century England and Wales* (1982), p.23.
8. *1st AR, LGB*, Appendix.D, BPP 1872 (c516), XXVIII, p.451, and *7th AR, LGB*, Appendix.D, BPP 1878 (c2130), XXXVII, p.383.
9. W. Chance, *op. cit.*, p.3.
10. *First AR, LGB*, BPP 1872 (c516), XXVII, p.xvii.
11. *2nd AR, LGB, Appendix 31*, BPP 1873 (c748), XXIX.I, pp.67–8.
12. *Ibid.*
13. *2nd AR, LGB, Appendix 32*, BPP 1873 (c748), XXIX, p.71.
14. *Ibid.*, p.72; also *3rd AR, LGB, Appendix 11*, BPP 1874 (c1071), XXV, p.121.
15. *Ibid.*, p.70. Brackets as in the original.
16. Pat Thane, 'Women and the Poor Law in Victorian and Edwardian England', *History Workshop*, Vol. 6 (1978), p.39.
17. *3rd AR, LGB, Appendix 11*, *op. cit.*, pp.124, 121 and 122.
18. *2nd AR, LGB, op.cit.*, p.74.
19. *Ibid.*, p.122.
20. *Ibid.*, p.123.
21. *Ibid.*, p.xix.
22. *3rd AR LGB, Appendix 11, op. cit.*, p.118.
23. *Ibid.*, p.119.
24. Bradfield Poor Law Union, Guardian Minutes, 5 March 1872.
25. *Guide to the Records of the New Poor Law and its successors in Berkshire 1835–1948* (Berkshire Record Office, 1984), p.4.
26. T. Bland-Garland, *Outdoor Relief* (1887), p.8.
27. *Ibid.*, p.10.
28. C.D. Francis, *The Injustice of the Poor Law in itself and its Demoralising effects* (Banbury 1872), p.5.
29. T. Bland-Garland, *From Pauperism to Manliness – the story of the Bradfield Union* (1891), COS Occasional paper No.21, p.2
30. T. Bland-Garland, *Outdoor Relief* (1887), p.13.
31. *Ibid.* p.2.
32. *Ibid.*, p.3
33. *Accounts and Papers*, BPP 1878, *op. cit.*, pp.5 and 9.
34. *Eighth AR, LGB, Appendix B*, BPP 1878–9 (c 2372), XXVIII.1, pp.138–9.
35. C.L. Elrington, 'Local Government and Public Services', *A History of the County of Warwick, Vol VII*, The Victoria History of the Counties of England (OUP, London, 1964), p.323.
36. *12th AR, Birmingham COS* (1881), p.6.
37. *13th AR, Birmingham COS* (1882), p.4.
38. *Accounts and Papers*, BPP 1886 (c58), LVI.431, p.78.
39. Reigate Poor Law Union, Board of Guardian Minutes, 15 November 1871, and 20 March 1872.
40. *The Surrey Advertiser and County Times*, 25 November 1871.
41. W. Chance, *op. cit.*, pp.96–7.
42. *20th AR, LGB, Appendix B*, BPP 1890–1 (c6460), XXXIII.I, p.231.

43. *Ibid.* p.232.
44. J.C. Cox, *op. cit.*, p.200.
45. *Ibid.* See also, *Royal Commission on the Aged Poor*, BPP 1895 (c7684), XV, pp.841–57.
46. Alexander McDougall Jnr, *Inquiry into the Causes of Pauperism in the Township of Manchester* (Manchester, 1884), p.10.
47. *20th AR, LGB, Appendix B*, BPP 1890–1 (c6460), XXXIII.I, p.235.
48. *20th AR, LGB*, BPP 1890/1, *op.cit.*, p.229.
49. *3rd AR, Birkenhead COS* (1874), pp.19–20.
50. *Accounts and Papers*, BPP 1886 (c58), LVI.43, pp.80–1
51. *19th AR, LGB*, BPP 1889–90 (c6141), XXXIII.I, p.109.
52. *Accounts and Papers*, BPP 1886 (c58), LVI.431, p.101.
53. *Ibid.*
54. Ruth H. Crocker, 'The Victorian Poor Law in Crisis and Change: Southampton 1870–1895', *Albion 19, 1* (Spring 1987), pp.23–4.
55. *Ibid.*, p.119.
56. *COReview*, November 1890, p.439.
57. BPP 1888, XV, *Report from Select Committee on Poor Law Relief; House of Lords*, para.516.
58. *COReview*, May 1888, p.222.
59. J.C. Cox, *Outdoor Relief: The Heritage of the Poor* (1900), p.23.
60. K. de Schweinitz, *op. cit.*, p.62.
61. *Plainwords on Out-relief* (pub. Knight and Co., London, 1893), pp.8–10.
62. *8th AR, LGB*, BPP 1878–9, *op. cit.*, pp.111 and 110.
63. *7th AR, LGB, Appendix A, No.11*, BPP 1878 (c2130), XXXVII.I, p.52
64. *Ibid.*, p.57.
65. *Seventh Annual Central Poor Law Conference*, 12 December 1877, p.323.
66. *20th AR, LGB*, BPP 1890–1 (c6460), XXXIII.I, p.226.
67. *8th AR, LGB, Appendix B*, BPP 1878–9 (c2372), XXVIII.1, p.139.
68. *Ibid.*, pp.142–7.
69. BPP 1910 (c5074), LII, Appendix Vol. XXI, p.60.
70. *Ibid.*
71. C.D. Francis, *The Injustice of the Poor Law itself and its demoralising effects* (Banbury, 1872), p.5.
72. *Plain Words on Out-relief, op. cit.*, p.39. See also Christopher Harvie, *The Lights of Liberalism* (1976), p.195, who refers to voters' 'hostility' and 'resentment' about the strictness of guardians at Oxford and Cambridge.
73. *Bradfield Poor Law Union, Administration, Pauperism and Expenditure Report*, 1 January 1890, p.20.
74. *Ibid.*,
75. *8th AR, LGB, Appendix B*, BPP 1878–9, *op. cit.*, p.107.
76. *3rd AR, LGB*, BPP 1874, *op. cit.*, p.171.
77. *Ibid.*
78. *17th AR, LGB*, BPP 1888 (c5526), XLIX.1, pp.64/5.
79. *3rd AR, LGB*, BPP 1874, *op. cit.*, p.173.
80. *Ibid.*
81. W. Chance, *op. cit.*, pp.78 and 113 (emphasis in original).
82. BPP 1909, *Majority Report on the Poor Laws* Appendix Vol. 1, Minutes of evidence (c4625), XXXIX Part 1, p.128, Item 2310.

83. James H. Treble, *Urban Poverty in Britain 1830–1914* (1979), p.52
84. *Majority Report of the Royal Commission on the Poor Laws, Part IV, Chapter 6*, BPP 1909 (c4625), XXXIX, p.193.
85. *Ibid.*, p.194.

CHAPTER 4

1. E.C. Midwinter, *Victorian Social Reform* (Harlow, 1986), pp.44–5.
2. Derek Fraser, *The Evolution of the British Welfare State*, 2nd edn (Basingstoke, 1986), p.71.
3. Gertrude Williams, *The State and the Standard of Living* (1936), p.8.
4. P. Burke, *Sociology and History* (1980), pp.81–2.
5. H. Spencer, 'The Coming Slavery', *The Contemporary Review, Vol XLV*, April 1884, p.461.
6. *Ibid.*, p.461 and p.482.
7. E.C.P. Lascelles, 'Charity in Early Victorian England', G.M. Young (ed.), *Early Victorian England, 1830–1865, Vol. 2* (1934), pp.320–1.
8. T.H. Marshall, 'Citizenship and Social Class', in David Held *et al.* (Eds), *States and Societies* (Oxford, 1983), p.252.
9. 'Out-door Relief', *Charity Organisation Reporter (COR)*, 29 March 1876.
10. J.R. Pretyman, *Dispauperization* (1876), p.42.
11. *First Annual Report: Local Government Board*, BPP 1872 (c516), XXVIII, pp.63–8.
12. *18th AR, London COS* (1885/6), p.4 (refers to comments made in 1870).
13. C.S. Loch, *The Charities Register and Digest* (1890), pp.iv–v.
14. J. Llewellyn Davies, *Macmillan's Magazine*, Vol. 15, December, 1866, cited in B. Dennis and D. Skilton (eds), *Reform and Intellectual Debate in Victorian England* (1987), p.44.
15. K. Woodroofe, *From Charity to Social Work* (1968), pp.17–18.
16. T. Mackay, *A History of the English Poor Law from 1834 to the Present Time*, Vol. III (New York, 1900), p.502.
17. Ian Williams, *The Alms Trade* (1989), pp.2–3.
18. G. Mosca, *The Ruling Class* (New York, 1939), p.50.
19. Geraint Parry, *Political Elites* (1969), p.37.
20. Melvin Richter, *The Politics of Conscience* (1964), p.331.
21. B. Webb, *My Apprenticeship* (1979 edn), pp.198–9
22. C.L. Mowat, *The Charity Organisation Society, 1869–1913: Its Ideas and Work*, p.114; '... steps for its restriction and ultimate abolition, *COR*, 2 June 1875, p.84; and 'a prospective abolition of out-relief seems to me the only solution to the difficulty', *COR*, 24 July 1879, p.188.
23. Antonio Gramsci, *Selections from the Prison Notebooks*, edited and translated Q. Hoare and G. Nowell-Smith (1971), pp.181–2
24. C. Trevelyan, *Three Letters on London Pauperism* (1870), p.32.
25. C.S. Loch, *Charity Organisation* (2nd edn, 1892), p.6.
26. J.R. Pretyman, *Dispauperization* (1876), p.158.
27. *AR, Brighton Provident and District Society* (1831), p.13.

28. *Ibid.*, p.11.
29. *Ibid.*, p.7 and p.16.
30. *Ibid.*, p.7 (emphasis in the original).
31. *Ibid.*, Rule 12. Another contemporary publication suggests that a provident society in suburban London was even more generous in certain circumstances: see *Provident Societies Recommended* (1833), pub. J.G. and F. Rivington, p.10.
32. William Davis, *Hints to Philanthropists* (1821, Irish University Press/edition 1971), p.142.
33. *AR, Brighton P and DS* (1831), pp.9, 8 and 11.
34. *AR, Liverpool PDS* (1834), Rule 12, p.10.
35. Revd. A. Campbell, *Intended as a Manual for the formation of similar Institutions* (Liverpool PDS, 1834), Preface.
36. *AR, Liverpool PDS* (1834), p.6.
37. *Ibid.*, pp.5–7.
38. The *Porcupine*, 17 May 1862, p.52.
39. *AR, Liverpool PDS* (1834), p.7 and pp.5–6.
40. The *Porcupine*, 17 May 1862, p.52.
41. Joan Gaddum, *Family Welfare Association of Manchester and Salford, A Short History, 1833–1974* (Manchester, 1974), p.5.
42. *Ibid*, pp.6–7.
43. *Report, Society for Relief of Distressed Travellers* (Oxford, 1814).
44. C.L. Mowat, *op. cit.*, p.11.
45. J.R. Green, *Edward Denison – In Memorium*, undated, Goldsmith's Library, University of London Press, FWA 248.
46. Baldwyn Leighton, *Letters of Edward Denison* (1872), p.47.
47. S. and B. Webb, *English Local Government 8, English Poor Law History, Part 2.1*, (1963 edn), pp.457–9; and K. Woodroofe, *op. cit.*, pp.45–7.
48. For example, Stewart J. Brown, *Thomas Chalmers and the Godly Commonwealth in Scotland* (Oxford, 1982), pp.122–294; and Revd. W. Hanna, *Memoirs of the Life and Writings of Thomas Chalmers, D.D.*, 4 Vols (Edinburgh, 1849–52).
49. K. de Schweinitz, *England's Road to Social Security* (South Brunswick, 1975), p.148.
50. Stewart J. Brown, *op.cit.*, pp.140–1.
51. B. Kirkham Gray, *Philanthropy and the State, or Social Politics* (1908), p.88.
52. Olive Checkland, *Philanthropy in Victorian Scotland* (1980), p.300.
53. M.T. Furgol, 'Thomas Chalmers' poor relief theories and their implementation in the early nineteenth century', (PhD thesis, Edinburgh University, 1987), p.410.
54. *Ibid.*, pp.406 and 403.
55. For exposition of the Elberfeld experiment and a critique on its cost, visitors, integration and public/ private expenditure relationships, see M.E. Rose, 'Poor Relief and Scientific Charity', unpublished paper (Manchester, c.1986).
56. J.R. Green, *Stray Studies, 2nd Series*, (1904), p.170.
57. Eleanor F. Rathbone, *William Rathbone: A Memoir* (1905), pp.370–4; and R.V. Holt, *The Unitarian Contribution* (1938), p.33.

58. G. Browne, 'The Elberfeld System of Poor Relief', *West Midlands Poor Law Conference*, May 1889, p.36.
59. W. Chance, 'The Elberfeld and English Poor Law Systems: A Comparison', *Economic Journal*, 7 (1897), p.332.
60. *First AR, LGB, Appendix 35, op. cit.*, p.235.
61. Chapter 1, footnote 21.
62. S. and B. Webb, *English Local Government 8, English Poor Law History, op. cit.*, p.456.
63. In 1885, *COR* was replaced by the monthly *Charity Organisation Review* (*COReview*).
64. *5th AR, London COS* (1874), pp.5–6; *1st AR, London COS* (1870), p.6
65. Thomas Hawksley, *The Charities of London and some errors in their Administration* (1869), p.16. A 'highly arrogant plan': B. Rodgers, *The Battle against Poverty Vol.1, From pauperism to human rights* (1968), p.45.
66. C.L. Mowat, *op. cit.*, pp.61–2.
67. G. Kitson Clark, *Churchmen and the Condition of England 1832–1885* (1973), p.272.
68. *6th AR, London COS* (1876), Appendix IV, pp.24–5.
69. *Ibid.*
70. Examples: Emily S. Maurice, *Octavia Hill* (1928); E.M. Bell, *Octavia Hill* (1942); C.L. Mowat, *op. cit.* on Charles C. Loch; H.O. Barnett, *Canon Barnett, His Life, Work and Friends* (1919); H. Bosanquet, *Social Work in London, 1869–1912* (1914), on her husband Bernard and colleagues.
71. Unitarians included Revd. H.S. Solly, Octavia Hill (later received into the C. of E.), Helen Dendy Bosanquet and James Stansfeld (president of the LGB at the launch of the crusade against out-relief). Reforming provincial Unitarians such as Joseph Chamberlain in Birmingham, the Rathbones in Liverpool and the Philips family in Manchester are referred to in Chapter 5. See R.V. Holt, *The Unitarian Contribution* (1938), pp.23, 45–6, 235, 253, 331, etc.
72. Examples: *Report of the COS Special Committee*, 'Training of the Blind' (1876); *Report of the COS Special Committee*, 'Education and Care of Idiots, Imbeciles, and harmless Lunatics' (1877); BPP 1889, *Report of the Royal Commission on the Blind and Deaf and Dumb of the UK*, XIX.1 and XX.1.
73. C.S. Yeo, 'Introduction to H. Bosanquet', *Social Work in London 1869–1912* (Brighton, 1973 edn), p.xiv.
74. Margaret E. Paisley, 'Social Provision for Crippled Children: 1850–1900', *Case Conference Vol.12, No.1* (May 1965), pp.18–23.
75. Helen M. Lynd, *England in the Eighteen Eighties* (1968), p.74.
76. D. Owen, *English Philanthropy, 1660–1960* (1965), p.243.
77. *COReview*, January 1891, p.1.
78. B. Harrison, 'Philanthropy and the Victorians', *Victorian Studies* (June 1966), p.368.
79. *Ibid.*, p.15.
80. G. Wagner, 'Dr Barnardo and the Charity Organisation Society ...' (LSE, University of London, PhD thesis, 1977), p.2.
81. *Ibid.*, p.178/9.

82. H. Stuart Hughes, *op. cit.*, p.4.
83. G. Stedman Jones, *Outcast London* (Peregrine edn, 1984), pp.301/14.

CHAPTER 5

1. H. Perkin, *The Rise of Professional Society: England since 1880* (1989), p.6 and p.8.
2. For example, Brixworth Union assumed local charity would take 'an organised form'. *2nd AR, LGB, Appendix 32*, BPP 1872 (c748), XXIX.1, p.72.
3. *COReview*, July 1891, p.292.
4. *Ibid.*, pp.292–3; see also 'Off the rails; or, a so-called COS', *COReview*, April 1887, pp.157–9,
5. Ramsay Muir, *A History of Liverpool* (1907), SR Publishers reprint 1970, p.306.
6. C.S. Loch, *The Charities Register and Digest* (1890), pp.v/vi.
7. Ramsay Muir, *op. cit.*, pp.307–8; also F.G. D'Aeth, 'Liverpool' in H. Bosanquet (ed.), *Social Conditions in Provincial Towns* (1912), pp.36–50.
8. David Owen, *English Philanthropy 1660–1960* (Camb. Mass., 1964), pp.4545.
9. Margaret Simey, *Charitable Effort in Liverpool in the Nineteenth Century* (Liverpool, 1951), pp.86–7.
10. David Owen, *op. cit.*, p.457.
11. William Rathbone, *Social Duties: considered in Reference to the Organisation of Effort in Works of Benevolence and Public Utility; by a man of Business* (1867), pp.129–30.
12. M. Simey, *op. cit.*, p.91.
13. *Ibid.*, p.94.
14. *The Times*, Monday, 21 June 1875.
15. D. Owen, *op. cit.*, p.463.
16. *Ibid.*, p.454.
17. *COR*, 7 June 1884, p.192.
18. *Ibid.*
19. *Ibid.*
20. Cited in Jose Harris, *Unemployment and Politics. A Study in English Social Policy 1886–1914* (Oxford, 1972), p.120.
21. M. Simey, *op. cit.*, p.92 and p.94
22. *Ibid.*, pp.95-6.
23. *COReview*, November 1890, p.428; also letter W. Grisewood to John Polson, Paisley, 27 November 1886.
24. Alan J. Kidd, 'Outcast Manchester: Voluntary Charity, Poor Relief and the Casual Poor, 1860–1905', in Alan J. Kidd and K.W. Roberts (eds), *City, Class and Culture* (Manchester, 1985), p.50.
25. F. Engels, *The Condition of the Working Class in England* (1844), reprint 1984, p.111
26. W.E. Chadwick, *The Church, The State, and the Poor* (1914), p.175; see also Revd. R. Parkinson, *On the Present Condition of the Labouring Poor with Hints for Improving It* (London and Manchester, 1841).

27. F. Scott, 'The Conditions and Occupations of the People of Manchester and Salford', *Transactions of the Manchester Statistical Society* (1888–9), pp.93–116.
28. H.C. Irvine, *The old D.P.S. 1833-1933* (Manchester, 1933), p.6.
29. Alan J. Kidd, 'Charity organisation and the unemployed in Manchester, 1870–1914', *Social History, 9* (1984), p.47.
30. R.V. Holt, *The Unitarian contribution* (1938), pp.45–6, 253 and 331. Also Alan J. Kidd, 'Introduction', in A.J. Kidd and K.W. Roberts (eds), *op. cit.*, pp.10–11.
31. Alan J. Kidd (1984), *op. cit.*, p.54.
32. Joan Gaddum, *Family Welfare Association of Manchester and Salford, A Short History 1833–1947* (Manchester, 1974), pp.8–9; also W.O. Henderson, *The Lancashire Cotton Famine, 1861–1865* (Manchester, 1934) for background to famine and resulting social tensions.
33. Joan Gaddum, *op. cit.*, p.9.
34. *Manchester and Salford DPS*, General Committee Minutes (1875).
35. H.C. Irvine, *op. cit.*, p.6.
36. *Manchester and Salford DPS*, General Committee Minutes, Thursday, 14 June1877.
37. Cited in W. Allen, *The Black Country* (1946), p.40.
38. D. Read, *The English Provinces, 1760–1960* (1964), pp.174–5.
39. Asa Briggs, *Victoria History of the County of Warwick, Vol.7,* (1964) pp.223–5.
40. *1st AR, Edgbaston Mendicity Society*, period ending Lady Day 1871, pp.3 and 6.
41. *6th AR, Birmingham COS* (1875), p.6.
42. *COReview*, November 1890, p.419.
43. E.W. Gilbert, *Brighton* (1954), p.89.
44. *Victoria History of the County of Sussex, Vol.2* (1907), pp.235–7 and pp.262–3.
45. E.W. Gilbert, *op. cit.*, p.175 and p.187.
46. C. Musgrave, *Life in Brighton* (1981 edn), p.319.
47. *COR*, 27 November 1872, p.177.
48. *2nd AR, Brighton COS* (1873), pp.4–5.
49. *Ibid.*
50. For example, *2nd AR, Brighton COS* (1873), p.3.
51. The *Brighton Daily News*, 25 November 1873, p.6. See the *Brighton Herald*, 2 December 1876, for comment about a later annual COS meeting being 'influentially, though not numerously, attended'.
52. *15th AR, Brighton COS* (1886), p.3.
53. W.E. Darwin, *COReview*, November 1890. Note the similar phraseology used in the article, *COR*, 9 August 1883, pp.256–7, on 'Charity Organisation in the Provinces: Southampton', suggests that the author using the pseudonym 'X' may possibly also have been W.E. Darwin.
54. R.H. Crocker, 'The Victorian Poor Law in Crisis and Change: Southampton, 1870–1895', Albion, 19,1 (Spring 1987), p.42.
55. *Southampton Times and Hampshire Express*, 24 May 1890, p.8.
56. *COR*, 8 December 1875, p.152.
57. *Southampton Times and Winchester Express*, 11 December 1875, p.4.

58. *Ibid.*, 15 January 1876, p.8
59. *COR*, 15 November 1877, p.181.
60. *Ibid.*
61. *7th AR, Southampton COS* (1882), p.8.
62. *6th AR, Southampton COS* (1881), p.8.
63. *10th AR, Southampton COS* (1885), p.7.
64. T.B. Dudley, *A Complete History of Royal Leamington Spa* (RLS, 1896), p.11.
65. David C. Ward, 'Deformation of the Gift: The Charity Organisation Society in Leamington Spa', MA thesis (Warwick University, 1975), p.25.
66. *COR*, 24 November 1875, p.142.
67. George Morley, *History of Royal Leamington Spa* (Leamington Spa,1877/9), p.136.
68. *COR*, 21 June 1877, p.105
69. *COR*, 10 July 1879, p.178.
70. David C. Ward, *op. cit.*, p.107.
71. For example, *6th AR, Leamington COS*, (1881), p.7.
72. *COR*, 30 November 1882, p.355.
73. *8th AR, Leamington COS* (1883), p.8.
74. *Leamington Chronicle*, 3 March 1890.
75. W.R.S. McIntyre, *Birkenhead – Yesterday and Today* (Liverpool, 1948), p.92.
76. *Birkenhead and Cheshire Advertiser*, March 1881.
77. *Ibid.*
78. *1st Annual Meeting, Birkenhead Provident and Benevolent Society*, 26 February 1864.
79. *1st AR, Birkenhead Provident and Benevolent Society* (1863–4), p.10.
80. *Circular*, 8 January 1872, pub. by Birkenhead Provident and Benevolent Society, and *5th AR, Birkenhead COS* (1876).
81. *1st AR, Birkenhead Provident and Benevolent Society* (1863–4), p.4.
82. *Ibid.*, p.10.
83. *Ibid.*, p.12.
84. *10th AR, Birkenhead COS* (1881), p.7.
85. *17th AR, Birkenhead COS* (1888), p.6.
86. *The Birkenhead News*, 23 February 1884.
87. *Liverpool Mercury*, 1 October 1876.
88. *Victoria History of Oxford, Vol.2* (1907), p.225; also C.V. Butler, 'Oxford', in H. Bosanquet (ed.), *Social Conditions in Provincial Towns* (1912), pp.60–72.
89. *COR*, March 1872, p.47; also *COReview*, November 1890, p.439.
90. *COR*, March 1872, p.47; and *COR*, 12 June 1872, p.111.
91. *COR*, June 1872, p.111.
92. Cited in *COR*, 5 March 1873, pp.39–40.
93. *COR*, 26 November 1873, p.164.
94. *COR*, 3 December 1873, p.168.
95. *AR, Oxford COS*, 9 months ending 30 September 1874, pp.6–7.
96. *AR, Oxford COS*, 12 months ending 30 September 1879, p.4.
97. *AR, Oxford COS*, 12 months ending 30 September 1888, p.6.
98. *COReview*, November 1890, p.439.

Notes

99. D. Phillips, *The Story of Reading* (Reading, 1980), pp.116–21.
100. M. Hinton, *A History of the Town of Reading* (1954), p.158.
101. A.L. Bowley and A.R. Burnett-Hurst, *Livelihood and Poverty* (1915).
102. *COR*, 25 February 1874, p.213.
103. *3rd AR, Reading COS* (1876), p.4.
104. *First AR, Reading COS* (1874–5), pp.3–5,
105. *7th AR, Reading COS* (1880–1), p.3.
106. *8th AR, Reading COS* (1881–2), p.3.
107. Stephen Yeo, *Religion and Voluntary Organisations in Crisis* (1976), pp.219–20.
108. *7th AR, Reading COS* (1880–1), pp.3 and 6.
109. For an example refer to *12th AR, Reading COS* (1886), p.3. London COS accepted that 'at Reading the work is falling off': *COReview*, July 1885, p.331.
110. *14th AR, Reading COS* (1887–8), p.3.
111. *COR*, 11 May 1882, pp.142–3.
112. *First AR, LGB, Appendix 29*, BPP 1872 (c516), XXVIII, pp.88–104.
113. *COR*, 12 June 1872, p.111.
114. *COR*, 23 December 1874, pp.347–8.
115. *COReview*, November 1890, p.439.
116. *AR, Oxford COS*, 12 months ending 30 September 1882, p.5.
117. *AR, Oxford COS*, 12 months ending 30 September 1887, p.7.
118. *AR, Oxford COS*, 12 months ending 30 September 1888, p.10.
119. For example, *7th AR, Reading COS* (1880–1), p.10.
120. *Annual Reports, Reading COS* (1874–90).
121. *11th AR, Birmingham COS* (1880), p.5.
122. *13th AR, Birmingham COS* (1882), p.4.
123. *COReview*, November 1890, p.420.
124. BPP, 1888, XV, *Report of the House of Lords Select Committee on Poor Law Relief*, para. 516.
125. *47th AR, Manchester and Salford DPS* (1879), p.6.
126. *Ibid.*, p.7.
127. *1st AR, Birkenhead COS* (1872), p.10, and, for example, *10th AR* (1883), pp.16/17.
128. *15th AR, Brighton COS* (1886), p.3; *16th AR* (1887), p.4; and *19th AR* (1890), p.4.
129. *COReview*, November 1890, pp.450–1.
130. *Southampton Times*, 4 March 1876, p.6.
131. R.H. Crocker,'The Victorian Poor Law in Crisis and Change: Southampton, 1870–1895', Albion, 19, 1 (Spring 1987), pp.24–5.
132. *COReview*, November 1890, p.422.
133. *COReview*, November 1890, p.441
134. *COReview*, November 1890, pp.442–3.
135. *COR*, 11 May 1882, p.142.
136. C.L. Mowat, *The Charity Organisation Society, 1869–1913* (1961), pp.22–3.
137. *COReview*, November 1890, p.451.
138. *2nd AR, Edgbaston Mendicity Society*, 12 months ending Lady Day 1872, p.4 (emphasis in the original).

139. *10th AR, Birmingham COS* (1880), p.5.
140. Similarly, re Oxford COS; *COReview*, November 1890, p.439.
141. *COR*, 21 June 1883, p.207. Also refer to M. Simey, *op. cit.*, p.99.
142. *26th AR, Liverpool CRS* (1888/Sol.9), p.9.
143. *23rd AR, Liverpool CRS* (1885–6), p.8.
144. The *Liverpool Review*, 16 April 1887, p.11.
145. H.C. Irvine, *The old D.P.S., 1833–1933* (Manchester, 1933), p.14.
146. The *Manchester Guardian*, 25 May 1886, and *Manchester and Salford DPS*, Monthly Committee Minutes, 2 June and 7 July, 1886.
147. *COR*, 24 April 1879, p.112.
148. *16th AR, Brighton COS* (1887), pp.3–4.
149. *17th AR, Brighton COS* (1888), p.4.
150. *COR*, 14 December 1876, p.175.
151. *3rd AR, Southampton COS* (1878), p.7.
152. *12th AR, Birmingham COS* (1881), p.3.
153. *COReview*, November 1890, p.447 and p.439.
154. *COR*, 14 June 1877, p.102.
155. *COReview*, November 1890, p.421 and p.427.
156. B. Webb, *My Apprenticeship* (Cambridge, 1879 edn), p.198.
157. C.S. Loch, *The Charities Register and Digest* (1890), p.xiii.
158. For example, *19th AR, Birkenhead COS* (1890), p.1 and pp.13–15.
159. *COR*, 26 December 1878, pp.227–8.
160. Calvin Woodard, 'The COS and the Rise of the Welfare State', (PhD thesis, University of Cambridge, 1961), p.204; and R.H. Crocker, 'The Victorian Poor Law in Crisis and Change: Southampton, 1870–1895', Albion, 19, 1 (Spring 1987), p.39.
161. H. Bosanquet, *Social Work in London, 1869–1912* (1914), p.69.
162. Mrs B. Bosanquet, *Rich and Poor* (1899), p.226
163. *COR*, 18 May 1882, p.150.
164. *19th AR, London COS* (1886/7), 2nd edn, p.6.
165. Mrs B. Bosanquet, *Rich and Poor* (1899), p.201.
166. *18th AR, London COS* (1885–6), p.4, refers to Trevelyan's 1870 comments.
167. *COReview*, May 1890, p.205.
168. *AR, Liverpool CRS* (1879–80), p.7.
169. *CRS Minute Book*, 7 March 1879.
170. *AR, Liverpool CRS* (1878/9), p.9, and *COR*, 22 March 1877, p.47.
171. *COR*, 22 March 1877, p.47.
172. *COR*, 21 June 1877, p.104.
173. *COR*, 15 November 1877, p.182, *5th AR, Southampton COS* (1880), p.8; also *4th AR, Southampton COS* (1879), p.4; *COR*, 9 August 1883, p.257; *10th AR, Southampton COS* (1885), p.6; and *COReview*, January 1886, p.18.
174. *12th AR, Brighton COS,* (1883), p.4.
175. *AR, Oxford COS* (1874), p.7.
176. *COR,* 26 April 1883, p.135; and 10 May 1883.
177. *COR*, 25 February 1874, p.214. Clergy coolness also reported by Exeter COS and Worthing COS *COR*, 26 May 1881, p.126.
178. Cited in Anthony Miller, *Poverty Deserved?* (Birkenhead, 1988), p.34.
179. *COR*, 11 May 1882, p.143.
180. *COR*, 30 August 1884, p.287.

Notes 191

181. *COR*, 26 April 1876, p.80.
182. *COR*, 8 August 1878, p.157.
183. *COR*, 1 May 1872, p.84; *COReview*, November 1890, pp.466–8.
184. J. Gaddum, *Family Welfare Association of Manchester and Salford, A Short History, 1833–1974* (Manchester 1974), p.9.
185. *COR*, 2 April 1873, p.64.
186. *COReview*, November 1890, pp.466–8; Leicester Provident Dispensary had 25 000 paying members in 1880, but distanced itself from any idea of amalgamating with the Leicester COS: *COR*, 15 July 1880, p.173.
187. For example, *ARs, Leamington COS* (1879 and 1882); *AR, Oxford COS* (1876), pp.5–6; (1879), p.4.; and C. Violet Butler, *Social Conditions in Oxford* (1912), pp.198–206; *15th AR, Brighton COS* (1886), p.4, and *21st AR, Brighton COS* (1892), p.4.
188. David C. Ward, 'Deformation of the Gift: The COS in Leamington Spa' (MA thesis, University of Warwick, 1975), p.107.
189. R.H. Crocker, *op. cit.*, p.35.
190. *COReview*, June 1886, pp.203–4.
191. *COReview*, June 1890, pp.250–1.
192. *COR*, 29 October 1873, p.147.
193. *Ibid.*
194. *Brighton Daily News*, Thursday, 25 February 1875.
195. *COR*, 2 December 1874, p.334.
196. *21st AR, Brighton COS* (1892), p.4.
197. *53rd AR, Manchester and Salford DPS* (1885), pp.13–14.
198. *COReview*, May 1890, pp.181–2.
199. *COR*, 7 February 1884, p.52.
200. *COReview*, May 1890, p.182; for similar frustration at Southampton: *COReview*, November 1890, p.480.
201. *COR*, 26 May 1881, p.125.
202. *COR*, 7 February 1884, p.52.
203. *COR*, 7 February 1884, p.52. A further example was Chester COS's pension fund, criticized by London as 'in danger of becoming a carcass': *COReview*, April 1887, p.175.
204. *COReview*, July 1885, p.331. See data and discussion in Chapter 6 below.
205. *Ibid.*
206. *Objects of the Society for Organising Charitable Relief and Repressing Mendicity*, published annually 1869–1890.
207. *Rules of the 'Liverpool Central Relief Society'*, and after 1874, 'The Liverpool Central Relief and Charity Organisation Society', published as a forward to their Annual Reports.
208. *AR, Liverpool CRS* (1876/.7), p.9.
209. *COR*, 8 September 1881, p.183.
210. David Owen, *op. cit.*, p.462.
211. *COReview*, April 1887, p.174.
212. *23rd AR, Liverpool CRS* (1885/6), p.9 and p.44
213. *COR*, 7 February 1884, p.52.
214. Alan J. Kidd, 'Charity Organisation and the unemployed in Manchester, c.1870–1914', *Social History*, 9 (1984), p.53.
215. *12th AR, Birmingham COS* (1881), p.4.

216. *COR*, 30 March 1882, p.89.
217. *COR*, 29 November 1877, p.189–90.
218. *COR*, 30 March 1882, p.89.
219. *COR*, 25 May 1882, p.154.
220. *The Brighton Herald*, Saturday, 27 November 1875.
221. *COR*, 8 April 1880, p.82, and *COR*, 20 January 1881, p.19.
222. *COR*, 30 March 1882, p.89.
223. *COR*, 29 June 1882, p.199.
224. *COR*, 20 December 1883, p.385.
225. *COReview*, 1887, p.216.
226. D.C. Ward, *op. cit.*, pp.97 and 103.
227. *COR*, 25 March 1880, p.79.
228. *COReview*, February 1890, p.72.
229. *COReview*, November 1890, p.444.

CHAPTER 6

1. *COR*, 29 October 1873, p.146
2. *COR*, 26 May 1881, p.125.
3. *19th AR, Birkenhead COS* (1890), p.5.
4. (Baron) H. Snell, *Men, Movements and Myself* (1936), p.70.
5. *Southampton Times*, 15 January 1876, p.8.
6. Mrs B. Bosanquet, *Rich and Poor* (1899), pp.226–7.
7. *12th AR, Leamington COS* (1887), p.9.
8. *19th and 20th ARs, Birmingham COS* (1888–9), p.4.
9. For example, a 'great deal of imposture' was detected by Oxford COS's 'rigid investigation': *COR*, 30 November 1876, p.176.
10. *Reports from Secretaries of Charity Organisation Societies as to the classes of Applicants to which aid is given.* London COS, December 1886.
11. B. Webb, *My Apprenticeship* (1979 edn), pp.202–3.
12. *13th AR, Southampton COS* (1888), p.5.
13. *AR, Oxford COS*, 12 months ending 30 September 1890, p.3.
14. *COR*, 1 January, 1879, p.2.
15. C. Violet Butler, *Social Conditions in Oxford* (1912), p.195.
16. BPP 1890 (c303), LXIII, p.17; and (c.i.303), LXIII, p.17.
17. K. Williams, *From Pauperism to Poverty* (1981), pp.126–7 and 214–16.
18. *ARs, Manchester and Salford DPS* (1872–84).
19. *COReview*, November 1890, p.433.
20. *Annual Meeting Proceedings, Friends of the Liverpool PDS*, 20 May 1834, p.11.
21. For example, *10th AR, Reading COS* (1884), case 2050, p.4; *12th AR, Reading COS* (1886), case 3151, p.4; *8th AR, Brighton COS* (1879), p.21. When longer-term support was envisaged the case became the subject of a Special Fund or Collection: e.g. *13th AR, Birmingham COS* (1882), p.6. See also, pp.122–5.

22. Data provided annually by their Relief and Begging Letter Department in DPS annual reports. Others have estimated there were 4.6 persons in the average 1891 English household: Peter Laslett, *Household and Family in Past Time* (Cambridge, 1972), pp.130–3.
23. Mrs B. Bosanquet, *Rich and Poor* (1899), p.161 and p.200. Also Francis Peek, *The Uncharitableness of Inadequate Relief*, Exeter Hall, 20 May 1879; C.S. Loch, *How to Help Cases of Distress* (1883), pp.6–9; Sophia Lonsdale, *The Evils of a Lax System of Out-door Relief*, paper read to COS Conference, 30 April 1895.
24. *The Minority Report of the 1909 Poor Law Commission, Part I*, 'Break up the Poor Law and Abolish the Workhouse', Fabian Society edn (1909), pp.36–7; Anne Digby, *Pauper Palaces* (1978), pp.161–2. The average weekly dole per outdoor pauper, including men, women and children, throughout England and Wales, between 1870 and 1889, was one shilling, nine and a half pence: K. Williams, *From Pauperism to Poverty* (1981), Table 4.6, p.170.
25. C. Booth, *Life and Labour of the People of London*, Vol.1, (1902 edn), p.33; and B.S. Rowntree, *Poverty, A study of Town Life* (1922 edn), p.351.
26. BPP 1910 (c5074), LII, pp.60–1.
27. *AR, Liverpool CRS* (1890), p.8.
28. *19th and 20th ARs, Birmingham COS* (1888 and 1889), p.5.
29. *COR*, 2 April 1873, p.63; and *COReview* November 1890, p.422 and p.425.
30. Examples: *21st AR, Brighton COS* (1892), p.5, *10th AR, Southampton COS* (1885), p.10, and *14th AR, Leamington COS* (1889), p.10.
31. P. Johnson, *Saving and Spending – The Working-class Economy in Britain, 1870–1939* (Oxford, 1985), pp.178–9.
32. B.S. Rowntree, *Poverty, A Study of Town Life* (1922 edn), p.355.
33. C. Booth, *Life and Labour of the People of London*, Vol.I (1902 edn), pp.33–5.
34. *The Brighton Herald*, Saturday, 27 November 1875.
35. *21st AR, Brighton COS* (1892), p.3.
36. For example, *11th AR, Leamington COS* (1886), pp.9–10.
37. *The Brighton Herald*, 27 November 1875.
38. *53rd AR, Manchester and Salford DPS* (1885), p.10.
39. *8th AR, Leamington COS* (1883), p.9.
40. *Ibid.*, p.10.
41. *Leamington Spa Courier*, 29 March 1890, p.3.
42. 'Minute Books, Birkenhead COS', 9 May 1882: see also 6 January 1879 and 19 May 1879 for earlier complaints against Mr Banks.
43. *11th AR, Birkenhead COS* (1882), p.5.
44. *13th AR, Birkenhead COS* (1886), p.6.
45. C.S. Loch (1890), *op. cit.*, p.ix.
46. Melvin Richter, *The Politics of Conscience* (1964), p.332.
47. C.S. Loch, *The Charities Register and Digest* (1890), p.ix. The 'minute investigation' into the 'circumstances and antecedents' applied to applicants at anti-outdoor relief Poor Law unions can be seen as a precursor for these COS procedures: B. Leighton, *Pauperization: Cause and Cure* (Shrewsbury, 1871), pp.4–5.
48. *COR*, 26 May 1881, p.124.

49. *12th AR, Birkenhead COS* (1883), p.7. For an impression of COS investigations in the USA, see M.B. Katz, *In the Shadow of the Poorhouse* (New York, 1980), pp.75–7.
50. *Leamington COS Record Book 1879–1893*, and David C. Ward, 'Deformation of the Gift: The COS in Leamington Spa' (Warwick University, MA thesis, 1975), pp.34–6.
51. *COR*, 26 May 1881 p.125; see also *Leicester COS*, Minute Book, 22 July 1878, and Judith Fido, 'The COS and Social Casework in London 1869–1900', A.P. Donajgrodzki (ed.), *Social Control in Nineteenth Century Britain* (1977), pp.227–8.
52. *12th AR, Reading COS* (1886), p.4.
53. *13th AR, Reading COS* (1887), p.6. For details of cases provided with a 'wringing machine', see *44th and 45th ARs, Manchester and Salford DPS* (1876–7), pp.16–17.
54. *AR, Oxford COS* (1882), p.7.
55. *19th AR, Birkenhead COS* (1890), p.5.
56. *8th AR, Brighton COS* (1879), p.21.
57. *Ibid.*
58. *COReview*, April 1887, p.174.
59. *Report of COS Special Committee Soup Kitchens, Children's Breakfasts and Dinners, and Cheap Food Supply* (1887), p.19–20; earlier COS Reports on these subjects included those in 1871 and 1877.
60. *The Charities Register and Digest* (1882), p.26.
61. K. Woodroofe, *From Charity to Social Work* (1962), p.39.
62. H. Bosanquet, *Social Work in London 1869 to 1912* (1914), p.64.
63. *4th AR, Southampton COS* (1879), p.6.
64. *COR*, 2 January 1879, p.6.
65. Letter from C.T. Gostenhofer to John Polson of Westmount, Paisley, 3 December 1886 (loc. Birkenhead Council for Voluntary Services).
66. *14th AR, Birkenhead COS* (1885), p.6.
67. Robert Humphreys, 'The Poor Law and Charity: The Charity Organisation Society in the Provinces, 1870–1890' (LSE, University of London, PhD thesis, 1991), p.332.
68. Letter from C.T. Gostenhofer, *op. cit.*
69. *COReview*, November 1890, p.441.
70. *Ibid.*
71. *COReview*, November 1890, p.419.
72. *13th AR, Birmingham COS* (1882), p.8.
73. *AR, Oxford COS*, 12 months ending 30 September 1879, p.12.
74. *Oxford Chronicle*, Supplement, 28 November 1885.
75. *AR, Oxford COS*, 12 months ending 30 September 1887, p.23, and 12 months ending 30 September 1890, p.26 (numerical error of applicants in original document).
76. E.H. Hunt, *Regional Wage Variations in Britain, 1850–1914* (Oxford, 1973), p.20 and p.62.
77. *AR,Oxford COS*, 12 months ending 30 September 1888, p.3.
78. *AR, Oxford COS*, 12 months ending 30 September 1890, pp.3–4.
79. *The Charities Register and Digest* (1890), p.cliii.
80. For example, *3rd AR, Horsham COS* (1876), p.4.

81. For example, Liverpool CRS loans in 1887–8 totalled £18, which was less than 1 per cent of all relief. *25th AR, CRS* (1887–8), p.7.
82. K. Woodroofe, *From Charity to Social Work* (1968), pp.38–9.
83. *55th AR, Manchester and Salford DPS* (1887), p.20.
84. *COReview*, November 1890, p.429.
85. *COReview*, November 1890, pp.422, 427, 428 and 441. Also *COR*, 26 May 1881, p.126, regarding difficulties with loans at Exeter COS, whereas, p.127, Aberdeen found loans 'very useful'.
86. *First AR, Reading COS* (1874–5), pp.3–4.
87. *COR*, 14 July 1875, p.501.
88. *Ibid.*
89. *9th AR, Reading COS* (1882–3), pp.6–7.
90. *12th AR, Reading COS* (1885/6), p.3.
91. *4th AR, Southampton COS* (1879), p.3.
92. *5th AR, Southampton COS* (1880), p.7.
93. *Eleventh AR, Southampton COS* (1886), p.7.
94. *8th AR, Leamington COS* (1883), p.11.
95. *AR, Oxford COS* (1876), p.4.
96. *AR, Oxford COS* (1878), p.4.
97. *COReview*, November 1890, pp.438–9.
98. *Report of Accounts: Kingston-on-Thames COS* (1888/9/90), p.3.
99. *Provident Societies Recommended* (1883), p.9, publisher: J.G. and F. Rivington. Also *Minutes of the Society for the Relief of the Aged and Industrious Poor of Oxford*, 22 November 1827.
100. *Birkenhead COS, ARs* (1883–7), *Birmingham COS, ARs* (1878–9), *11th AR, Southampton COS* (1886): and *Manchester and Salford DPS, ARs* (1870–85).
101. *9th AR, Birmingham COS* (1878), p.5.
102. *10th AR, Birmingham COS* (1879), p.7.
103. *12th AR, Leamington COS* (1887), pp.12–13.
104. Leamington Spa Courier, 29 March 1890, p.3.
105. For example, *ARs, Oxford COS* (1875), p.4; (1877), p.4; (1884), pp.6–7.
106. *COR*, 2 March 1882, p.61.
107. Lynedoch Gardiner, *Duty of the Church to Paupers and Vagrants* (1882), p.13.
108. *COR*, 17 May 1877, pp.88–9
109. *AR, Liverpool CRS* (1873–4), pp.7–8.
110. *56th AR, Manchester and Salford DPS* (1888), p.8.
111. *57th AR, Manchester and Salford DPS* (1889), p.12.
112. *Ibid.*
113. *AR, Oxford COS* (1887), pp.8–9
114. *AR, Oxford COS*, 12 months ending 30 September 1885, p.5.
115. *AR, Oxford COS*, 12 month ending 30 September 1885, p.5.
116. *AR, Oxford COS*, 12 months ending 30 September 1877, p.4.
117. *AR, Oxford COS*, 12 months ending 30 September 1890, p.23.
118. *4th AR, Southampton COS* (1879), pp.7–8.
119. *12th AR, Southampton COS* (1887), p.6.
120. *8th AR, Leamington COS* (1883), pp.10–11, and David C. Ward, *op. cit.*, pp.48–9.

121. *15th and 16th ARs, Birmingham COS* (1884) and (1885), p.4.
122. *COReview*, November 1890, p.420 and p.419.
123. *19th and 20th ARs, Birmingham COS* (1888–9), p.4.
124. *13th AR, Birmingham COS* (1882), p.6.
125. Mrs B. Bosanquet, *Rich and Poor* (1899), pp.221–5, and C.L. Mowat *op. cit.*, p.98.
126. BPP 1895 (c7684), XIV, Minutes of Evidence: Report of the Royal Commission on the Aged Poor (1895), para. 4081.
127. *AR, Oxford COS*, 12 months ending 30 September 1890, p.4.
128. *Ibid.*
129. *COReview*, November 1890, p.427.
130. *COReview*, November 1890, p.422.
131. *First AR, Reading COS* (1874–5), pp.5–6; see also private correspondence from C.T. Gostenhofer of Birkenhead COS, *op. cit.*
132. 'Charity and Food', *Report of the Special Committee of the COS upon Soup Kitchens, Children's Breakfasts and Dinners and Cheap Food supply* (1887).
133. *COR*, 10 July 1879, p.178.
134. *4th AR, Leamington COS* (1879), p.9; also, for details of special appeal to 'acquire and fit up a permanent and convenient kitchen', *6th AR, Leamington COS* (1881), p.9.
135. *7th AR, Leamington COS* (1882), p.10.
136. *8th AR, Liverpool CRS* (1870–1), p.8; also *17th AR, Liverpool CRS* (1879–80), p.9, for details of soup distribution in the adverse winter. Croydon COS operated soup kitchens, 'one penny being charged for a quart of soup and two pounds of bread': *COReview*, November 1890, p.441.
137. The *Liverpool Lantern*, 1 March 1879, p.323.
138. *17th AR, Liverpool CRS* (1879–80), p.7
139. *AR, Liverpool CRS* (1870–1), p.8.
140. The *Liverpool Lantern*, Saturday, 18 January 1879, p.227.
141. *Ibid.*
142. *5th AR, Birkenhead COS* (1876), p.7, reported speech by Ribton Turner.
143. For example, *12th AR, Birkenhead COS* (1883), p.7.
144. For example, *4th AR, Leamington COS* (1879), p.10.
145. *8th AR, Birkenhead COS* (1879), p.9.
146. *Kingston COS*, Report of Accounts (1878–9) and (1880), p.3.
147. *COR*, 26 May 1881, p.125.
148. *12th AR, Leamington COS* (1887), p.11.
149. *Ibid.* As mentioned in Chapter 5, Liverpool CRS were also among the societies favouring migration and emigration assistance. In the three years 1871–4 they helped 781 poor persons with fares to manufacturing districts. *AR, Liverpool CRS* (1873–4), p.8.
150. *AR, Oxford COS*, 12 months ending 30 September 1883, pp.3–4.
151. *Ibid.*
152. *Seventh AR, Southampton COS* (1882).
153. *Eleventh AR, Southampton COS* (1886), p.6.
154. *13th AR, Southampton COS* (1888), p.7.
155. For example, *3rd AR, Leicester COS* (1879), p.5, for their scheme of 'country-lodgings' for convalescents.

Notes 197

156. *44th and 45th AR, Manchester and Salford DPS* (1876 and 1877), pp.6–7.
157. *Ibid.*, p.8
158. J. Gaddum, *Family Welfare Association of Manchester and Salford, A Short History 1833–1933* (Manchester, 1974), p.11.
159. *58th AR, Manchester and Salford DPS* (1890), p.14.
160. *8th AR, Birkenhead COS* (1879), p.7.
161. *10th AR, Birkenhead COS* (1881), p.7; see also Birkenhead COS Minute Book, for Birkenhead Provident Society Card.
162. *8th AR, Birkenhead COS* (1879), p.7.
163. *5th AR, Birkenhead COS* (1876), p.12. For further difficulties in retaining visitors see, for example, *16th AR, Birkenhead COS* (1890), p.8.
164. *COReview*, April 1887, pp.174–5.
165. *AR, Oxford COS* (1874), p.7.
166. *AR, Oxford COS*, 12 months ending 30 September 1881, p.5.
167. *38th and 39th ARs Manchester and Salford DPS* (1871–2), p.8, and *58th AR* (1890), p.23.
168. G. Stedman Jones, *Outcast London* (Penguin, 1984), p.246.
169. B. Kirkham Gray, *Philanthropy and the State, or Social Politics* (1908), p.119.
170. *11th AR, Birmingham COS* (1880), p.4.
171. *Ibid.*, pp.4–5.
172. *15th and 16th AR's, Birmingham COS* (1885), p.3.
173. *COReview*, November 1890, pp.420–1.
174. J. Gaddum, *Family Welfare Association of Manchester and Salford, A Short History, 1833–1974* (Manchester, 1974), p.11.
175. *11th AR, Southampton COS* (1886), p.5
176. *8th AR, Birkenhead COS* (1879), p.6
177. *14th AR, Birkenhead COS* (1885), p.5.
178. *15th AR, Birkenhead COS* (1886), p.3.
179. *COReview*, January 1886, letter dated 18 December 1885 from C.T. Gostenofer, Hon. Sec., Birkenhead COS.
180. *COReview*, January 1886, pp.14–15.
181. *COReview*, November 1890, p.439.
182. *AR, Oxford COS*, 12 months ending 30 September 1881, p.3.
183. Keith Gregson, 'Poor law and organised charity: the relief of exceptional distress in north-east England, 1870-1910', in M.E. Rose (ed.), *The Poor and the City: The English Poor Law in its Urban Context, 1834–1914* (Leicester, 1985), p.108.
184. *Ibid.*, p.109.
185. *Report of a Special Committee of the COS on the best means of dealing with exceptional distress*, COS pamphlet (1886), p.iv. Brighton COS considered it their duty to be even more alert at 'times of severe depression' to discriminate between the deserving and 'the unhappily large class which gains its living by fraud, falsehood, and mendicity' *16th AR, Brighton COS* (1887), p.4.
186. *Social Notes*, No. 29, 21 September 1878, pp.461–2 (question mark in the original).
187. BPP 1888, *Report: House of Lords Select Committee on Poor Law Relief*, XV, para. 1680.

Notes

188. Liverpool CRS Minutes, 28 January 1863.
189. *AR, Liverpool CRS* (1890–1), p.37.
190. *COR*, 15 November 1877, p.182.
191. *8th AR, Southampton COS* (1883), p.6; see also S. and H. Barnett, *Practicable Socialism* (1895 edn), pp.212–15 for other impressions of who the COS considered to be 'ineligible' and 'not requiring relief'.
192. *13th AR, Southampton COS* (1888), p.5.
193. *14th AR, Southampton COS* (1889), p.5.
194. *11th AR, Southampton COS* (1886), p.6.
195. 'Waste in Charity', a tract to accompany *The Cautionary Card*, COS Form no.51.
196. Another notorious case was *Waller v. Loch, COR*, 8 September 1881, p.183, and 1 December 1881, p.227.
197. *COR*, 1 December 1875, pp.147–8.
198. *COR*, 16 June 1875, p.92.
199. *11th AR, Southampton COS* (1880), p.10.
200. *Ibid.*, p.7.
201. *6th AR, Birkenhead COS* (1877), p.8.
202. *13th AR, Reading COS* (1887), pp.5–6.
203. *14th AR, Reading COS* (1887–8), p.5.
204. H.O. Barnett's speech, reprinted in S. and H. Barnett, *Practicable Socialism* (1895 edn), p.211.
205. H. Bosanquet, *Social Work in London, 1869 to 1912* (1914), p.54 and p.56.
206. *COR*, 15 February 1877, pp.26–7.
207. *Ibid.*, p.26.
208. K. Woodroofe, *From Charity to Social Work* (1968), pp.42–3.
209. Mrs B. Bosanquet, *op.cit.*, p.8.
210. For example, *14th AR, Leamington COS* (1888), p.10.
211. *10th AR, Birkenhead COS* (1881), p.7.
212. *16th AR, Birkenhead COS* (1887), p.6. For further example see *19th AR, Birkenhead COS* (1890), p.8. For similar problems at Leicester and their inability to attain committee quorums see: *14th AR, Leicester COS* (1890), p.7.
213. *Birkenhead News*, Saturday, 20 February 1886.
214. *COR*, 8 October 1873, p.134.
215. *44th and 45th ARs, Manchester and Salford DPS* (1876–7), p.13.
216. M. Simey, *op. cit.*, p.95.
217. Gilbert Slater, *Poverty and the State* (1930), pp.25–6
218. *COR*, 23 February 1882, p.51.
219. *COReview*, November 1890, p.413.
220. For example, *COR*, 20 October 1875, p.123, and *COR*, 19 July 1876, p.126.
221. *COR*, 7 July 1881, p.162
222. *AR, Oxford COS* (1878), p.6.
223. Francis Peek, *The Uncharitableness of Inadequate Relief*, May 1879, p.11.
224. *The Brighton Herald*, 2 December 1876.
225. *Ibid.*
226. *The Liverpool Lantern*, January 4, 11, 18, 25; February 1, 22; March 1, 1879.

Notes

227. *The Liverpool Review*, 16 April 1887, p.11.
228. *Ibid.*
229. *8th AR, Birkenhead COS* (1879), pp.8 and 15.
230. *Statement of Accounts, Dorking Poor Law Union*, 12 months ending Lady Day, 25 March 1882, p.8.
231. *8th AR, London COS* (1877), p.16.
232. *8th AR, Birkenhead COS* (1879), p.7
233. *The Birkenhead News*, 2 August and 16 August 1879.
234. *The Birkenhead News*, 23 February 1884, p.2.
235. *5th AR, Edgbaston CO and Mendicity Society* (1874), p.5.
236. *13th AR, Birmingham COS* (1882), pp.6–7.
237. R. Humphreys, *op. cit.*, p.345.
238. W.B. Stephens (ed.), *A History of the County of Warwick, Vol.VII*, The Victoria History of the Counties of England (OUP, London, 1964), pp.556/67.
239. R. Humphreys, *op. cit.*, p.350.
240. *AR, Oxford COS*, 12 months ending 30 September 1890, p.23.
241. R. Humphreys, *op. cit.*, p.346.
242. *21st AR, Brighton COS* (1892), p.5.
243. *46th AR, Manchester and Salford DPS* (1878), p.4.
244. *10th AR, Southampton COS* (1885), p.10.
245. *14th AR, Southampton COS* (1889), p.6.
246. *11th AR, Southampton COS* (1886), p.10.
247. R.H. Crocker, *op. cit.*, p.38.
248. *Report of the Committee on the Bristol Poor* (1884), p.214.
249. *10th AR, Leamington COS* (1885), p.13.
250. *14th AR, Leamington COS* (1889), p.10.
251. *6th AR, London COS* (1875), p.11.
252. *Reading Mercury*, 21 February 1874.
253. *7th AR, Reading COS* (1880–1), p.3. Reading were not alone in their privations. For example, Eton COS repeatedly struggled against insolvency in spite of tight financial controls: *17th AR, Eton COS* (1888–9), p.5. also Leicester COS Minute Book, December 1882, and *14th AR, Leicester COS* (1890), p.6.
254. R. Humphreys, *op. cit.*, p.351.

CHAPTER 7

1. *COR*, 23 February 1882, p.51.
2. *COR*, 4 May 1882, p.83; for the same theme repeated eight years later, see *COReview*, November 1890, pp.414–15.
3. *COR*, 23 February 1882, p.51.
4. C.L. Mowat, *The Charity Organisation Society, 1869–1913* (1961), pp.63–81.
5. *Ibid.*, p.81.
6. C.S. Loch, *Charity Organisation* (2nd edn, 1892), p.106.

7. *COR*, 26 May 1881, p.124; and E.W. Benson, 'The Science of Charity', *COS Occasional Paper No.19*, 23 April 1891.
8. *COS Occasional Paper No.19*, p.1 and p.2.
9. C.S. Loch, *The Charities Register and Digest* (1890), p.xiii
10. Thomas Chalmers, *The Christian and Civic Economy of Large towns*, 3 Vols (Glasgow, 1821–6), II, pp.36–7.
11. C.S. Loch, *The Charities Register ...* , *op. cit.*, pp.xiii and ix.
12. The *Birkenhead News*, 23 February 1884, p.2.
13. H. Bosanquet, *The Strength of the People* (2nd edn, 1903), p.208 (emphasis in original).
14. *Ibid.*
15. *COR*, 26 May 1881, p.124.
16. Examples: R.C.K. Ensor, *England 1870–1914*, (Oxford, 1936); R.H.Gretton, *A Modern History of the British People* (1913), p.11; A.V. Dicey, *Law and Public Opinion in England during the Nineteenth Century* (2nd edn, 1914); H. Lynd, *England in the Eighteen Eighties* (1968); A. Briggs and A. Macartney, *Toynbee Hall* (1984); G. Stedman Jones, *Outcast London* (Penguin edn 1984), pp.xix/xx; and E.P. Hennock, 'Poverty and social theory in England: the experience of the eighteen-eighties', *Social History, 1* (1976), p.69, for the argument that changes arose out of the 'crisis of the 1860s'.
17. G. Stedman Jones, *op. cit.*, p.271.
18. *COReview*, January 1889, p.25.
19. BPP 1887, *16th Annual Report, LGB* (c5131), XXXVI.I
20. *COReview*, June 1891, p.265.
21. BPP 1888, *Report: Select Committee of House of Lords on Poor Law Relief*, XV, para. 4174, and Helen Bosanquet, *op. cit.*, p.330.
22. B. Bosanquet, *The Philosophical Theory of the State* (1899, reprint 1965), p.185.
23. *COReview*, March 1886, p.100.
24. Thomas Chalmers, *Christian and Civic Economy*, Vol II, (1823), pp.36–7.
25. G.D.H. Cole, 'A Retrospect of the History of Voluntary Social Service', in A.F.C. Bourdillon (ed.), *Voluntary Social Services: Their place in the Modern State* (1945), p.20.
26. A. Mearns, *The Bitter Cry of Outcast London* (1883 – Leicester, 1970 edn), *Squalid Liverpool*, reprint from *The Liverpool Daily Post* (Liverpool, 1883), and A. Lady, *Afternoons in Manchester Slums* (Manchester, 1887).
27. For 1880s social tensions see: H.M. Lynd, *England in the Eighteen-Eighties* (1968), pp.23–60, and G. Stedman Jones, *op. cit.*, pp.281–314.
28. *COReview*, January 1891, p.53.
29. C. Booth, *Life and Labour of the People of London*, 17 Vols, (1889–1903); S.B. Rowntree, *Poverty: A Study of Town Life* (1901); F. Scott, 'The Conditions and Occupations of the people of Manchester and Salford', *Transactions of the Manchester Statistical Society* (1888–9), pp.99–116; and a report on J. Stopford Taylor's survey of Liverpool overcrowding, *COR*, 7 June 1884, p.192.
30. C.S. Loch, *Charity Organisation* (2nd edn, 1892), p.101.
31. B. Kirkham Gray, *Philanthropy and the State, or Social Politics* (1908), p.117.
32. *The Times*, 1 December 1890.

33. C. Woodard, 'The COS and the Rise of the Welfare State' (University of Cambridge, PhD thesis, 1961), p.180.
34. G.H. Sabine, *A History of Political Theory* (New York, 1963), p.737.
35. Melvin Richter, *The Politics of Conscience: T.H. Green and His Age* (1964), p.269–70.
36. Alfred Marshall, *Principles of Economics* (2nd edn, 1891), p.3.
37. Helen Bosanquet (1903), *op. cit.*, pp.70–1.
38. G. Stedman Jones, *op. cit.*, p.147.
39. Melvin Richter (1964), *op. cit.*, p.334.
40. G. Williams, *The State and the Standard of Living* (1936), p.20.
41. G. Sabine, *op. cit.*, p.732.
42. Michael Freeden, *The New Liberalism* (Oxford, 1986 edn) pp.171–2.
43. A. Toynbee, *Lectures on the Industrial Revolution* (1887), p.xi.
44. Helen M. Lynd, *op. cit.*, p.147.
45. B. Kirkham Gray, *op. cit.*, p.116.
46. *Ibid.*, p.119.
47. T. Hawksley, *The Charities of London* (1869), p.19.
48. B. Bosanquet, *The Philosophical Theory of the State* (1899, reprint 1965), pp.140–1.
49. *Ibid.*, p.178.
50. *Ibid.*, p.179.
51. T.H. Green, 'The Principles of Political Obligation', para. 220, in R.L. Nettleship (ed.), *Works of Thomas Hill Green, Vol.II* (1886).
52. L.T. Hobhouse, 'The Historical Evolution of Property, in Fact and in Idea', in Bishop Charles Gore (ed.), *Property its Duties and Rights* (1913), p.31.
53. *Ibid.*
54. Hastings Rashdall, 'The Philosophical Theory of Property', in Charles Gore (ed.), *op. cit.*, pp.63–4.
55. T.H. Green, 'The Principles ... ', *op. cit.*, para. 209.
56. *Ibid.*, paras 209 and 210.
57. B. Bosanquet, *The Civilization of Christendom* (1893), pp.vi–vii.
58. *Ibid.*, p.vii.
59. T.H. Green, 'On the Different Senses of "Freedom" ... ', in R.L. Nettleship ed., *Works of Thomas Hill Green, Vol.II* (1886), p.314.
60. T.H. Green, 'Principles of Political Obligation', op. cit., para. 154.
61. B. Bosanquet (1899), *op. cit.*, p.268n.
62. *Ibid.*, p.269n.
63. *Ibid.*, p.271.
64. *Ibid.*, p.270n.
65. *AR, Oxford COS* (1890), pp.18–21.
66. H.D. Bosanquet, *The 'Poverty Line'*, COS Occasional Paper No. 11.
67. S.B. Rowntree, *The 'Poverty Line'*, undated reply to H.D. Bosanquet's, 'The Poverty Line' (Goldsmith's Library, University of London, FWA B425). Emphasis in original.
68. H. Bosanquet, (1903), *op. cit.*, p.114.
69. Melvin Richter, (1966), *op. cit.*, p.19.
70. Michael Freeden, *The New Liberalism* (Oxford, 1986 edn), pp.170–94.
71. Melvin Richter, *The Politics of Conscience* (1964), p.121 and p.297.
72. Melvin Richter, (1966), *op. cit.*, p.4.

73. G. Stedman Jones, *op. cit.*, p.9.
74. E.J. Urwick, 'Settlement Ideals', *COReview*, Vol.XIX (1903).
75. S.A. Barnett,'Practicable Socialism', *The Nineteenth Century Vol.* April 1883, pp.554/5.
76. S.A. Barnett, 'University Settlements', in S. and H. Barnett, *Practica Socialism* (1895 edn), p.165.
77. *Ibid.*, p.174.
78. S.A. Barnett (April 1883), *op. cit.*, p.554–5.
79. *COR*, 5 April 1883, p.105.
80. *Ibid.*
81. *COReview*, March 1886, p.100.
82. *Ibid.*
83. Melvin Richter (1966), *op. cit.*, p.ii.
84. *COReview*, August 1895, pp.338 and 343.
85. *Ibid.*, p.362.
86. *Ibid.*, p.365.
87. Gillian Darley, *Octavia Hill* (1990), pp.322–3.
88. H.D. Bosanquet, *Social Work in London 1869–1912*, (1914), p.76.
89. *COReview*, Vol. III (1898), p.331; and *COReview*, Vol. I (1897), p.50.
90. Gareth Stedman Jones, *op. cit.*, pp.290–1.
91. Fabian Tract No.1, *Why are the Many Poor?* (1884).
92. A.M. McBriar, *An Edwardian Mixed Doubles, the Bosanquets versus the Webbs* (Oxford, 1987).
93. B. Semmel, *Imperialism and Social Reform* (1960), p.24.
94. *COR*, 21 February 1884, p.63.
95. BPP 1872, *First AR, LGB, Appendix 20* (c516), XXVIII, pp.63–8; *COR*, 14 February 1872, p.16; and *3rd AR, London COS*, (1872), pp.13–4.
96. For example, *11th AR, London COS* (1879–80), pp.4–7.
97. *24th AR, London COS* (1892), p.53.
98. *10th AR, Southampton COS* (1885), p.7.
99. See *COReview*, November 1890; for example, Bristol COS admitted it was not 'strong enough to get its voice listened to … ', p.425.
100. BPP 1872, *First AR of the LGB, Appendix 20* (c516), XXVIII, p.66.
101. C.S. Loch, *The Charities Register and Digest* (1890), p.ix.
102. Anthony Miller, *Poverty Deserved?* (Birkenhead 1988), pp.5–6. More generally on the charity of the poor to the poor: F.K. Prochaska, 'Philanthropy', in F.M.L. Thompson (ed.), *The Cambridge Social History of Britain, 1750–1950, Vol.3* (1990), pp.362–6.
103. T.S. Simey, *Principles of Social Administration* (1937), p.136; and for examples of COS claimed successes see *14th AR, Brighton COS* (1885), pp.29–30; *10th AR, Southampton COS* (1885), pp.8–9.
104. Thomas Hawksley, *The Charities of London and Some of the errors in their Administration* (1869), p.16.
105. *COR*, 27 March 1872, p.59.
106. H. Bosanquet (1914), *op. cit.*, p.232.
107. C.S. Loch, *Charity Organisation* (2nd edn, 1892), p.30.
108. A.W. Vincent, 'The Poor Law Reports of 1909 and the social theory of the Charity Organisation Society', *Victorian Studies, 27* (1983–4), pp.361 and 363.
109. *12th AR, Southampton COS* (1887), p.5

Notes 203

110. *COReview*, November 1890, p.445.
111. R. Humphreys, *op. cit.*, pp.335–43.
112. Octavia Hill, 'The Charity Organisation Society', *COS Occasional Paper No.15*, pp.1–4.
113. S. and B. Webb, *English Poor Law History, Part II* (1929), p.456.
114. *The Charities Register and Digest* (1882), p.102.
115. C.S. Mowat, *op. cit.*, pp.127–31.
116. Emily Townshend, 'The Case against the COS', *Fabian Tract 158*, p.6.
117. G. Stedman Jones, *op. cit.*, p.xx.
118. Calvin Woodard, *op. cit.*, p.9.
119. C.S. Yeo, 'Introduction', to Helen Bosanquet, *Social Work in London, 1869–1912* (Brighton, 1973 edn), p.xi.
120. *COReview*, January 1891, pp.52–3. The criticisms of Samuel Barnett, discussed earlier, provide another well-publicised example of drifting COS support.
121. B. Harrison, 'Philanthropy and the Victorians', *Victorian Studies*, IX, (1966), p.360.
122. Mrs Bernard Bosanquet, *Rich and Poor* (1899), p.156.
123. B. Webb, *My Apprenticeship* (1979 edn), p.201.
124. H.D. Bosanquet, *Social Work in London, 1869–1912* (1914), p.16.
125. Edward Shils, *The Intellectuals and the Powers* (Chicago, 1972), p.42. COS Unitarians would have been experienced in holding views that 'made them intensely unpopular among all other groups of those who professed themselves Christians': R.V. Holt, *The Unitarian Contribution ...* (1938), p.275.
126. B. Webb (1979 edn), *op. cit.*, p.206.
127. Brian Harrison, *op. cit.*, p.366.
128. H.O. Barnett, 'What has the COS to do with Social Reform', in S. and H. Barnett, *Practicable Socialism* (1895 edn), pp.211–12.
129. F.K. Prochaska, 'Philanthropy', in F.M.L. Thompson (ed.), *The Cambridge Social History of Britain, 1750–1950, Vol.3*, (1990), p.357, and N. Gash (ed.), *The Long Debate on Poverty* (1974 edn), p.xxi.
130. For example, *7th AR, Reading COS* (1880–1), p.7, shows Mr W.G. Hayward contributed 5s. Also, *8th AR, Birkenhead COS* (1879), comparison between p.2 and pp.10–3 suggests some committee members made no financial contribution.
131. D.F. Fraser (ed.), *The New Poor Law in the Nineteenth Century* (1976), p.11, and N. Gash (ed.), *op. cit.*, (1974), p.xxi.
132. *The Concise Oxford Dictionary* (Oxford 1990), p.894.
133. N. Gash (ed.), *op. cit.*, p.xxi.
134. C.L. Mowat, *The Charity Organisation Society, 1869–1913: It's Ideas and Work* (1961), p.93; *COR*, 26 May 1881, p.124; and H. Bosanquet, *Social Work in London 1869–1912: A History of the COS*, (1914), p.392.
135. C.S. Loch, *COS Occasional Paper No.40* (1893), p.4.
136. *COReview*, November 1890, p.415.
137. *Ibid.*, p.414.
138. *Ibid.*
139. W.L. Burn, *The Age of Equipoise* (1964), p.127.
140. *COR*, 17 February 1881, p.36, and 24 March 1881, p.70.
141. *COR*, 17 February 1881, p.36.

Bibliography

ARCHIVE COLLECTIONS

The British Library: Humanities and Social Sciences

Provident Societies Recommended (1833), publishers: J.G. and F. Rivington, London.
Reports of London COS and Provincial Societies (1874/5/Sol.6) and (1890/1). Contains reports for Birkenhead, Birmingham (Edgbaston), Brighton, Liverpool, Oxford, Reading and Southampton.
Family Welfare Association (formerly the COS) Reports etc:
Model Rules for Provident Dispensaries (June 1878).
Charities Register and Digest (1882, 1884, and 1890).
The Charity Organisation Society and the Reynolds-Barnado Arbitration (1878).
Dwellings of the Poor, Report of Dwellings Committee (1873).
Report of Special Committee of the COS on the Education and Care of Idiots, Imbeciles and Harmless Lunatics, etc. (1877).

Berkshire County Record Office

Papers/pamphlets (1870/1908).
Bradfield Poor Law Union, Board of Guardian Minutes

Birkenhead Council for Voluntary Service

Annual Reports, *Birkenhead Provident and Benevolent Society* (1864–1871).
Annual Reports, *Birkenhead Association for Organising Relief and Repressing Mendicity* (1872–1897).
Minute Books, *Birkenhead Association for Organising Relief and Repressing Mendicity*, Quarterly Meetings (1872–1906).
Letter C.T. Gostenhofer to John Poulson, Westmount, Paisley. 3 December 1886.

Birmingham: City Libraries, Local Records Department

Annual Reports, *Edgbaston Mendicity Society* (1870–1873).
Annual Reports, *Edgbaston Charity Organisation and Mendicity Society* (1873–1875).
Annual Reports, *Birmingham Charity Organisation Society* (1875–1890).

The Bodleian Library, Oxford

Annual Reports, *Oxford Society for the Suppression of Mendicity* (1869–1871).

Bibliography 205

Annual Reports, Oxford Anti-Mendicity and Charity Organisation Association (1873–1885).
Society for the Relief of Distressed Travellers and others, printed notice (1814).
Minutes of an 'adjourned meeting', reference the formation of *Society for the Relief of Distressed Travellers and others*, 1 April 1814.
Report of Society for the Relief of the Aged and Industrious Poor of Oxford, 23 November 1827.
Minutes of inaugural meeting of *Office for the Suppression of Mendicity*, 3 December 1827.

Brighton: City Reference Library

Annual Reports, Charity Organisation Society for Brighton, Hove and Preston (1873, 1876 and 1892).
Brighthelmston Jubilee Benevolent Fund, establishment document, 25 October 1809.
Report of Brighton Provident and District Society (1831), bound with psalms, hymns and anthems.

British Library of Political and Economic Science

Reports, Charity Organisation Societies of the United Kingdom (Provincial) (1878/80–1890). Societies included vary from year to year.
Reports, London Charity Organisation Society (1873–1940).
Charity Organisation Reporter, Volumes 1–13 (1872–1884).
Charity Organisation Review, Volumes 1–NS XII (1885–1938).
Social Notes, Volume 1 (March–August, 1878).
Poor Law Conferences (1876–1911).
Charity Organisation Papers, Nos 1–14.
Statistics of Middle-class Expenditure, pamphlet (c.1896), HD6/D267.
Family Welfare Association (formerly the COS) Reports etc.:
  Conference on Night Refuges (1870).
  Co-operation of District Committees of COS with Guardians (1879).
  An Examination of 'General' Booth's Social scheme (1890).
  Manual of Society for Organising Charitable Relief and Repressing Mendicity (1870).
  On the Best Means of Dealing with Exceptional Distress, Report of a Special Committee (1886).
  Outdoor Relief (1889).
  Report upon Metropolitan Charities known as Soup-kitchens and Dinner-tables (1871).
  Reports, leaflets and press-cuttings relating to the Association for the Prevention of Pauperism and crimes in the Metropolis, later the Society for Organising Charitable Relief and Repressing Mendicity, afterwards the COS.
  Occasional Papers, 9, 11, 13–33, 36–59.
  Report of Special Committee upon Soup Kitchens, Children's Breakfasts and Dinners, and Cheap Food Supply (1887).

The Goldsmiths' Library: University of London

Family Welfare Association (formerly the COS):
Catalogue of the Library of the Charity Organisation Society, compiled by D.H. Knott, 1963. (The contents of the London COS Library are now in the Goldsmiths' Library, other than Reports of Committees and general operational data relating to London, which are located in the Greater London Record Office.)
Included in the Goldsmiths' Library collection are:
G.C.T. Bartley, 'The Poor Law in its Effects on Thrift', paper to the British Assoc. for Advancement of Science, Bradford, 22 September 1873.
William Fowler, 'The Poor Law and its Administration in the Aston Union', Birmingham 1873.
Francis W. Fox, 'On the Necessity for New Poor Law Administration', Bristol 1870.
Revd. C.D. Francis, 'The Injustice of the Poor Law in itself..', Banbury 1872.
Charles Lamport, 'Charity, Pauperism, and Self-Help', 1875.
Revd. L.R. Phelps, 'Poor Law and Charity', Oxford 1887.
Additional *Family Welfare Association* publications:
Cautionary Information Card, published by the COS, Form no. 51 (1887).
The Charity Organisation Society's Almanack, a poster (1873).
The Confessions of an Old Almsgiver; Or Three Cheers for the COS (1871).
Effects of Charities Illustrated (1880).
'Outdoor relief and charity', proof for members of the COS Council only (1877).

Leicestershire County Record Office

Minute Books, *Leicester Charity Organisation Society*, 24 April 1876 to 3 January 1881, and 7 January 1881 to 31 December 1885.

Liverpool Record Office

Annual Reports, Liverpool Central Relief and Charity Organisation Society (1863–1924).
Minute Books of *Liverpool CRS* and Executive Committee, January 1863–September 1881, and March 1892–September 1915.
Relief Committee Minute Book of *Liverpool CRS*, June 1863–March 1864.
An Account of the Liverpool District Provident Visiting Society (1834), includes prefatory remarks by Revd. A. Campbell, 'Intended as a Manual for the Formation of Similar Societies'.
Proceedings of the Friends of the Liverpool District Provident Society, 20 May 1834.
Report of the Committee of the Liverpool District Provident Society (1834).
Liverpool Mercury, articles by W. Grisewood, with comments and letters thereon (1899).
Liverpool CRS, newspaper-cuttings: 22 January1862 to 23 December 1884.
Liverpool Review, editorial on Liverpool CRS, 16 April 1887, p.11.

The Liverpool Lantern, series of articles and letters on the Liverpool CRS, January, February and March 1879.

Manchester: City Central Library

Local Studies Department
Annual Reports, Manchester and Salford District Provident Association (1833/1920). From 1894 called the District Provident and Ch~ rity Organisation of Manchester and Salford.
From 1877 includes reports of the Manchester and Salford Provident Dispensaries Association.
Committee Minutes, West Hill Convalescent Home, Southport, 1879/1959.
Newspaper cuttings: social, welfare and medical services, charities.

Archives Department
'Special Distress Fund', established 1878 by DPS to deal with trade depression and severe winter.
DPS, General Committee Minutes, 5 July 1866 to 23 August 1878 (includes accounts, reports, letters, etc.).
DPS, Monthly Committee Minutes, 7 July 1880 to 5 May 1897.

Southampton Civic Record Office

Minute Books, Southampton Board of Guardians (1869–1890).
Southampton Incorporation Accounts (1870–1890).
Workhouse Committee, Weekly return of paupers.
Newspaper cuttings: social conditions, the COS, etc.

Warwick County Record Office

Royal Leamington Spa Charity Organisation Society. Charity Organisation Society Casebooks. CR 51/1877-1882.
Royal Leamington Spa Charity Organisation Society. Clipping Book. CR 51/1883.

UNPUBLISHED THESES

B.K. Adams, 'Charity, Voluntary Work and Professionalism in Late Victorian and Edwardian England, with Special Reference to the COS and Guilds of Help' (MA thesis, University of Sussex, 1976).
J.E. Burditt, 'Philanthropy and the Poor Law: A Study of the Relief of Poverty in the Romford Union, 1795–1914' (MPhil thesis, Birkbeck College, University of London, 1978).
F.F.S. Driver, 'The English Bastille: Dimensions of the Workhouse System, 1834–1884' (PhD thesis, University of Cambridge, 1988).

L.J. Feehan, 'The Relief of Poverty in Liverpool, 1850–1914' (PhD thesis, University of Liverpool, 1988).
Stephen Flavell, 'Charity Organisation Society in Leicester, 1876–1914' (MA thesis, University of Leicester, 1972).
M.T. Furgol, 'Thomas Chalmers' Poor Relief Theories and Their Implementation in the Early Nineteenth Century' (PhD thesis, University of Edinburgh, 1987).
Michael R. Gibson, 'The Treatment of the Poor in Surrey under the Operation of the New Poor Law between 1834 and 1871' (PhD thesis, University of Surrey, 1979).
Robert Humphreys, 'The Poor Law and Charity – The Charity Organisation Society in the Provinces, 1870–90' (PhD thesis, LSE, University of London, 1991).
Mary E. MacKinnon, 'Poverty and Policy: The English Poor Law, 1860–1910' (DPhil thesis, University of Oxford, 1984).
Stephen Page, 'Poverty in Leicester' (PhD thesis, University of Leicester, 1987).
Y.J. Potter, 'Economic Change, Poverty and Poor Relief: The Able-bodied Pauper and the New Poor Law in North Yorks, 1834–1900', (MA thesis, University of Durham, 1980)
D.W. Thomson, 'Provision for the Elderly, 1830–1908' (PhD thesis, University of Cambridge, 1980).
M.C. Satre, 'Poverty in Berkshire' (PhD thesis, New York University, 1978).
Gillian Wagner, 'Dr. Barnardo and the COS: A Re-assessment of the Arbitration Case of 1877' (PhD thesis, University of London, 1977).
David C. Ward, 'Deformation of the Gift: The COS in Leamington Spa' (MA thesis, University of Warwick, 1975).
Calvin Woodard, 'The Charity Organisation Society and the Rise of the Welfare State' (PhD thesis, University of Cambridge, 1961).

PARLIAMENTARY PAPERS

Royal Commission of Inquiry into the Administration and Practical Operations of the Poor Laws, BPP 1834 (c44, 251and 313), XXVII to XXXIX incl., plus appendices.
Reports to the Local Government Board by H.M. Secretary of State for Foreign Affairs, 'Poor Laws in Foreign Countries', BPP 1875 (c1255), LXV.I.
Report from the Select Committee of the House of Lords on Poor Relief, BPP 1888 (c363), XV.
Report of the Royal Commission on Poor Law Relief in the case of Destitution by Incapacity for Work from Old Age, BPP 1895 (c7684), XIV and XV.
Report of the Royal Commission on the Poor Laws, BPP 1909 (c4499), XXXVII, plus appendices.
Annual Reports of the Poor Law Board (PLB), 1st AR (1849) to 23rd AR (1871), *Subject Catalogue of the House of Commons Parliamentary Papers, 1801–1900, Vol. III* (Cambridge, 1988), pp.580/1.
Annual Reports of the Local Government Board (LGB), 1st AR (1871/2) to 24th AR (1894–5), *ibid.*, pp.581–2.
Accounts and Papers on Poor Relief, *ibid.*, pp.589–98.

Bibliography 209

NINETEENTH-CENTURY PUBLICATIONS AND PAMPHLETS

Anon, *Plain Words on Out-Relief* (London, 1894).
Joseph Arch, *Joseph Arch: The Story of his Life, Told by Himself* (1898).
P.F. Aschrott, *The English Poor Law System, Past, and Present* (1888 edn).
Eliz. B. Bailey, *Edward Denison* ... (1884).
S. and H. Barnett, *Practicable Socialism* (1895 edn).
E.W. Benson (Archbishop of Canterbury), 'The Science of Charity', *COS Occasional Paper No. 19* (1891).
W.G. Blaikie, *Leaders in Modern Philanthropy* (1884).
T. Bland-Garland, *Outdoor Relief* (1887).
Charles Booth, 'First Results of an Enquiry based on the 1891 Census', *Journal, Royal Statistical Soc.*, LVI (1893).
Charles Booth, *Old Age Pensions and the Aged Poor, A proposal* (1899).
Charles Booth, *Life and Labour of the People of London*, 17 Volumes (1902).
William Booth, *In Darkest England and the Way Out* (1890).
B. Bosanquet, *Knowledge and Reality: A Criticism of F.H. Bradley's Principles of Logic* (1885).
B. Bosanquet, *'In Darkest England', on the wrong track* (1891).
B. Bosanquet, *The Civilization of Christendom* (1895).
B. Bosanquet (ed.), *Aspects of the Social Problem* (1895).
B. Bosanquet, *Philosophical Theory of the State* (1899).
Mrs Bernard Bosanquet, *Rich and Poor* (1899).
C.B.P. Bosanquet, *The Organisation of Charity* (1874).
C.B.P. Bosanquet, *A Handy Book for Visitors of the Poor in London* (1874).
C.B.P. Bosanquet, *London: Some Account of its Growth, Charitable Agencies and Wants* (1868).
Lord Brabazon, *Social Arrows* (1886).
Thomas Chalmers, *The Christian and Civic Economy of Large Towns, 3 vols* (Glasgow,1821/6).
William Chance, *The Better Administration of the Poor Law* (1895).
W. Chance, 'The Elberfeld and English Poor Law Systems: A Comparison', *Economic Journal*, 7 (1897).
M.E. Chudleigh, *Charity in Essence and Operation* (1882).
J.C. Cox, 'Outdoor Relief ...', *Poor Law Conferences*, 1889–90 (1890).
A.C. Crowder, *The Administration of the Poor Law* (1888).
T.B. Dudley, *A Complete History of Leamington Spa* (Leamington, 1896).
F. Engels, *The Condition of the Working Class in England* (1973 edn)
T.H.S. Escott, *England: Its People, Polity and Pursuits* (1886).
Fabian Tract No. 1, 'Why are so many Poor?' (1884).
Baldwyn Fleming, *Pauperism and Relief* (1890).
T.W. Fowle, *The Poor Law, The Friendly Societies, and Old Age Destitution* (1892).
Lynedoch Gardiner, 'The Supplementation of Poor Law Out-Relief', *COR* (26 December 1878).
Lynedoch Gardiner, *Duty of the Church to Paupers and Vagrants* (1882).
Henry George, *Progress and Poverty* (1880).
C. Gore, *Lux Mundi* (1899).

J.R. Green, *Stray Studies, 1st series* (1876).
T.H. Green, *Prolegomena to ethics* (ed. A.C. Bradley, Oxford 1884).
T.H. Green, *Works of T.H. Green*, 3 Volumes (ed. R.L. Nettleship, 1885/8).
W.T. Greene, *Population and Pauperism* (1891).
W. Grisewood, *The Poor of Liverpool: Notes on their Condition* (1897).
Revd. S. Humphreys Gurteen, *A Handbook of Charity Organisation* (Buffalo, 1882)
Thomas Hawksley, *The Charities of London* (1869).
Thomas Hawksley, *Objections to the History of the Society* (1875).
G.M. Hicks, *A Contribution Towards the History of the Origin of the COS* (1875).
Octavia Hill, *Homes of the London Poor* (1883, reprint 1970).
Octavia Hill, 'The Charity Organisation Society', *COS* Occasional Paper No. 20 (1891).
J.A. Hobson, 'Is Poverty Diminishing?', *Contemporary Review* (April 1896).
J.A. Hobson, 'The Social Philosophy of Charity Organisation', *Contemporary Review* (November 1896); B. and H. Bosanquet's reply, *Contemporary Review*, (January 1897).
J.R. Hollond, 'The Principles of Charitable Relief', *COR* (27 March 1872).
J. Hornsby-Wright, *Thoughts of a Charity Organisationist* (1878).
W.A. Hunter, 'Outdoor Relief: Is It so Very Bad?', *Contemporary Review, LXV* (1894).
H.M. Hyndman, 'English Workers as They Are', *Contemporary Review* (July 1887).
Thomas Kirkup, *An Inquiry into Socialism* (1888).
A. Lady, *Afternoons in Manchester Slums* (Manchester, March 1887)
Baldwyn Leighton (ed.), *Letters and other writings of the late Edward Denison, M.P.* (1872).
C.S. Loch, *A New Chapter in Charity Organisation* (1885).
C.S. Loch, 'Introduction' to *The Charities Register and Digest* (1890).
C.S. Loch, *An Examination of 'General' Booth's Social Scheme* (1890).
C.S. Loch, *Criticisms of General Booth's Social Scheme* COS pamphlet (1891).
C.S. Loch, 'Charity Organisation', *COS Occasional Paper No. 40* (1893).
Sophia Lonsdale, *The Evils of a Lax System of Out-door Relief* (1895).
Josephine S. Lowell, *Public Relief and Private Charity* (New York, 1884).
Alexander McDougall, Jnr, *Inquiry into the Causes of Pauperism in the Township of Manchester* (Manchester 1884).
Thomas Mackay, *The English Poor* (1889).
Thomas Mackay, 'The Abuse of Statistics', *Quarterly Review, 179* (1894).
Thomas Mackay, *Methods of Social Reform* (1896).
Thomas Mackay, *The State and Charity* (1898).
Thomas Mackay, *A History of the English Poor Law, Vol. III* (1899).
Alfred Marshall, *The Future of the Working Class* (1873).
Alfred Marshall, *Principles of Economics* (1891).
(Revd.) C. Marson, *The Charity Organisation and Jesus Christ* (1897).
Harriet Martineau, *Illustrations of Political Economy*, 9 volumes (1832–4).
C.F.G. Masterman, *The Heart of the Empire: Discussion of Problems of Modern City Life in England* (New York, 1873).
(Revd.) A. Mearns, *The Bitter Cry of Outcast London* (1883).

(Revd.) Herbert V. Mills, *Poverty and the State or Work for the Unemployed* (1886).
R.S. Mitchison, 'The Advantages of Outdoor Relief', *Central Poor Law Conference* (1891).
M.W. Moggridge, *Method of Almsgiving: A Handbook for Helpers* (1882).
George Morley, *History of Royal Leamington Spa* (1887).
W. O'Hanlon, 'Our Medical Charities and their Abuses', *Transactions of the Manchester Statistical Society* (1872/3).
Robert T. Paine, *Pauperism in Great Cities: Its 4 Great Causes* (Chicago, 1893)
(Revd.) Richard Parkinson, *On the Present Condition of the Labouring Poor with Hints for Improving It* (Manchester and London, 1841).
Francis Peek, *The Uncharitableness of Inadequate Relief* (1879).
J.R. Pretyman, *Dispauperization* (1876).
Provident Societies Recommended, pub. J.G. and F. Rivington, London (1833).
John Rae, *Contemporary Socialism* (New York, 1884).
W. Rathbone, *Social Duties Considered* (1867).
Report of the Committee to inquire into the condition of the Bristol poor (1884).
B.W. Richardson, *The Health of the Nation* (1887)
D.G. Ritchie, *The Moral Function of the State* (1887).
D.G. Ritchie, *The Principles of State Interference* (1891).
Fred Scott, 'The Conditions and Occupations of the People of Manchester and Salford', *Transactions of the Manchester Statistical Society* (1888/9), pp.93/116.
Samuel Shaen, *The Assault of Lambeth Workhouse* (1869).
Samuel Smiles, *Self-Help* (1859).
(Revd.) H. Solly, *How to Deal with the Unemployed Poor of London, and with its Roughs and Criminal Classes* (1868).
(Revd.) H. Solly, *These Eighty Years* (1893).
H. Spencer, 'The Coming of Slavery', *The Contemporary Review, Vol. XLV* (1884).
Squalid Liverpool, reprint from *Liverpool Daily Post* (1883).
J.H. Stallard, 'Pauperism, Charity, and the Poor Laws', *National Association for the Promotion of Social Sciences* (1869).
W.M.T., 'The Charity Organisation Society', *Social Notes, No. 29* (21 September 1878).
Arnold Toynbee, *Are Radicals Socialists?* (1884 edn).
W. Vallance, 'The Influence upon the Poor of a Wise and Strict Administration of Out-door Relief', *Poor Law Conferences* (1881).
N. Wiseman, *Some Eminent Christian Workers in the Field of Philanthropy*, undated.
J. Hornsby Wright, *Thoughts and Experiences of a Charity Organisationist* (1878)
G.U. Yule, 'An investigation into the causes of changes in pauperism in England ...', *Royal Statistical Society Journal*, cxii (1899), pp.249/86.

CONTEMPORARY NEWSPAPERS AND MAGAZINES

Birkenhead and Cheshire Advertiser
Birkenhead News

Birmingham Daily Mail
Birmingham Daily Post
Brighton Daily News
Brighton Herald
Charity Organisation Reporter
Charity Organisation Review
Leamington Spa Courier
Leamington Chronicle
Liverpool Lantern
Liverpool Mercury
Liverpool Review
Manchester Guardian
Manchester Evening News
Oxford Chronicle
Oxford Gazette
Reading Mercury
Reading Observer
Social Notes
Southampton Times and Winchester Express
Southampton Times and Hampshire Express (after 10.4.1875)
The Times

SECONDARY SOURCES

J.H. Abraham, *The Origins and Growth of Sociology* (1973).
P. Abrahams, *The Origins of British Sociology* (Chicago, 1968).
B.A. Abrams and M.D. Schmitz, 'The Crowding Out Effect of Governmental Transfers on Private Charitable Contributions', *Public Choice, No. 1* (1978), pp.28–30.
Paul Adelman, *Victorian Radicalism, The Middle-class Experience 1830–1914* (1984).
J.L. Amond, *The Elberfeld System* (Edinburgh, 1907).
P.D. Anthony, *John Ruskin's Social Theory* (Cambridge, 1983).
David Ashforth, 'Settlement and Removal in Urban Areas: Bradford 1834–71', M.E. Rose (ed.), *The Poor and the City: The English Poor Law and Its Urban Context 1834–1914* (Leicester, 1985).
T.S. Ashton, *Economic and Social Investigation in Manchester, 1833–1933* (1934).
C.R. Attlee, *The Social Worker* (1920).
Peter Bachrach and Morton S. Baratz, 'The Two Faces of Power', *American Political Science Review, 56* (1962), pp.947–52.
Charles F. Bahmueller, *The National Charity Company: Jeremy Bentham's Silent Revolution* (Berkeley, 1981).
W.A. Bailward, *The Poor Law and Charity* (1902).
Paul Barker (ed.), *Founders of the Welfare State* (1984).
Annie Barnes, *Tough Annie: From Suffraggette to Stepney Councillor* (1980).
Henrietta Barnett, *Canon Barnett: His Life, His Work, His Friends* (1919).

Bibliography 213

Francois Bedarida, *A Social History of England, 1851–1975*, translated by A.S. Forster (1979).
George K. Behlmer, 'The Gypsy Problem in Victorian England', *Victorian Studies*, 27 (1983–4).
E. Moberley Bell, *Octavia Hill* (1942).
W. Beveridge, *Unemployment* (1930).
Eugene C. Black, *The Social Politics of Anglo-Jewry, 1880–1920* (1988).
Charles Booth, *Life and Labour of the People of London*, 17 Vols (1902).
H. Bosanquet, *The Strength of the People* (1903 edn).
Mrs Bernard (Helen) Bosanquet (ed.), *Social Conditions in Provincial Towns* (1912).
Helen Bosanquet, *Social Work in London 1869–1912: A History of the COS* (1914).
A.F.C. Bourdillon (ed.), *Voluntary Social Services, Their Place in the Modern State* (1945).
A.L. Bowley and A.R. Burnett-Hurst, *Livelihood and Poverty* (1915).
R.H. Bremner, *From the Depths: The Discovery of Poverty in the United States* (New York, 1956).
Asa Briggs, *Victorian Cities* (1968).
Asa Briggs, *Victorian People* (1954).
Asa Briggs and Anne Macartney, *Toynbee Hall, The First Hundred Years* (1984).
Stewart J. Brown, *Thomas Chalmers and the Godly Commonwealth in Scotland* (Oxford, 1982).
A.E. Brown (ed.), *The Growth of Leicester* (Leicester, 1970).
Maurice Bruce, *The Coming of the Welfare State* (1961/8).
M. Bulmer (ed.), *Essays on the History of British Sociological Research* (Cambridge, 1985).
W.L. Burn, *The Age of Equipoise* (1964).
C. Violet Butler, *Social Conditions in Oxford* (1912).
Maurice Caplan, 'The New Poor Law and the Struggle for Union Chargeability', *International Review of Social History, XXIII* (1978).
W.E. Chadwick, *The Church, The State and the Poor* (1914).
W. Chance, *Poor Law Reform: The Case for the Guardians* (1910).
Olive Checkland, *Philanthropy in Victorian Scotland* (1980).
Katherine Chorlry, *Manchester Made Them* (1950).
R.A. Church, *The Great Victorian Boom 1850–1873* (1975)
G. Kitson Clark, *The Making of Victorian England* (1962).
G. Kitson Clark, *Churchmen and the Condition of England, 1832–1885* (1973).
Peter Cockton, *Subject Catalogue of the House of Commons Parliamentary Papers, 1801–1900, Part III* (Cambridge, 1988).
N. Cohn, *The Pursuit of the Millenium* (1957).
Stefan Collini, 'Hobhouse, Bosanquet and the State: Philosophical Idealism and Political Arguments in England, 1880–1918', *Past and Present, 72* (August, 1976).
Stefan Collini, *Liberalism and Sociology: L.T. Hobhouse and Political Argument in England 1880–1914* (Cambridge, 1979).
Stefan Collini, 'Political Theory and the "Science of Society" in Victorian Britain', *Historical Journal, Vol. XXIII* (1980).
V. Cormack, *The Welfare State* (1954).

Peter Clarke, *Liberals and Social Democrats* (Cambridge, 1978; paperback edn 1981).
Rosalind Coward and John Ellis, *Language and Materialism* (1977).
Ruth H. Crocker, 'The Victorian Poor Law in Crisis and Change: Southampton 1870–1895', *Albion, 19.1* (Spring 1987).
A. Dale, *Fashionable Brighton, 1820–1860* (1967).
Gillian Darley, *Octavia Hill* (1990).
B. Dennis and S. Skilton, *Reform and Intellectual Debate in Victorian England* (1987).
C.J. Dewey, 'Cambridge Idealism ...', *Historical Journal, xvii*, (1974), pp.63–78; reply from S. Collini, *ibid., xviii* (1975), pp.171–7.
Anne Digby, *Pauper Palaces* (1978).
Anne Digby, *The Poor Law in Nineteenth Century England and Wales* (1982).
Anne Digby, *British Social Policy: From Workhouse to Workfare* (1988).
A.D. Elliott, *The Life of G.J. Goschen, First Viscount Goschen, 1831–1907*, 2 Vols (1911).
Malcolm Elliott, *Victorian Leicester*, London (1979).
I.C. Ellis, *Records of Nineteenth Century Leicester* (privately printed 1935).
R.C.K. Ensor, *England, 1870–1914* (Oxford, 1936).
E.J. Evans, *Social Policy 1830–1914* (1978).
Judith Fido, 'The Charity Organisation Society and Social Casework in London, 1869–1900', in A.P. Donajgrodzki (ed.), *Social Control in Nineteenth Century Britain* (1977)
S.E. Finer, *The Life and Times of Sir Edwin Chadwick*, London (1952).
R.S. Fitton and A.P. Wadsworth, *The Strutts and the Arkwrights* (Manchester, 1958).
D. Fraser, *The Evolution of the British Welfare State* (1973, revised 1986).
D. Fraser (ed.), *The New Poor Law in the Nineteenth Century* (1976).
Michael Freeden, *The New Liberalism: An Ideology of Social Reform* (Oxford, 1986 reprint).
Joan Gaddum, *The Family Welfare Association, A Short History 1833–1974* (Manchester, 1974).
John A. Garraty, *Unemployment in History: Economic Thought and Public Policy* (New York, 1978).
N. Gash (ed.), *The Long Debate on Poverty* (1974).
Jessica Gerard, 'Lady Bountiful ...', *Victorian Studies, 30 (2)* (1987), pp.183–210.
Charles Gore, *The New Theology and the Old Religion* (1907).
Charles Gore (ed.), *Property, Its Duties and Rights* (1913).
P.L.J.H. Gosden, *Self-Help* (1973).
A. Gramsci, *Selections from the Prison Notebooks of Antonio Gramsci*, edited and translated by Quinton Hoare and Geoff Nowell-Smith (1971).
B. Kirkham Gray, *Philanthropy and the State or Social Politics* (1908).
R.Q. Gray, 'Bourgeois hegemony in Victorian Britain', J. Bloomfield (ed.), *Papers on Class, Hegemony and Party* (1977).
J.R. Green, *Stray Studies, 2nd Series* (1903).
Keith Gregson, 'Poor Law and Organised Charity: the relief of exceptional distress in North East England, 1870–1910', in M.E. Rose (ed.), *The Poor and the City: The English Poor Law in the Urban Context* (Leicester, 1985).
R.H. Gretton, *A Modern History of the British People* (1913).

Jose Harris, *Unemployment and Politics: A Study of English Social Policy, 1886–1914* (Oxford, 1972).
Brian Harrison, 'Philanthropy and the Victorians', *Victorian Studies* (June 1966).
J.F.C. Harrison, 'The Victorian Gospel of Success', *Victorian Studies* (December 1957).
Christopher Harvie, *The Lights of Liberalism* (1976).
Kathleen Heaseman, *Evangelicals in Action* (1962).
W.O. Henderson, *The Lancashire Cotton Famine, 1861–1865* (Manchester, 1934).
E.P. Hennock, 'Poverty and Social Theory in England: The Experience of the 1880's', *Social History 1* (1976).
Ursula Henriques, *Before the Welfare State* (1977).
Octavia Hill, *Letters to My Fellow Workers* (1907).
Boyd Hilton, *The Age of Atonement* (Oxford 1988).
G. Himmelfarb, *The Idea of Poverty* (1984).
G. Himmelfarb, *Victorian Values and Twentieth-century Condescension* (1987).
L.T. Hobhouse, *The Metaphysical Theory of the State* (1918).
Eric Hobsbawm, *The Age of Empire, 1875–1914* (1987).
Raymond V. Holt, *The Unitarian Contribution* (1938).
Pamela Horn, 'Labour Organisations', in G.E. Mingay (ed.), *The Victorian Countryside*, Vol. 2 (1981).
Humphry House, *The Dickens World* (1950).
E.H. Hunt, *Regional Wage Variations in Britain, 1850–1914* (Oxford, 1973)
Ideas and Beliefs of the Victorians, BBC Publication (1949).
Hugh Colley Irvine, *The Old DPS 1833–1933* (Manchester, 1951).
Paul Johnson, *Saving and Spending: The Working-Class Economy in Britain, 1870–1939* (Oxford, 1985).
Andrew Jones, *The Politics of Reform* (Cambridge, 1972).
Gareth Stedman Jones, *Outcast London* (1984).
Gareth Stedman Jones, *Languages of Class* (1985).
P.A. Jones, *The Christian Socialist Revival 1877–1914* (1968).
R. Jowell, S. Witherspoon and L. Brook (eds), *British Social Attitudes, 7th Report* (Aldershot, 1990).
Michael Katz, *Poverty and Policy in American History* (New York, 1983).
Michael Katz, *In the Shadow of the Poor House* (New York, 1986).
P. Keating (ed.), *Into Unknown England* (1976).
S.E. Keeble, *The ABC Annotated Bibliography of Social Questions* (1907).
R.A. Kent, *A History of British Empirical Sociology* (Aldershot, 1981).
Alan J. Kidd, 'Charity Organisation and the unemployed in Manchester, 1870–1914', *Social History, 9* (1984), p.47.
Alan J. Kidd and K.W. Roberts (eds), *City, Class and Culture* (Manchester, 1985).
T. Kirkup, *The History of Socialism* (5th edn 1913).
G. Lansbury, *My Life* (1928).
Lynn H. Lees, *Poverty and Pauperism in Nineteenth Century London* (Leicester, 1988).
C. Levi-Strauss, 'The Principle of Reciprocity', in L. Coser and B. Rosenberg (eds), *Sociological Theory,* (New York, 1965).
Jane Lewis, 'Social Facts, Social Theory and Social Change', paper to O.U. symposium on Charles Booth (1988).
C. Lloyd, *Explanations in Social History* (Oxford 1986).

M.E. Loane, *The Queen's Poor* (1905).
C.S. Loch, 'Statistics of Population and pauperism in England and Wales, 1861–1901', *Royal Statistical Society Journal, lxix* (1906), pp.289–312.
Steven Lukes, *Individualism* (1973).
Steven Lukes, *Power* (1974).
Steven Lukes (ed.), *Power* (1986).
Helen M. Lynd, *England in the Eighteen Eighties* (1968).
A.M. McBriar, *An Edwardian Mixed Doubles: The Bosanquets and the Webbs* (Oxford, 1987).
N. McCord, 'The Poor Law and Philanthropy', in D. Fraser (ed.), *The New Poor Law in the Nineteenth Century* (1976).
O.R. McGregor, 'Social Research and Social Policy in the 19th century', *British Journal of Sociology, VIII* (1957).
Ross McKibbon, *The Ideologies of Class* (Oxford, 1990).
Alasdair MacIntyre, *Secularization and Moral Change* (Oxford, 1967).
Mary Mackinnon, 'Poor Law Policy, Unemployment and Pauperism', *Explorations in Economic History, 23* (1986).
Mary Mackinnon, 'English Poor Law Policy and the Crusade against Out-Relief', *The Journal of Economic History*, Vol. XLVII, No. 3 (September 1987).
Mary Mackinnon, 'The Use and Misuse of Poor Law Statistics', *Historical Methods, Vol. 21*, No. 1 (Winter 1988).
Hugh McLeod, *Class and Religion in the Late Victorian City* (1974)
J. Martineau, *The English Country Labourer and the Poor in the Reign of Queen Victoria* (1901).
John W. Mason, 'Thomas Mackay: The Anti-Socialist Philosophy and the COS', in K.D. Brown (ed.), *Essays in Anti-Labour History* (1974).
John W. Mason, 'Political Economy and the Response of Socialism in Britain, 1870–1914', *The Historical Journal, 23,3* (1980).
C.E. Maurice (ed.), *Life of Octavia Hill* (1913).
Emily Maurice, *Octavia Hill: Early Ideals* (1928).
M. Mauss, *The Gift*, translation Ian Cunnison (1970).
Standish Meacham, *Toynbee Hall and Social Reform 1880–1914* (Yale, 1987).
Gary S. Messinger, *Manchester in the Victorian Age: The Half-known City* (Manchester UP, 1985).
W.J. Mommsen (ed.), *The Emergence of the Welfare State in Britain and Germany* (1981).
Charles Loch Mowat, *The Charity Organisation Society 1869–1913: Its Ideas and Work* (London, 1961).
Charles A. Murray, *In Pursuit of Happiness and Good Government* (1988).
Charles A. Murray, *The Emerging British Underclass* (1990).
Clifford Musgrave, *Life in Brighton* (1985).
Howard Newby, 'The Deferential Dialectic', *Comparative Studies in Society and History*, Vol. 17, No. 2 (April 1975).
T.R. Malthus, *An Essay on Population* (1914 edn).
J.H. Muirhead (ed.) *Bernard Bosanquet and his Friends* (1935).
Charles A. Murray, *The Emerging British Underclass* (1990).
A Survey of the Social Services in the Oxford District British Library ref. OXFORD, Barnett House, Survey Committee, *A Surrvey of the Social Services in the Oxford District* (OUP, 1938).

Bibliography 217

J. Edwin Orr, *The Second Evangelical Awakening in Britain* (1949).
David Owen, *English Philanthropy 1660–1960* (Cambridge, Mass., 1964).
Robert Owen, *The Life of Robert Owen by Himself* (1920 edn).
Stephen J. Page, 'A new source for the historian of urban poverty: the use of charity records in Leicester, 1904–29', *Urban History Year Book* (1987).
G. Parry, *Political Elites* (1969).
E.F. Paul, F.D. Miller *et al.* (eds), *Beneficence, Philanthropy, and the Public Good* (Oxford, 1987).
Harold Perkin, 'Individualism versus Collectivism in Nineteenth-century Britain: A False Antithesis', *Journal of British Studies*, XVII (1977).
Harold Perkin, *The Rise of Professional Society: England since 1880* (1989).
A.C. Pigou (ed.), *Memorials of Alfred Marshall* (1927).
J.A.R. Pimlott, *Toynbee Hall* (1935).
Robert Pinker, *English Hospital Statistics, 1861–1938* (1966).
Robert Pinker, *The Idea of Welfare* (1979).
F.K. Prochaska, *Women and Philanthropy in Nineteenth Century England* (Oxford 1980).
F.K. Prochaska, 'Philanthropy', in F.M.L. Thompson (ed.), *The Cambridge Social History of Britain, 1750–1950, Vol. 3* (1990).
Peter Quennell (ed.), *London's Underworld* (1950).
Eleanor F. Rathbone, *William Rathbone: A Memoir* (1905).
A. Redford, *Labour Migration in England 1800–1850* (1926).
Mrs M. Pember Reeves, *Round about a Pound a Week* (1913).
Melvin Richter, 'T.H. Green and his Audience: Liberalism as a Surrogate Faith', *Review of Politics*, Vol. 18 (1958), pp.444–72.
Melvin Richter, *The Politics of Conscience: T.H. Green and His Age* (1964)
Melvin Richter, 'Intellectual and Class Alienation: Oxford Idealist Diagnoses and Prescriptions', *Archives Européenes Sociologie*, VII (1966).
L.C. Robbins, *The Theory of Economic Policy in English Classical Political Economy* (1952).
D. Roberts, *The Victorian Origins of the Welfare State* (1963).
D. Roberts, *Paternalism in Early Victorian England* (1979)
Robert Roberts, *The Classic Slum* (Manchester, 1971).
Russell D. Roberts, 'A Positive Model of Private Charity and Public Transfers', *Journal of Political Economy, 921*, (Feb./June 1984).
Brian Rodgers, *The Battle against Poverty: Vol. 1 – From Pauperism to Human Rights* (1968).
Madeline Rooff, *A Hundred Years of Family Welfare* (1972).
Lionel Rose, *Rogues and Vagabonds: Vagrant Underworld in Britain 1815–1985* (1988).
M.E. Rose, 'The Respectable Poor and the Residuum: The Victorian Crisis of Poor Relief', *Social History Society Newsletter, Vol. 4* (Spring 1979).
M.E. Rose (ed.), *The Poor and the City: The English Poor Law in the Urban Context* (Leicester, 1985).
M.E. Rose, 'Poor Relief and Scientific Charity: The Elberfeld System and its Influence', unpublished paper, (*c.* 1986).
M.E. Rose, 'The disappearing pauper: Victorian attitudes to the relief of the Poor', in E.M. Sigsworth (ed.), *In Search of Victorian Values* (Manchester UP, 1988).
Seebohm B. Rowntree, *Poverty: A Study in Town Life* (1901).

Seebohm B. Rowntree, 'The Poverty Line', reply to H. Bosanquet, *The ⅃ Line*, COS Occasional Paper No. 11.
G. Sabine, *A History of Political Theory* (New York, 1963).
John Saville, *Rural Depopulation in England and Wales 1851–1951* (1957)
Barry Schwartz, 'The Social Psychology of the Gift', *The American Journa. Sociology*, Vol. 73, No. 1 (July 1967).
Karl de Schweinitz, *England's Road to Social Security* (1975).
E. Shils, *The Intellectuals and the Powers, and Other Essays* (1972).
T.S. Simey, *Principles of Social Administration* (1937).
Margaret B. Simey, *Charitable Effort in Liverpool in the Nineteenth Century* (Liverpool, 1951).
T.S. Simey and M.B. Simey, *Charles Booth, Social Scientist* (1960).
Gilbert Slater, *Poverty and the State* (1930).
(Baron) H. Snell, *Men, Movements and Myself* (1936).
Paul Spiker, *Stigma and Social Welfare* (1984).
Denis Smith, *Conflict and Compromise: Class Formation in English Society, 1830–1914* (1982).
R.N. Soffer, 'The Revolution in English Social Thought 1880–1914', *American Historical Review, LXXV* (1970), pp.1938–64.
P. Stanworth and A. Giddens, *Elites and Power in British Society* (1974).
W. Stark, *The History of Economics in its Relation to Social Development* (1944).
W.B. Stephens (ed.), *Victoria County History, Warwick, Vol.7: The City of Birmingham* (Oxford UP, 1964).
E.C. Wingfield Stratford, *The Victorian Sunset* (1932).
R.H. Tawney, *Poverty in an Industrial System* (1913).
R.H. Tawney, *Social History and Literature* (Cambridge, 1950).
A.J. Taylor, *Laissez Faire and State Intervention in Nineteenth-century Britain* (1972).
P. Thane (ed.), *The Origins of British Social Policy* (1978).
P. Thane, 'Women and the Poor Law in Victorian and Edwardian England', *History Workshop*, Vol. 6 (Autumn 1978).
P. Thane, *The Foundations of the Welfare State* (1982).
David Thomson, 'Workhouse to Nursing Home', *Ageing and Society, 3* (1983).
David Thomson, 'I am not my father's keeper', *Law and Society Review*, 2 (1984).
David Thomson, 'Welfare and the Historians', in L. Bonfield, R.M. Smith and K. Wrightson (eds), *The World We Have Gained* (Oxford, 1986).
F. Tillyard, 'Three Birmingham Relief Funds, 1885, 1886, and 1905', *Economic Journal, 15* (December 1905).
Peter Townsend, *Family Life and Old People* (1957).
Mrs E. Townshend, *The Case against the COS*, Fabian Tracts 158 (1911).
James H. Treble, *Urban Poverty in Britain 1830–1914* (1979).
'Urban History and Local History', Editorial: *History Workshop, 8* (1979).
W.R. Ward, *Victorian Oxford* (1985).
F. Vigier, *Change and Apathy: Liverpool and Manchester in the Industrial Revolution* (Cambridge, Mass., 1970).
Andrew Vincent and Raymond Plant, *Philosophy, Politics and Citizenship* (Oxford, 1974).

Bibliography 219

A.W. Vincent, 'The Poor Law Reports of 1909 and the Social Theory of the Charity Organisation Society', *Victorian Studies, 27* (1983–4).
Andrew Vincent (ed.), *The Philosophy of T.H. Green* (Aldershot, 1986).
Gillian Wagner, *Barnardo* (1979).
James Walwin, *Victorian Values* (1987).
S. and B. Webb, *English Poor Law Policy* (1910).
Sidney and Beatrice Webb, *English Local Government 8, English Poor Law History, Part II* (1929).
R.K. Webb, 'Reflections on writing the Social History of Victorian England', *Journal of Modern History, 58, 3* (1986).
Beatrice Webb, *My Apprenticeship* (Cambridge, 1979 edn).
Earl Morse Wilbur, *A History of Unitarianism* (Cambridge, Mass., 1945).
Gertrude Williams, *The State and the Standard of Living* (1936).
Ian Williams, *The Alms Trade* (1989).
Karel Williams, *From Pauperism to Poverty* (1981).
F.F. Wilson, *How Best to Reduce the Rates, or Dr Chalmers and the Elberfeld System of Relief* (1907).
K. Woodroofe, *From Charity to Social Work in England and the United States* (1962).
K. Woodroofe, 'The COS and the origins of social case-work', *Historical Studies, Australia, and New Zealand, IX* (1959–61), pp.19–29.
R. Woods, 'Mortality and Sanitary Conditions in the Best Governed City in the World – Birmingham 1870–1910', *Journal of Historical Geography, Vol. 4, No. 1* (1978), pp.35–46.
C.S. Yeo, introduction to Helen Bosanquet, *Social Work in London 1869–1912* (Brighton, 1973 edn).
C.S. Yeo, *Religion and Voluntary Organisations in Crisis* (1976).
G.M. Young, *Victorian England: Portrait of an Age* (1953).
A.F. Young and E.T. Ashton, *British Social Work in the Nineteenth Century* (1967).

Index

Able-bodied paupers
   male, 17, 22–5, 31, 37–9, 42–3, 160
   female, 25, 31, 34, 37
Affiliated societies, 9, 65, 96, 99, 135
Agricultural areas, 3, 15, 28, 47, 65, 68, 79, 81; *see also* Rural areas
Anson, Revd Adelbert, 53
Armed Forces, 17, 60
Aristocracy, 9, 18, 60, 67, 71, 167
Artisans, 35, 93–4, 127, 146, 156
Ashton 7, 57
Aston Poor Law Union, 26, 46
Atcham Poor Law Union, 26–7, 30, 32, 38, 45, 65
Audits (financial), 24, 118, 141

Badger, Richard, 76
Baines, Colonel, 110
Baldwyn Fleming, 48
Balliol College, Oxford, 149, 154
Banbury Poor Law Union, 34
Banks, Mr R.J., 111
Barnardo, Dr Thomas, 62, 63, 135 146
Barnett, Canon Samuel, 32, 61, 136, 155–7
Barnett, Henrietta, 61, 136, 157, 168
Barrington, R., 157
Barton Regis (Bristol) Poor Law Union, 84, 86
Beggars, 57, 64, 99, 104, 111, 131, 147, 157; *see also* Mendicants
Benefit clubs, 33
Benevolent societies, 73, 82, 98, 109
Bettesworth, Fred, 28
Birkenhead, 77–9
   COS (Association for Organizing Charitable Relief and Repressing Mendicity), 9, 30, 65, 78–9, 86, 99, 100–7, 111, 115–18, 120–1, 126, 129, 132, 137–41
   COS Provident Department, 78, 129
   Ladies' Sanitary Society, 79
   Poor Law Union, 41, 42
   Provident and Benevolent Society (PBS), 78
Birkenhead and Cheshire Advertiser, 111
Birkenhead News, 141
Birmingham, 71–2, 131
   COS, 9, 35, 61, 65, 71–2, 85–7, 90, 95, 98, 104–9, 115–21, 124, 131, 139, 141

medical charities, 93–5, 109
City Relief Fund Committee, 131
Poor Law Union, 30, 35, 41, 71, 85, 175
Birtley, T.H., 142
Bible women, 136
Bismarck, 158
Bland-Garland, T., 34
Blanket funds, 117, 121–2
Blissard, Revd J.C., 71
Booth, Charles, 3, 46, 109–10, 148
Booth, William, 62
Booth, J. Sclater, 28
Bourgeoisie, 138
Bosanquet, Bernard, 61, 147, 149–54, 167
Bosanquet, Helen, 6, 49, 61, 136, 145–6, 154, 162, 166–7, 171
Bowley, A.L., 81
Boyle, Courtenay, 45
Bradford, 59
Bradfield Poor Law Union, 27–9, 34–8, 45–6, 65, 81
Briggs, Asa, 71
Brighthelmston Provident Institution, 56, 73
Brighton, 56, 72–3
   COS (Brighton, Hove and Preston Charity Organisation Society), 9, 30, 65, 73–4, 83, 86, 89, 93–9, 105–11, 115–17, 135–9, 142, 169
   Jubilee and Accident Fund, 89
   Provident and District Society (P and DS), 56
   Poor Law Union, 35, 41–3, 83, 107
Brighton Daily News, 73
Briston COS, 86, 90, 109, 119, 125, 142
Brixworth
   Poor Law Union, 30–8, 45, 65, 86
   Out-Relief Association, 180n64
Brown, Stewart J., 58
Brown, Sir William, 134
Browne, Colonel Granville, 59
Bruce, M., 22
Burns, Cleland, 96
Burrows, Sir Cordy, 95
Bury, Revd W., 32–4, 38
Burnett-Hurst, A.R., 81
Businessmen, 1, 64, 67–9, 74–8, 86, 97

Cambridge guardians, 182n72
Caird, Edward, 154

220

Index

Canterbury, Archbishop of, 145
Carmarthen Poor Law Union, 35
Case studies
   COS deserving applicants, 114
   COS non-deserving applicants, 80, 135–6
   COS special cases, 124
   CRS, 140
Casual labour, 47, 54, 58, 66, 69, 74, 77, 79
Cautionary procedures, 101, 104, 133–4
Cavenagh, General, 73
Chadwick, Edwin, 50
Chalmers, Revd Dr Thomas, 9, 32, 58, 70, 145–7
Chamberlain, Joseph, 4, 11, 35, 49, 71, 146–7
Chance, William, 29, 32, 49, 59
Chargeability Act (1875), 18–20
Charity: traditional, haphazard, indiscriminate, 4, 5, 9, 50, 58, 77, 87, 90, 98, 108, 157, 170, 174
Charity Officer, 140
Charity Organisation Reporter (COR), 60, 89, 96, 98, 144, 156, 174
Charity Organisation Review (*COReview*), 65, 96, 97, 129, 132, 138, 157–9, 175
Charity trustees, 63, 88, 90
Charwomen, 94, 95, 111–14, 126, 127
Checkland, Olive, 58
Chorlton Poor Law Union, 41
'Church of Charity', 145
Church of England, 64, 74, 78, 167
City Missionaries, 136
Civil servants, 174
Close parishes, 18
Clothing, cast-offs, 117
Coal Fund tickets, 117, 122
Cocoa rooms, 97, 117
College domestics, 80
Congestion, urban, 68
Contemporary Review, 158
Convalescent homes, 70, 117, 127–8, 131, 139
COS, cooperation with
   charities, 87–90
   clergy, 90–3
   guardians, 83–6
   provident dispensaries, 93–5
Cotton famine, 131
COS Council, 6, 9, 62, 165, 173
Country lodgings, 117
Cox, Revd Dr J.C., 38
Cross, Revd J.A., 125
Croydon COS, 86, 118–19, 125
Culley, George, 26–7

Cunnew, G., 76

Dansey, R. I., 36
Darlington COS, 96, 133
Darwin, Charles, 51
Davies, Revd Llewellyn, 54
Davey, J.S., 49
Dawson, Dr, 95
Debauchery, 54
Debt recovery, 120–1
Demographic changes, 27, 79
Denison, Edward, 32, 166
'Deserving' applicants to charities, 4, 7, 10, 50, 55, 57, 60, 65–76, 80, 84, 97, 101–27, 132, 135–6, 151, 161–6, 172–4
'Deserving' applicants to Poor Law, 5, 15, 21, 30, 53, 105–7
Destitutes, 22–3, 34–6, 49, 52, 68, 112–14, 120, 133–7
Deterrence, doctrine of, 22, 28
Digby, Anne, 22
Dinners, free or 'penny', 66, 97–8, 116–17
Disease, 2, 3, 26, 68, 128, 166
Disraeli, Benjamin, 50
Dockers, 20, 43, 58, 66, 74, 77, 126, 132
Doles, Poor Law, 8, 10, 46–7, 86, 101, 106–9, 118, 124, 162, 170, 173
Domestic missionaries, 91
Domestic servants, 79–80, 93–5, 127
Dorking (Surrey), 169
Doyle, Andrew, 59
Drunkenness, *see* Intemperance

Economic change, 1, 2, 4, 12, 20, 31, 63
Economic uncertainties, 4, 9, 11, 14–15, 28, 50
Edgbaston (Birmingham) Mendicity Society, 71
Edgbaston ratepayers, 72
Elberfeld, 9, 59, 67–8, 75
Employment register, 126
Endowed charities, 87, 90, 173
Environment (vs character), 2–4, 11–12, 36, 71, 148, 151–6, 163–5, 174
Errand boys, 127
Evangelicals, 62–3
Exceptional distress, 19, 39, 70, 78, 85–7, 98, 101, 115, 118, 130–3, 141
Expenditure
   COS, 12, 109, 139–41, 168
   CRS, 109
   Poor Law, 18–20, 24–6, 44–5

Index

Fabian Society, 159
Family
  responsibilities, 1, 16, 26, 42, 68, 89–93, 110–14, 126, 130, 140, 145, 152
  segregation, 15, 18, 33, 48
  size, 22, 108–9, 118, 124
  values, 5, 6, 64, 111, 153, 160–1
Faringdon Poor Law Union, 81
Fawcett, Henry, 73
Le Feuvre, Sheriff, 134
Fever epidemic, 33, 68
Finances, *see* Expenditure
Fishing industry, 47, 72
Fire-lighter factories, 97, 126
Fitzroy, Major C.C., 138, 173
Fleming, H., 24–5, 28, 36, 45
Flowers for the poor, 124
Footwear, children's, 120
Fortnightly Review, 158
Fowler, William, 26
Francis, Revd C.D., 34
Fraud, 15–16, 49, 61, 90, 136
Free hospitals, 95
Furgol, M.T., 58

Gambling, 154
Gardiner, General Sir Lyndoch, 90, 122
Gaskell, Mrs, 57
Gateshead, 133
General Inspectors, 84
Gilliland, J., 76
Gladstone, William E., 50
Gloucester COS, 82
Gordon, Revd S.C., 142
Goschen, G.J., 5, 8, 9, 14, 21, 27, 30, 41–2, 49, 53, 60, 80, 83, 159, 165, 172
Gostenhofer, C.T., 118
Graham, Alan, 148
Gramsci, Antonio, 55
Grants, COS, 7, 11, 84, 100, 103–9, 117–22, 132, 176
Green, Thomas Hill, 1, 149, 152–4
Griffin, Dr R.W.W., 43, 74
Griffiths, Henry Jnr, 131
Grisewood, William, 69, 88
Gurney, Russell, 75

Hall, A. W., 44
Hamilton, Revd Dr, 110
Hannah, Revd Dr J., 73
Harlock, Miss G., 46, 109
Harris, Jose, 7
Harrison, B., 62
Hawksley, Thomas, 60, 151

Headington (Oxford) Poor Law Union, 44, 106
Heathcote, J.M., 140
Henley, J. J., 46, 84
Heywood, Oliver, 94
Hill, Octavia, 32, 49, 61, 91, 133, 151, 157, 166–7
Hobson, J.A., 154
Home Colonial Society, 68
Hooper, Revd, 100
Hospitals, 52, 78, 87, 93, 95, 117, 122, 127, 135, 157
Hospital Sunday, 91
House of Lords Select Committee on Poor Law Relief (1888), 133
Housing reforms, 151
Hungerford Poor Law Union, 36
Hungry applicants, 43, 45, 131
Huntley & Palmer Ltd, 81
Hyde (Greater Manchester), 57
Hyndman, H. M., 158

Idealism, 1–2, 148–55
Immorality, 12, 14, 52, 54, 61, 152
Independent Labour Party, 158
Indigent classes, 53, 128
Individualism, 1–2, 4, 6, 11–12, 46, 50–1, 60, 67, 70, 93, 119, 127, 147–9, 150–3, 156, 159–74
Industrial conditions, 1–3, 18, 27–8, 71, 81, 148–51
Industrial profit, 64
Insanity, *see* Lunatics
Intellectuals, 12, 60, 167
Intemperance, 27, 54, 80, 87, 95, 134–5
Interventionism, 2, 4, 7, 11–12, 55, 149–59, 164, 174
Investigation, COS methodology, 110–14
Invalid Children's Aid Association, 62
Invalids, 123

Jackson, William, 78
Jenkinson, Revd J.H., 81
Jersey, Lord, 81
Jewellers, 75
Johnson, Paul, 109

Kensington Poor Law Union, 35
Kidd, Alan J., 69, 98
Kingston-on-Thames COS, 121, 126, 169
Kitchen, Very Revd G.W., 139
Knight, Sarah, 34

Labour Test Order, 46
'Ladies', *see* Visitors
'Lady Bountiful', 129
Laird, John, 71
Lambert, John, 45
Langton, William, 69
Laundresses, 94–5, 126
Lawyers, 1
Lazy poor, 147, 160
Leamington, 76–7
  COS (Charity Organisation and Relief Society), 9, 30, 65, 75, 94, 99, 105, 107, 112, 115–17, 120–7, 137–9, 142, 163
Leamington Chronicle, 77
Leamington News, 77
Leamington Spa Courier, 111, 122
Leeds
  COS, 86, 90, 119, 125
  Poor Law Union, 86
Legacies, 109
Leigh, Lord, 76
Leigh, Revd J.W., 76
Leisured classes, 74
Leith COS, 121
Liberals, 1–2, 68–71, 78
Lichfield, Earl of, 60
Liverpool, 59, 66–9
  CRS (Central Relief Society), 9, 59, 61, 65–70, 78, 85, 88, 91, 95–8, 105–9, 115–19, 125–30, 134, 138–9, 148, 175
  Poor Law Union, 30, 42, 43
  Provident District Society (PDS), 56–7, 106
Liverpool Lantern, 126, 140
Liverpool Review, 88, 140
Loans, COS
  defaulting, 11, 97, 116–18, 120–2, 163
  numbers, 105, 119–21
  popularity, 11, 117–21, 163
  value, 108, 119–21
Local Government Board (LGB), 8, 23–32, 34, 39–49, 53, 59, 83–4, 106, 146, 159, 160–2, 167, 175
Loch, C.S., 49, 59, 61, 66–8, 86, 90, 116, 145–50, 154–7, 162, 165–7, 172
London
  COS (Society for Organising Charitable Relief and Repressing Mendicity), 6, 7–10, 57–61, 64–6, 69–70, 79–82, 91, 95–100, 115–19, 125–6, 130, 133–7, 142–4, 150–1, 164, 171–2

East End, 20, 100, 146
Ethical Society, 154
Lord Mayor, 133
Longe, F.D., 41
Longley, Henry, 27, 48
Lonsdale, Sophia, 65–6
Lunatics, 22, 40–1, 175
Lung diseases, 68
Lynd, Helen M., 150

McDougall, Alexander, 39
Mackgill, Revd Campion, 86
McKinnon, Mary, 21
Makin, Mr William, 111
Malthus, T.R., 1, 4, 51
Manchester, 69–70, 148
  families, 148
  Poor Law Union, 9, 35, 39, 40–2, 95, 105
  School, 149
Manchester Guardian, 89, 138
Manchester and Salford DPS (District Provident Society), 9, 57, 61, 65–6, 69–70, 78, 85, 89, 93, 98, 105–8, 111, 115–22, 129–31, 138–9, 142, 175
  DPS Sick Relief Fund, 69, 71
  Provident Dispensary Association (PDA), 30, 57, 69, 94–5
Mangles (or wringing machines), 119
Mansion House Funds, 130, 157
Marjoribanks, W., 99
Marshall, Alfred, 1, 149
Mathews, Mrs Elizabeth, 121
Mechanics, 43, 95
Medical Charities, 33, 93–5, 109, 128–9, 153, 170
Medical Poor Law relief, 25, 33–4, 37, 74, 156
Mendicants, 5, 56–8, 60, 70–3, 78, 127, 144; *see also* Beggars
Mersey Ferry Committee, 126
Middlesbrough, 133
Migration, 83, 85, 117, 127, 157
Mills, Revd Herbert V., 68
Moggridge, M.W., 127
Moneylenders, 163
Moore, John, 6
Moorhouse, Bishop, 89
Mowat, C.L., 7
Muir, Ramsey, 67
Murray, Charles, 6

Nantwich Poor Law Union, 36
Nettleship, R.L., 154

Newcastle upon Tyne COS, 133
New Liberals, 4, 11, 49, 52, 152–3, 158, 161
New Unionists, 137, 174
Night-shelters, 98
Nineteenth Century, 158
Not able-bodied paupers, 31–2, 37–9, 160
Nurses, 95, 126

Occasional papers, COS, 136
O'Hanlon, William, 94
Orphans, 22, 32, 52, 123
Outdoor relief
   numbers and cost, 8, 14, 54, 58, 65, 72, 105–6, 124, 144, 153, 159, 160–2, 171, 175
   categories, 15, 17, 21–2, 160
Owen, David, 7, 67, 97
Oxford, 79–81
   COS (Anti-mendicity and Charity Organisation Association), 9, 44, 57, 65, 80–4, 90–4, 100, 104–10, 115–27, 130–3, 138–41, 149–50, 154–6, 172
   Incorporated Parishes Poor Law Union, 9, 44, 83, 106, 107
   Society for the Relief of Distressed Travellers, 57
   Working Women's Benefit Society, 94
Oxford University Press, 79
Oxford Undergraduates Journal, 80

Page, J., 76
Pamphlets, COS, 9, 65, 130, 144, 148
Parasitical classes, 137
Parish officers, 15, 43
Parochial Assessment Bill (1862), 18
Paupers
   aged, 15, 23, 53, 171, 175
   female able-bodied, 15, 18, 22, 31
   infirm, 16, 17, 31, 37, 53, 106, 171, 175
   male able-bodied, 15, 18, 22–4, 31–2, 37
   women with dependent children, 15, 17, 23, 45, 124
Pawnbrokers, 109, 163
Peek, Francis, 140
Pell, Albert, 32, 37, 86
Penny Savings Bank, 94, 130
Pensions, 11, 84, 105–8, 113, 117, 122–5, 135, 142, 157, 174–6
Pernicious poor, 71
Phelps, Revd L.R., 81, 90
Philadelphia COS (USA), 111
Philips, Herbert, 94

Poor Law Conferences, 26, 29
Poor Law
   costs, 14, 33, 45, 175
   'orthodox policy', 29
   unit relief, 55, 84, 93, 101, 105, 107, 158
Poor Law Acts
   Amendment (1834), 14–7
   Prohibitory Order (1844), 17
   Regulation Order (1852), 17
   Amendment (1867), 19
   Metropolitan Minute (1869), 8
   Circular on outdoor relief (1871), 8, 24
   Majority and Minority Reports (1909), 46, 49, 109
Poor rates, 14, 17, 33, 45, 170
Poplar Poor Law Union, 35
Population growth, 1, 19–20, 24, 31, 50, 74, 77, 81, 152
Positive freedoms, 150
Postance, Revd H., 92
Post Office Savings Bank, 130
Poverty-line, 1, 10
Practicable socialism, 156
Premiums on provident investments, 56
Pretyman, J.R., 53
Prince of Wales, 72
Professionals, 64, 70, 74–8, 102, 159, 173
Propagandism, 144
Property speculators, 75
Provident societies, 56, 73, 78, 93–5, 103, 106, 121, 129, 130, 137, 184n31; *see also* Manchester and Salford DPS
Provident dispensaries, 93–5
Prudential agent, 129
Public health, 50, 71, 147
Public works, 165
Purey-Cust, Revd A.P., 92

Quarrying, 79
Queen's Hospital Birmingham, 95

Railways, 3, 66
Railway servants, 95
Railway tickets, 117
Randall, Alderman, 80
Rashdall, Revd Hastings, 152
Ratepayers, 46, 72, 74, 160
Rathbone, William, 59, 67
Raynor, Joseph, 67, 68, 77
Reading, 81–2, 136
   COS, 9, 65, 81–2, 84, 105, 107, 110, 115–17, 120, 136, 139, 143
   Destitute Children Aid Committee, 120
   Poor Law Union, 30, 39, 105

Index 225

Reagan, Ronald, 6
Record books, COS, 136
Referred applicants, COS, 100, 112–13, 115–16, 138, 176
Reformers of charity, 50–1
Reigate Poor law Union, 35–6
Relatives, responsibility of, 27–8, 33–5, 46, 54, 101, 111–13, 123
Relief methods, COS, 114–30
Religion, 34, 60, 68, 82, 168
Relieving Officers, 18, 25, 32, 35, 43–7, 74, 110–13, 136, 141, 173
Rowntree, Seebohm, 3, 46, 109, 110, 148, 154
Royal Commissions
  Poor Laws (1832), 14
  Aged Poor (1895), 124
  Poor Laws (1905), 46, 49, 175
Royal Family, 167
Royden, T.B., 88
Rumney, Thomas, 46
Ruskin, John, 60, 148
Ruthin Poor Law Union, 35

Sackville West, Hon W.E., 80
Salaried staff, COS, 70, 103, 139, 142
Salford, *see* Manchester and Salford DPS
Salford Poor Law Union, 85
Salvation Army, 62
Sanitation, 33, 50, 147
Scarlatina, 68
Scientific methodology of charity, 1, 5–7, 10, 12, 49–55, 59–63, 90, 94, 100–5, 114–17, 136, 144–6, 156–7, 161, 166–8, 172–3
Scott, Fred, 69
Scripture readers, 91, 136
Seamen, 43, 117
Seasonal work, 69, 79
Secretaries, COS, 66, 76, 88, 89, 103, 118, 121, 127–8, 165, 172
Segregation in workhouses, 8, 15–18, 53
Self-aggrandisement, COS, 165–9
Servants, 64, 93, 95, 127
Settlement and Removal legislation, 15–16
Settlements, University, 154–8, 175
Shaftesbury, Lord, 11, 156
Sheffield, 59
Shrewsbury Poor Law Union, 30, 38, 65
Shuttleworth, Dr James Kay, 69
Sick clubs, *see* Provident societies
Sidgwick, Henry, 1, 149
Simey, Margaret, 3, 67–8, 138, 161
Slums, 69, 71–2, 151, 166

Smiles, Samuel, 1, 24, 51, 147, 159–60, 168
Smith, Adam, 1, 15
Smith, C. Crowther, 43, 74
Smith, James, 70, 85, 127–8, 135
Smith, Revd W. Saumerez, 78
Social
  change, 1, 3–9, 11, 18, 20, 27–8, 47, 50–2, 59–61, 72, 146, 150, 153–4
  control, 53, 62, 64, 70, 77, 99–100, 137, 146, 152, 158
  'physicians', attempts, 56, 58, 62, 76, 104, 138, 145–6, 149, 153
Social Democractic Federation (SDF), 158
Social Science Association, 167
Socialism, 2, 6, 11, 26, 52, 137, 148–50, 156–8
Society for Organising Charitable Relief and Repressing Mendicity, *see* London COS
Soup kitchens, 78, 97–8, 117, 125–6, 133
Southampton, 73–5, 127
  COS, 9, 43, 65, 86, 90–2, 99, 102, 105–8, 115–17, 120–3, 127, 132–4, 139, 142, 169
  Poor Law Union, 30, 43, 105, 107
  Provident Dispensary, 92
Southampton Times, 74
Spas, 75–6, 120
Special cases, 11, 122–5, 139–42
Speenhamland, 14
Spencer, Herbert, 51
Spooner, Revd W.A., 100
Squalor, 3, 46, 111, 138, 148, 165–6
Stansfeld, James, 59
Stigmatization, 7, 34–6, 44–6, 53–5, 147, 158
Stretford, Manchester, 57
'Strict' Poor Law Unions, 8–9, 15, 26–41, 46, 65, 84
Subscriptions, COS, 138–43
Surrey Poor Law Unions, 36
Sutton Seed Company Ltd, 81

Taylor, Dr J.S., 68
Thatcher, Mrs M., 6
Thrift, 5, 33, 45, 47, 51, 56–8, 66, 69–70, 75–9, 93, 102, 110, 119, 125, 138, 152–3, 156, 174
Tickets
  COS, 72, 80, 122, 127
  tradesmen's, 97–9, 118, 122, 135
The Times, 148
Town Missionaries, 91
Toxteth Relief Society, 88

Toynbee, Arnold, 150, 155
Toynbee Hall, 156, 158
Treble, James H., 49
Trevelyan, Sir Charles, 53, 91, 122, 146
Turner, C. J. Ribton, 79

'Undeserving' poor, 5, 10, 72, 99, 104, 110–12, 121, 133–7, 161–3, 168, 172–4
Unemployment, 20, 22, 28, 35, 49, 54, 69, 126, 131, 137, 146–7, 152, 165
Unitarians, 10, 57, 59, 61, 68, 70, 90
University College, Oxford, 150
Unskilled labour, 43, 47, 66
Urbanization, 1, 3, 11, 15–18, 30, 35, 50, 83, 100, 110, 148, 157, 160, 164, 167, 174

Vagrants, *see* Beggars and Mendicants
Victorian charity, 3–4, 13, 50, 62, 144, 147, 155, 166, 169–70
Vigilance Association, 77
Villiers, C.P., 18
Vincent, A.W., 7, 162
Visitors, COS, 7, 11, 57–9, 64, 68, 77–9, 103, 123, 128–30, 133–8, 145, 162, 166, 173

Wages, 3, 14, 16, 23, 27, 43, 53–4, 74, 81, 85, 93, 104, 111–13, 119, 125–30, 147
Walker, H., 56
Wallas, Graham, 154
Wallingford Poor Law Union, 29, 38, 65, 81

Walrond, Revd M.S.A., 136
Washerwomen, 127
Webb, Beatrice, 29, 60, 158, 166, 168
Webb, Sidney, 29, 60, 158
Welfare benefits, 13, 158, 164
Welfare state, 12, 22, 61, 163, 174
West Hartlepool COS, 133
West Midlands, 41, 46, 118, 146
Whatley, Archbishop, 57
Whitechapel, 155–6
Whiteley, Edward, 67
Whitcombe, George, 87
Whitehurst, Revd T.B., 76
Wilberforce, Revd Canon, 134
Willes, William, 76
Williams, Karel, 21
Winchester, Dean of, 75
Winter comforts, 124
Wirral (Cheshire), 77, 99, 141
Wodehouse, E.H., 23, 53
Woodroofe, K., 7
Workhouse
  infirmary, 95, 106
  inmates, 8, 17–20, 32, 36–41, 45–6, 53, 161
  'offer of', 15, 39, 53
  'well regulated', 15, 17
Worsley, R., 82
Wringing machines, *see* Mangles

Yarmouth, Lord, 76
Young, A.F., 7